LITERACY STRONG

ALL YEAR LONG

LITERACY STRONG

ALL YEAR LONG

Powerful Lessons for Grades 3–5

VALERIE ELLERY

LORI OCZKUS

TIMOTHY V. RASINSKI

ASCD

Alexandria,
Virginia USA

INTERNATIONAL LITERACY ASSOCIATION

Newark,
Delaware USA

1703 N. Beauregard St. • Alexandria, VA 22311-1714 USA
Phone: 800-933-2723 or 703-578-9600
Fax: 703-575-5400
Website: www.ascd.org
E-mail: member@ascd.org
Author guidelines: www.ascd.org/write

INTERNATIONAL LITERACY ASSOCIATION

PO Box 8139
Newark, DE 19714 USA
Phone: 800-336-7323 • Fax: 302-731-1057
Website: www.literacyworldwide.org
E-mail: customerservice@reading.org

Deborah S. Delisle, *Executive Director*; Stefani Roth, *Publisher*; Genny Ostertag, *Director, Content Acquisitions*; Julie Houtz, *Director, Book Editing & Production*; Darcie Russell, *Editor*; Judi Connelly, *Associate Art Director*; Georgia Park, *Senior Graphic Designer*; Keith Demmons, *Production Designer*; Mike Kalyan, *Director, Production Services*; Shajuan Martin, *E-Publishing Specialist*; Kelly Marshall, *Senior Production Specialist*

Copublished simultaneously by ASCD and the International Literacy Association.

PAPERBACK ISBN: 978-1-4166-2616-9 ASCD product # 118013 n8/18
Quantity discounts are available: e-mail programteam@ascd.org or call 800-933-2723, ext. 5773, or 703-575-5773. For desk copies, go to www.ascd.org/deskcopy.

Library of Congress Cataloging-in-Publication Data

Names: Ellery, Valerie, 1964- author. | Oczkus, Lori D., author. | Rasinski, Timothy V., author.
Title: Literacy strong all year long : powerful lessons for grades 3-5 / Valerie Ellery, Lori Oczkus, and Timothy V. Rasinski.
Description: Alexandria, Virginia, USA : ASCD, [2018] | Includes bibliographical references and index.
Identifiers: LCCN 2018008383 | ISBN 9781416626169 (pbk.)
Subjects: LCSH: Language arts (Elementary) | Language arts (Elementary)--Activity programs.
Classification: LCC LB1576 .E4254 2018 | DDC 372.6--dc23 LC record available at https://lccn.loc.gov/2018008383

27 26 25 24 23 22 21 20 19 18   1 2 3 4 5 6 7 8 9 10 11 12

To all the strong and courageous grades 3–5 teachers who work hard to equip and empower their students to be *Literacy Strong*!

LITERACY STRONG

ALL YEAR LONG

Powerful Lessons for Grades 3–5

Acknowledgments ix

Introduction xi

1. Starting the School Year Literacy Strong 1

2. Beating the Midyear Blahs 83

3. Ending the School Year Literacy Strong. 170

4. Stopping the Summer Slide 254

Study Guide. 347

References. 353

About the Authors 357

Acknowledgments

I will be forever grateful to my husband, Gregg, our adult children, Nick (Beth), Derek, Jacey (Wayne), and Brooke (Joel), and our two grandchildren, Evelyn and Wyatt, for sharing me with the literacy world. I am blessed to have so many who believe in me and inspire me daily, including my mother, Laurie Hill, who is my prayer warrior, and Dr. Janie Hull, who worked faithfully with me on this writing journey.

—Valerie

Thanks to my husband, Mark, and our young adult children Bryan, Rachael, and Rebecca for keeping me literacy strong! Also, love and gratitude to my parents, Bruce and Barbara Dutton, for their faith and encouragement.

—Lori

Thanks to my parents, Laura and Chester Rasinski, who, in their own special ways, helped my brother, sister, and me to become literacy strong.

—Tim

We are grateful to the ASCD staff, and especially to our editor, Darcie Russell, who brings a level of expertise to the profession to help promote literacy worldwide.

—*Literacy Strong* Team: Valerie, Lori, & Tim

Introduction

Literacy is at the heart of all learning! It comprises reading, writing, listening, speaking, and language competencies. Just like a heart is the most essential organ, pumping the vital necessities to all other areas of the body, literacy is the essential component that propels learning in all other content areas to function properly and bring lifelong learning. Therefore, students' level of learning is directly affected by their level of literacy knowledge and ability to access and apply that knowledge. To continue to strengthen the literacy skills of students in the intermediate grades for academic success, educators will need to integrate literacy through effective approaches such as:

- interdisciplinary, project- and concept-based learning to motivate and engage them, allowing for an inquisitive stance toward their learning process (Lanning, 2013; Strobel & van Barneveld, 2009);
- opportunities for collaborative conversations about their learning process;
- effective neuroscience and brain research connections into learning for a growth mindset (Caine & Caine, 2013; Dweck, 2006; Jensen, 2009);
- awareness of the importance of emotional and social health (Tomlinson, 2017); and
- acquiring a backward design process (Wiggins & McTighe, 2011).

Keeping literacy as the strong foundation is exactly what is needed to propel learning to higher, stronger grounds. A cohesive, comprehensive literacy experience gives students opportunities to make pertinent connections among the standards of learning. This learning is strengthened as the process and content spirals with a continuous cause-and-effect structure moving through the various seasons of a school year.

School-based seasons are very similar to our Earth's seasons. Both divide the year into quarters, marked by changes along the way. Most school-based seasons have a beginning of the school year, a midyear point, a closing of the school year, and a summertime. With every new season, there is a cause that launches it. Earth's seasons are caused by a tilt on its axis. Similarly, our school-based seasons are also caused by a tilt in the learner's mindset. We, the teachers, represent Earth, remaining steadfast on student achievement as we move around the ever-changing shifts in both learners' minds and the global field of education.

As we learn to effectively move through the various seasons of a school year, we need to give students ample opportunities to take in all that each season offers. Farmers would not expect to plant apple seeds during the first season and see fruit the next day. The apple seed needs time to take root and grow stronger to be able to produce flavorful apples. It takes a process to produce a product, and the same is true for our school-based seasons. There are times to plant, water, weed, prune, and harvest knowledge. We must first sow into the mind of a learner the amount of seed that is necessary to obtain the kind of harvest that allows the learner to be a productive citizen.

Each season is necessary for the strength, accumulation of knowledge, and longevity within the learner. "Practice that is distributed over longer periods of time sustains meaning and consolidates the learnings into long-term storage in a form that will ensure accurate recall and applications in the future" (Sousa, 2011, p. 106). Strong literacy students apply their newfound knowledge throughout the school year as lessons increase in complexity and remain relevant to their developmental needs.

The major goal of *Literacy Strong All Year Long: Powerful Lessons for Grades 3–5* is to empower and equip intermediate educators with ways to effectively keep literacy achievement strong and progressing in their classrooms. This resource allows educators to teach literacy strategy lessons that spiral across the entire school year, focusing on reaching various learning styles in today's diverse classrooms. The lessons motivate intermediate learners to accumulate literacy achievement for long-term retention by accessing and enhancing prior learning throughout the school year for a particular literacy strategy strand (e.g., analyzing words, questioning for close reading). These lessons create ample opportunities for previous learning to be applied in various situations throughout the seasons of the school year.

We hope this book captures our collaborative work as it builds on and extends research on how the brain makes connections between new and previous learning and helps students accumulate and strengthen literacy strategies for deeper learning (Anderson, 2009; Caine & Caine, 2013; National Research Council, 2012; Sousa, 2011; Wolfe, 2010). Every effort is needed to maintain the instructional cycle for layering deeper learning as educators assess, plan, implement, assess again, and reflect to maximize the quality of literacy instruction using a progression of literacy strategies. These strategies are presented in a lesson framework designed for developing a seamless flow of learning across the seasons of a school year.

Organization of This Book

Each chapter uses a season of the school year to center instruction with a focus on the English Language Arts Literacy Standards (National Governors Association Center for Best Practices and Council of Chief State School Officers, 2010) presented in 40 lessons that are conducive to deeper learning. Each chapter begins with a brief overview of the importance of keeping literacy strong during the specific season of the school year. The remaining portion of the chapter gives educators 10 Literacy Strands in comprehensive literacy lessons for applying literacy strategies within the English Language Arts Standards. Each Literacy Strand presented in Chapter 1 spirals throughout the remaining chapters, rising in complexity. This continuum gives educators the opportunity to use students' previous academic vocabulary and learning standards as a springboard. As learners gain knowledge, confidence, and independence over time, the sophistication of the standards also progresses. A comprehensive literacy lesson format (adapted from Ellery & Rosenboom, 2011) guides educators as they gradually release responsibility to students so they can become self-regulated, literacy-strong learners. The comprehensive literacy lesson format encompasses the following features.

Lesson Trailer

The lesson trailers are designed to fulfill the purpose of a movie or book trailer: they intend to attract the educator with the purpose of the lesson and to motivate him or her to teach the focused literacy lesson in the classroom.

Literacy Enhancer

The literacy enhancer gives an overview of each lesson with a focus on boosting literacy strength in one of the reading component areas of word work, vocabulary, fluency, and comprehension. A literacy strategy is also aligned to the highlighted reading component with the focus skill of the strategy noted (e.g., Comprehension: Determining Importance and Summarizing of key details and main idea).

Preparation

Every great lesson begins with preparation. This focus area of the lesson supports educators in answering the question: What resources are needed to accomplish the lesson with excellence? It is a time to prepare the materials, review the key academic vocabulary, focus on the big ideas and learning objectives, and establish essential questions. Every effort that is made for learning to occur signifies the value placed on establishing an environment that is conducive for learning.

Initiation

This initial phase of instruction develops student interest and motivation by creating an action (e.g., establish an anticipatory lead-in, hook, or attention grabber; inquiry-based learning; problem-based learning), which opens the mind of the learner and sets the stage for learning. This phase is intended to be accomplished in a short time period with interactive engagement between the teacher and students.

Demonstration

This modeling phase allows the teacher to explain clearly and concisely the what, how, and why of a task through explicit demonstration. It sets up the instruction so the teacher can unpack key learning points, with students having a view into the mind of the teacher through think-alouds and real-time examples.

Collaboration

This section provides instructional format and conversational coaching through shared experiences. It allows students to process information and apply accountable talk while responding to and further developing what others share in relationship to their own cognitive development from the content. The collaboration phase also allows learners to share text-dependent evidence through apprenticeship learning.

Application

Real-time practice is the key to this section of the lesson. During this instructional phase, learners can be with partners, in groups, or work independently to apply their newfound knowledge through approximations and active engagement experiences (e.g., guided small groups, literacy centers or stations, investigative labs).

Reflection

Intrapersonal perspective is the focus of this phase of the learning format. Students are provided a time to be self-regulated learners by considering and recording what they have learned and what they still want to learn (e.g., evaluating the feedback from monitoring progress toward a learning goal, learning logs, or written reflection journals).

Adaptation and Extension

This section of the lesson provides various ways to adapt and extend learning, allowing flexibility in meeting the diverse instructional levels and needs of learners in today's classrooms. The design of the lesson integrates many learning modalities to craft a rigorous lesson. This adaptation and extension phase recommends ways for instructors to reach as many of the learning styles and exceptional needs as possible.

Evaluation

Each lesson has "I can . . ." statements and behavior indicators to evaluate the process and product within the lesson. These tools are oriented to reflect what the student knows and still needs to know for intentional instruction as an integral part of the learning cycle, not just the end of the process.

Reproducible

These resources are designed to allow for collaboration and accountable talk, as well as for interpreting and applying previous learning to newfound knowledge by relating experiences and acquiring ownership of learning.

Chapter Overviews

Chapter 1: Starting the School Year Literacy Strong. The introduction of this chapter offers evidence on the importance of getting the school year off to a strong start by teaching literacy routines and setting expectations for students to become stronger readers and writers. Establishing benchmarks for future points of reference to gauge students' learning is addressed. Also, strategies are described on how to focus a literacy community on building rapport with students and empowering parents to help lay a solid literacy foundation for them. Ten comprehensive strategy lessons that are relevant for the beginning of the year form the core of Chapter 1. These lessons demonstrate the routines, expectations, assessments, and opportunities for collaboration as a literacy community.

Chapter 2: Beating the Midyear Blahs. The introduction of Chapter 2 highlights the importance of maintaining momentum at the halfway mark of the school year. This chapter focuses on progressing literacy learning through a time when learning can get stagnant. It offers ways for educators to maintain momentum and monitor expectations that were established at the beginning of the year. This season allows for strengthening the student–teacher–parent relationship because rapport has been built. The chapter also offers ways to continue evaluating literacy goals and benchmarks by monitoring progress in specific literacy components. Building on the lessons in Chapter 1, this chapter features the 10 comprehensive strategy lessons that are relevant in the middle of the year of their literacy journey. Each lesson spirals from the literacy enhancers (standards/literacy strategies) featured in Chapter 1.

Chapter 3: Ending the School Year Literacy Strong. The introduction highlights the importance of stepping up and finishing strong, not with a slow glide but with a strong climb, to give educators the endurance and ability to stay focused on learning through the end of the school year. This chapter provides practical ways to be intentional, with appropriate intensity levels that allow literacy goals to be achieved. Also, this chapter reminds educators of the influence that they have acquired as literacy leaders in their classrooms and how to use their influential stance to end the year literacy strong. Ten comprehensive strategy lessons that are relevant to skills acquired by the end of the year highlight the academic vocabulary from previous seasons of the school year found in Chapters 1 and 2.

Chapter 4: Stopping the Summer Slide. The introduction shares the importance of progressing literacy through the summer months. The focus is on continued reinforcement of the literacy strategies from the school year and on reading for pleasure, emphasizing summer reading lists, roles and responsibilities, and continued goal setting as students prepare for their next year's adventure. An extended summer break presents a unique challenge for educators and learners. The 10 comprehensive strategy lessons provide an independent and possibly tutorial learning environment. Each lesson continues to build off the key academic vocabulary within the standards featured in Chapters 1–3.

Literacy Strong All Year Long: Spiraling to Success

We designed the interactive literacy lessons in this book to support you, grades 3–5 educators, in guiding students throughout the seasons and cycles of the school year. When you put literacy at the heart of your classroom, students benefit from a strong foundation and joyfully engage in higher levels of reading and learning.

Lessons

For a quick look at all the lessons in this book, refer to Figure 1, which lists reading component strands, literacy strategy strands, and lesson titles. This chart will be beneficial as you plan throughout the school year.

FIGURE 1

40 Lessons at a Glance

Reading Component Strand	Literacy Strategy Strand	Chapter 1 Lesson	Chapter 2 Lesson	Chapter 3 Lesson	Chapter 4 Lesson
Word Study	Decoding	Vowel Teams, p. 13	Syllable Segmentation: Haiku, p. 92	Stressing over Syllables: Cinquain Poetry, p. 178	Syllable Scoop Search, p. 263
Vocabulary	Gaming with Words	Word Ladders, p. 21	Making and Writing Words, p. 101	Semantic Feature Analysis, p. 184	Family Wordo, p. 270
Vocabulary	Analyzing Words	Numerical Prefix Roots, p. 27	Functional Roots, p. 109	Land, Water, Stars Roots, p. 194	Finding Word Roots Throughout the Summer, p. 279
Vocabulary	Associating Words	Shades of Meaning and Colorful Words, p. 32	Like What? Similes and Metaphors Galore, p. 114	Wacky Wise Words, p. 199	Words and Their Crazy Relatives, p. 286
Fluency	Phrasing, Pacing, Expressing	Keep a Poem in Your Pocket and a Song in Your Heart, p. 42	Honoring President John F. Kennedy Through Oratory, p. 124	Readers Theatre: Make Text Come Alive, p. 210	Celebrating USA on Independence Day, p. 298
Comprehension	Previewing	Sneak Preview 1-2-3, p. 49	Informational Text Feature Tour!, p. 129	Text Trip Maps, p. 216	Preview Power, p. 309
Comprehension	Inferring and Drawing Conclusions	Making Predictions, p. 58	A Text with a View: Imagery with Reading, p. 137	Tableaux: Making Text Come to Life, p. 225	Summer Book Buddies, p. 318
Comprehension	Questioning for Close Reading	Top 5 Interrogative *W* Words for Speculative Talk, p. 64	Inference Dance Moves: Reading Between the Lines, p. 143	ARE You Ready to Rumble? Anticipating, Reacting, and Evaluating, p. 231	Question Generator, p. 324
Comprehension	Determining Importance and Summarizing, p. 69	Sifting What Matters: Digging Up Details, p. 69	Recount Recipe, p. 151	Getting the Gist: Circling Around the Main Idea, p. 239	Movie Message Madness, p. 330
Comprehension	Motivating Readers	Motivation with Book Logs, p. 75	Take Off and Partner Talk Bookmarks, p. 159	Ready, Set Goals, Read!, p. 245	Splash into Summer Reading!, p. 337

~1

Starting the School Year Literacy Strong

Children must be taught how to think, not what to think.
—Margaret Mead

Once you learn to read, you will be forever free.
—Frederick Douglass

What is your favorite sign or symbol that signals the start of school? Maybe it is the aroma of freshly sharpened pencils waiting to draft creative adventures and record student inquiries into exciting informational topics. Perhaps you love the stacks of new books that your class will break in as they get lost in the magic of reading and learning. As you pause to look at your classroom before the students enter, how do you feel? Even veteran teachers get butterflies preparing to meet their learners. Fortunately, the beginning of the school year invites students and teachers alike to start fresh and literacy strong!

Students and teachers in the intermediate grades need to set learning goals and address them using

- Strategies in comprehension, vocabulary, and fluency that allow access to more challenging texts (both fiction and informational).
- Strategies to more deeply comprehend the quantity and rigor of informational texts.
- Strategies to understand the difference between facts and opinions, find text evidence to support ideas, and write clearly to defend positions.

Success in the intermediate grades involves finding ways for students to take on the responsibility for "heavy lifting" in literacy learning with the expert support of the teacher. Fortunately, students in intermediate grades really enjoy working and talking with one another! Collaborative learning supports individual learning and helps students to learn social skills necessary for learning and employment. Small, flexible group instruction led by the teacher supports learning for all students, especially English language learners (ELLs) and struggling readers.

In addition to creating an inviting learning environment for students at the start of school, classroom management experts Harry Wong and Rosemary Wong (2009) advise explicitly teaching the behaviors that you expect from your students. From the moment the students step in the door, the Wongs suggest having students practice basic routines, such as lining up, visiting the classroom library, and turning in complete work.

Let's peek into classrooms in which teachers are working to help ensure students' success.

Literacy-Strong Classroom Scenarios

What does a literacy-strong intermediate grade classroom look like at the beginning of the year? Some words that come to mind are *student-centered, collaborative, interesting, rigorous,* and *joyful.* Here are some classroom stories for inspiration for the first few weeks of school that feature lessons from this chapter.

Motivation: The Class Book Club

Miss Fong leads her 4th graders in a discussion about the formal and informal clubs and organizations they are involved in, including scouts, churches, sports, and even a homespun neighborhood club that meets in a fort. Miss Fong invites her students to join the Room 17 Book Club and asks what they think membership will entail. Students suggest that everyone will belong to the club and will read the same books, talk about the books, and eat snacks related to the books. Miss Fong agrees and shares that the class will record information about the books that they read together and those she reads aloud to them. She explains that she will read aloud some classic 5th grade books, informational texts, and even fabulous picture books. Miss Fong begins reading *Harriet the Spy* by Louise Fitzhugh (because it was her favorite book as a 10-year-old). Students are spellbound and beg for more when the 15-minute read-aloud is over and are excited about watching the movie based on the book. Miss Fong asks students to share with partners what happened so far and what they think Harriet will do next. They talk about their favorite parts and record the title in their reading logs. Students study the rating system given on the log and explain to their partners how they rate the book based on their first impression. They list a "because" reason for their thinking and use the discussion frame "So far I give the book a _____ because_____." Later in the week students will fill out logs with books they are reading and rate them as well. The year is off to a reading start!

Comprehension: Sneak Preview 1-2-3

Students in Mrs. Proctor's 3rd grade take out their *Sneak Preview 1-2-3* bookmarks to use in reading the informational text *Animal Architects* by Timothy Bradley (2012). She has conducted a variety of lessons to guide students through the use of the bookmark as they make predictions. Students now know that bland, simplistic predictions such as "This is about animals that build," are not acceptable. Predictions need to be based on clues from the text and a deeper preview. The students work in pairs to follow the steps to previewing the text as outlined on the bookmark. First, they study the front and back covers to make predictions about what they will learn using the title, author, cover art, and back cover information. Next, they carefully flip through the book to study chapter titles, visuals, and text features to make deeper predictions. Lastly, students try a "puzzle, purpose, and point of view" preview of the text where they think about the author's purpose and point of view. Making logical predictions means spending time with purposeful text walks and talking with others. The students dive into the reading ready to learn!

Vocabulary: Shades of Meaning and Colorful Words

Mr. Jimenez's 5th grade students tap their toes and sway to the upbeat song "Happy" by Pharrell Williams as they listen for words that express emotion. Partners come up with synonyms for the word *happy* and add them to the class chart, which already includes the words *cheerful, elated,* and *excited*. Mr. Jimenez then invites a group of eight students to the front of the room to choose some of the words from the chart and stand in order of intensity from least to most happy. Students discuss whether they agree or disagree with the order. Students record the words in their literacy notebooks and sketch faces to illustrate each emotion. This initial lesson sparks interest in shades of meaning for emotions, and the class continues studying, discussing, and recording shades of meaning for the gamut of emotions from angry to frightened and sad. Mr. Jimenez's class begins building excitement around "word consciousness," which good readers need to delve deeply into complex texts.

Addressing Beginning-of-the-Year Challenges

Amid the excitement of the new school year, educators face many competing challenges. Three specific tasks that teachers need to tackle almost simultaneously are (1) getting to know students and parents to connect with them individually and as a community, (2) gathering and understanding baseline assessment information for each student, and (3) establishing classroom management procedures and routines. In this section are some suggestions for facing these challenges head-on to set the stage for learning.

Questions Teachers Ask to Address Beginning-of-the-Year Challenges

- What are the most essential literacy routines that I need to begin in my classroom?
- What are some ways to successfully train students in literacy routines?
- How do I keep track of student progress?
- How can I actively engage students in lessons?
- How can I establish a rapport with my students and their parents?
- How can I build a sense of community in my comprehensive literacy classroom?

Must-Haves for Starting Literacy Strong

1. Spark the Love of Reading

Set the stage for students to love reading by sharing some of your favorite childhood books. Tell why each of the books made your favorites list and be sure to include fiction, informational texts, and picture books. Ask students to record their list of all-time favorites in a literacy journal or notebook or in a folder for reading logs. Tell students they will be exposed to many great books that will inspire them to enjoy reading even more than they already do. Consider reading aloud a picture book such as Patricia Polacco's *Thank You, Mr. Falker* (1998), the story of how a teacher inspired the author when she was a young struggling reader.

2. Hold Day One Reading and Compliment Conferences

Principal and former 5th grade teacher Kathy Langham suggests inviting students into the classroom library to select a book on "day one" or the first day of school! Then circulate as each student whisper reads to you while you jot down informal notes about reading level, book choice, and interests, as well as any comprehension and fluency strategies. Talk to the students individually, briefly asking a few questions about what they read, allowing a few days to meet with all students. Mrs. Langham shares that this is a great way to begin to establish a relationship with your students and to begin to know them as readers.

Popular author and literacy consultant Jennifer Serravallo also suggests meeting individually with students early to discuss the books they've selected in what she calls 90-second compliment conferences. She suggests spending the first 30–45 seconds asking students a few questions and listening to them read aloud. If the students filled in their responses on sticky notes, glance at those as well. Then during the next 30 seconds give the students compliments about what they are doing well as readers. Only compliments and positive feedback—no instruction or corrections! Use statements like "I saw you responding to every page in some way by asking a question or making a connection. Doing that will help you stay engaged with any book that you read." Or "I see that you are jotting down some of the words you don't know. That means you are noticing where you may need to talk to others. That is a great strategy to use with any book." See video clips on Ms. Serravallo's blog that show her conducting 90-second compliment conferences (www.jenniferserravallo .com/blog/reading-teacher-priority-one-students-readers/).

3. Model Procedures and Literacy Routines for a Well-Run Classroom

At the start of school, model every positive behavior that you want from your students. They also need to know what is expected of them during classroom literacy routines such as procedures for read-alouds, independent reading, workstations, writers' workshop, and partner reading. Routines should be explained, modeled, and guided with some practice. Although it may take longer to roll out the necessary steps by modeling and discussing each one, the payoff is that students internalize and use the procedure (McEwan-Adkins, 2012). Spend about 10 minutes each day of the first few weeks of school modeling how to participate in literacy routines (Reutzel & Clark, 2011). If you roll out each routine in this way, students will understand what is expected of them. To establish a procedure in your classroom, follow these steps:

- Discuss and explain why the procedure is important.
- Demonstrate by role-playing how to perform the procedure properly.
- Invite a student to act out the steps of the procedure in front of the class.
- Guide as the class practices.
- Record the procedure (e.g., for listening to read-alouds or talking with partners) on a chart.
- Refer and return to the chart often to discuss and reflect on how well the class is following the steps.

4. Make Read-Alouds Interactive

Use a variety of engagement strategies during read-alouds to actively involve students and improve their reading comprehension.

- *Turn and talk:* Students turn to a partner and take turns responding throughout the read-aloud. To ensure success, provide a sentence stem, such as "My favorite part was _____ because _____," or "I think _____ will happen next because _____," or "I wonder why the character _____." Encourage students to use text evidence in their responses.

- *Quick jot:* Pause once or twice during a read-aloud for students to quickly write down their thoughts such as a favorite part, wondering, or other response to the book. Ask students to share their responses with their table teams. Read the responses for quick informal assessments, especially at the beginning of the year as you get to know students.

- *Act up:* Pause often and encourage students to use gestures and act out various parts of the reading and vocabulary words.

- *Sketch it:* Provide slates or strips of paper and pause during read-alouds to invite students to sketch what has happened so far in the reading or something that they learned from the text. Encourage students to share their responses with partners and the class.

5. Grow Independent Readers

Provide a classroom environment that encourages independent reading at various times throughout the day—using a variety of texts. Model how to read independently and build stamina so students can eventually read silently up to 45 minutes to an hour. Encourage students to read at least 30 minutes at home as well. Donalyn Miller (2009), author of *The Book Whisperer: Awakening the Inner Reader in Every Child,* suggests starting the day with independent reading for 5 to 10 minutes instead of other warm-up activities. This quiet reading time encourages students to enjoy reading and sets the tone for learning for the day. Use anchor charts as visual tools where teachers and students record the most essential information on a chart for display. Students then refer to the anchor charts as they self-monitor what they are learning and apply it independently. Conference often with students to encourage deeper comprehension. Create a simple interest inventory with your class. Ask students to create a list of questions and boxes to check to encourage wide reading. Use the inventories as students set new reading goals and when conferring with students to encourage them to read. Here is an example of a class interest inventory you can use with your students:

- What do you like to do for a hobby?
- What kinds of books do you like to read?
- What genres do you like to read? mysteries ___ fantasy ___ adventure ___ realistic fiction ___ funny books ___ nonfiction ___ history ___ historical fiction ___ how-to books ___ other ___

- Which topics are you interested in or do you want to learn about? sports ___ which sports? _____ drama ___ dance ___ community service (environment, people, animals) ___ wild animals ___ marine life ___ the ocean ___ pets ___ space ___ history ___ volcanoes ___ natural disasters ___ video games ___ travel ___ new places (name them) _____ pet or babysitting ___ plants ___

6. Create an Inviting Classroom Library

Set apart an inviting classroom library space with at least 10 books per student or 200 to 300 books (Reutzel & Fawson, 2002). Organize books in baskets or tubs and clearly label your classroom reading materials by genre, authors, themes, and topics that interest the age group you teach. Possibly provide comfortable bean bag chairs or crates with padding on top. Display some books with the covers facing out in stands or on shelves, including a mix of narrative and informational texts. Encourage students to keep track of their reading with reading logs, and model by recording class read-alouds on a class reading log (see Chapter 1, Lesson 10).

7. Build Literacy and Community with Poetry Routines

Chanting poetry together is a great way to build a sense of community at the beginning of the year and all year long. Students enjoy the rhythm, rhyme, and repetition that songs, poems, and cheers or chants offer. Try using a "poem a week" (Oczkus, 2012) as a classroom routine and learning opportunity. Read it every day together, display it for all to see, and make copies for students to put in a poetry notebook. For the first reading, read the poem aloud, and during subsequent readings, conduct shared readings using various formats (Oczkus & Rasinski, 2015) such as

- Echo reading: The teacher reads a line and students repeat it.
- Close reading: The teacher reads aloud and students follow along. As the teacher leaves out select words or phrases the students chime in to supply them.
- Alternate lines or stanzas: The teacher reads a line or stanza aloud and the class reads the next one aloud. Or groups of students read a designated stanza.
- Silly voices: The class reads the poem together using a whisper or silly voice such as mouse voice, monster voice, robot voice, or ghost voice.
- Partner reading: Student pairs work together to take turns reading lines or stanzas.

On subsequent days reread the poem and ask students to work in pairs to reread it. Students may illustrate their poems and select words to learn and highlight patterns they notice. At the end of the week, invite teams to perform their poetry (Oczkus, 2012; Oczkus & Rasinski, 2015).

8. Display Wacky Word Walls

Students need to learn 3,000 words per year! That's a ton of word learning! Luckily, wide reading supplies students with many opportunities to learn the words they need. However, we also know that students need to study words and develop "word consciousness."

Word walls are a great way to provide students with handy reference tools for both reading and writing. Word walls are simply groups of words selected to display in the classroom—posted on a bulletin board or chart paper or hung from the ceiling. Each category of words warrants its own wall or area. For example, the shades of meaning word wall might have sets of words for emotions. Students also may record the words in their literacy notebooks. Many of the lessons in this book provide you with a source of words to create word walls. Here are a few examples of words you can use to build word walls:

- High-frequency words
- Commonly misspelled words
- Content area words for science or social studies
- Latin and Greek root words (see Chapter 1, Lesson 3)
- Shades of meaning words (see Chapter 1, Lesson 4)
- Synonyms, antonyms, homographs (see Chapter 4, Lesson 4)

Encourage students to use the word walls as reference tools when they read and write. Model often how to do so. Play simple games with the word walls by asking students to work in pairs or teams to take turns providing definitions, acting out the words, and providing synonyms or antonyms while others match with the correct words. Students also can play a form of bingo called "Wordo" (See Chapter 4, Lesson 2) by choosing nine words from the wall to put into a blank Wordo card and covering the words with markers as each word is read by the teacher or leader.

9. Use Literacy Notebooks

Intermediate students grow their comprehension and deepen understanding of texts when they have the opportunity to write in response to reading. At the beginning of the year, model and guide students as they learn to record their thinking during and after reading. One option is to use notebooks with sturdy covers that students can personalize and decorate. Throughout the lessons in this book you will find suggestions for students to write in their literacy notebooks. Students may want to add sketches, sticky notes from their reading, copies of some of the reproducible images in this text folded and glued in, as well as lists of words from the word wall. The more "interactive" and colorful the notebook is the better! Encourage students to write and work neatly to help make their literacy notebooks become personal reflection and reference tools that they can be proud of. When you collect them to comment or grade, consider using sticky notes for your comments rather than writing directly on the notebooks.

10. Set Up Literacy Stations or Centers

The lessons in this book offer many suggestions for literacy stations or centers. You might set up areas of the room to best serve these functions: word work, library, literature circle, writing, and computer lab. Many activities in this book can fit into the "Daily Five" (Boushey & Moser, 2014), a management system divided into five categories: reading to self, reading to someone, listening to reading, working with words, and writing. All content and routines must be modeled and scaffolded so that students can work effectively and independently at the literacy stations or centers. A gradual release of independence increases academic success and gives students opportunities to be more responsible for their learning, which in turn creates self-reliant learners.

11. Differentiate Instruction for Intermediate Grades

Differentiating instruction in the intermediate grades requires finding ways to scaffold instruction to meet the needs of all students. By actively engaging students in movement, songs, games, and a wide variety of texts, you are providing opportunities for different types of learners. Collaborative learning and meeting with students in small, flexible groups are two other critical means of differentiating instruction in your classroom.

Collaborative Learning for Deeper Understanding

Students in intermediate grades enjoy talking and working together so collaborative learning is natural and enjoyable for them. Research supports cooperative learning and serves as a way for students to improve their comprehension. When students engage in conversations with one another about their reading, their comprehension deepens (Fisher & Frey, 2008). Provide opportunities for students to work in a variety of collaborative structures including partners, trios, and table teams.

Facilitating Small-Group Instruction

Another way to provide differentiation is to meet with small, flexible groups. After students complete any assignment in this book, "pile sort" (Oczkus, 2012) the papers into groups of "got it," "sort of got it," and "need help." Then meet with students to provide the assistance they need to learn the skill or strategy. Small, guided reading groups are not just for primary grades when students are first learning to read; reading with upper elementary grades is also important. Small teacher-led guided reading groups are a great way to use differentiated complex reading materials to guide and elevate the level of critical thinking and discussion. Groups can be formed by reading levels, strategy use, or interests. Some groups meet with the teacher once or twice weekly, while struggling readers and ELLs may need to meet twice weekly or more. Intermediate students benefit from the extra feedback, guided practice, and rich discussions that the teacher facilitates during small-group instruction. Any lesson in this book can be conducted in a small-group format.

12. Establish Informal and Formative Assessment Procedures

These days, we teach in an assessment-crazed world. The pressure to measure student performance is everywhere. Your school district likely requires tools such as beginning-of-year baseline assessments; ongoing assessments; and formal and informal district, state, and national tests. Planning assessment procedures is part of establishing purposeful literacy routines toward successful instruction. Determine what type of assessment is best for your classroom needs. Create a schedule to carve out time early in the beginning of the school year to assess, and establish a record-keeping system (e.g., assessment folder, digital file, composition notebook). Throughout the year, you'll also want to keep track of and monitor your students' progress as they grow and learn. The information you gain with these informal assessments is helpful in planning your instruction. One method for informal assessments is quick clipboard cruising. By taking quick notes during individual conferences, you can measure how students are doing. Take a quick, on-the-spot running record (Clay, 2000) by having the student read aloud while you note the words the student substitutes. Jot down the word in the book and the word the child substitutes, such as if the text reads *foe* and the child says *for*. Note whether the substitutions make sense or not. Record self-corrections as well. Look for patterns and overall comprehension.

Make note of the following details when talking to students about the books they are reading (Routman, 2003):

- What are you reading?
- Why did you pick up this book?
- Who are the main characters? (fiction)
- What is the problem? (fiction)
- What are your favorite parts and why?
- What is interesting, and why? (nonfiction)
- What do you want to learn? What are you learning? (nonfiction)

13. Make Parents Partners from the Start

Instead of waiting until a problem arises, call or e-mail parents to say hello in the beginning weeks of the school year. Share one compliment about their child that you can offer based on what you've seen so far. Ask the parents to share something positive about their child that you should know. Set up a video conference call for busy parents who can't make it for a classroom conference. You can also set up a digital portfolio and send periodic video feeds of students learning in action. Here is a list of popular read-aloud books that parents can use to motivate their child to read:

- *That Book Woman* by Heather Henson
- *Amber on the Mountain* by Tony Johnston
- *The Bee Tree* by Patricia Polacco
- *More Than Anything Else* by Marie Bradley
- *How to Read a Book* by Kate Messner

14. Beginning-of-the-Year Word Ladder

	Start with the contraction for "Let us"
Let's	Change one letter to make the opposite of more.
Less	Change one letter to make a word that is the opposite of tidy.
Mess	Change one letter to make a small green plant that lives in damp areas.
Moss	Change one letter to make a word that means to lightly throw something.
Toss	Change one letter to make several small children.
Tots	Take away one letter to make one small child.
Tot	Add one letter to make a word that means to run at a moderate pace.
Trot	Take away the vowel and replace with two vowels to make what children like to get on Halloween.
Treat	Change the last letter to make the part of a shoe or tire that touches the ground.
Tread	Take away one letter to make a word that describes what we want to do this year.
Read	Let's read!

Overview of Chapter 1 Lessons

Lesson 1. Word Study: Decoding—Vowel Teams

Lesson 2. Vocabulary: Gaming with Words—Word Ladders

Lesson 3. Vocabulary: Analyzing Words—Numerical Prefix Roots

Lesson 4. Vocabulary: Associating Words—Shades of Meaning and Colorful Words

Lesson 5. Fluency: Phrasing, Pacing, Expressing—Keep a Poem in Your Pocket and a Song in Your Heart

Lesson 6. Comprehension: Previewing—Sneak Preview 1-2-3

Lesson 7. Comprehension: Inferring and Drawing Conclusions—Making Predictions

Lesson 8. Comprehension: Questioning for Close Reading—Top Five Interrogative *W* Words for Speculative Talk

Lesson 9. Comprehension: Determining Importance and Summarizing—Sifting What Matters: Digging Up Details

Lesson 10. Comprehension: Motivating Readers—Motivation with Book Logs

LESSON 1. WORD STUDY: DECODING

Title **VOWEL TEAMS**

Trailer Teamwork makes the dream work! Unity is key to being on a winning team. Working together side by side is a vital trait. Letters and sounds can act as teams working toward a seamless flow of language. Students practice sorting and gliding with vowel digraphs and diphthongs!

Literacy Enhancer Word Study: Decoding—Vowel Digraph and Diphthongs

Key Academic Vocabulary

Decoding: The process of translating a printed word into its oral representation. In word decoding, readers use a variety of strategies including phonics (sound-symbol relationships), structural analysis (prefix, base word, suffix), and context.

Diphthong: A unit of sound gliding the vowel sound by the combination of a vowel digraph allowing the tongue to move and change

Vowel Digraph: A pair of vowel letters coming together to form a vowel team representing one sound

Learning Objectives

- Examine grade-level phonics and word analysis skills in decoding words.
- Apply combined knowledge of letter-sound correspondences for vowel digraphs.
- Identify spelling-sound correspondences for additional ambiguous vowel teams.

Essential Questions

- What strategies can I use to help me decode unknown words in my reading?
- How can I use vowel digraph patterns to determine the most likely correct spelling of a word?

STEP 1: PREPARATION

Organize Materials

- *Vowel Digraph Riddles* reproducible
- *"'Twas the Night Before School Starts"* reproducible
- *Vowel Digraph and Diphthong Sorting Cards* reproducible
- Multimodal text sets with samples of vowel digraphs
- Handheld mirrors (optional)

- Supplies to create a class Anchor Chart (e.g., chart paper, markers)
- Word Journals or Writing Notebooks

STEP 2: INITIATION

Teamwork Makes the Dream Work

Ask students to name different types of teams (e.g., sports: football, soccer; organizational: community, schools, political). Discuss the characteristics of what makes a good team. Share how teachers and parents act as a team. Highlight that a good team always works together as one unit. Read the poem "'Twas the Night Before School Starts" and have students listen for qualities of teamwork (i.e., working together, partnership, communication, grit, setting goals, meeting needs, winning, succeeding).

STEP 3: DEMONSTRATION

Vowel Teamwork

1. Revisit part of the poem, emphasizing the bold words as you read aloud. *Without this partnership victory would* **abstain**/ *For when the* **brain** *is nurtured/ there is much to* **gain!** Say the three words with the same *ai* vowel digraph (e.g., *abstain, brain, gain*). Use a handheld mirror to isolate the *ai* vowel digraph sound in each word. In addition, hold the outside of the mouth when isolating the vowel digraph. Describe the position of your mouth for that particular *ai* digraph (e.g., mouth is in one position slightly opened, tongue flat, some teeth showing, and hand does not move). Note that although the *ai* has two vowels, it only makes one sound as these letters form a vowel team.

2. Examine another section of the poem *'Twas the night before school starts, When all through the* **town**/ *The parents were smiling 'cause the children didn't* **frown**! Say the two words with the same *ow* vowel digraph sounds. Describe the position of your mouth for this particular digraph (e.g., mouth begins open slightly, tongue starts flat but moves, no teeth showing, hand moves when holding the cheeks).

3. Note that although the *ow* has two vowel letters, the mouth seems to glide and change position as the lips pucker more towards the end of the pronunciation of the vowel digraph *ow*. Explain how this sound is a diphthong, making a more complicated sound together as the mouth moves around to make the sound.

4. Compare the ambiguous vowel *ow* sound in "town" to the *ow* sound in "flow." These both have the *ow* vowel digraph pattern; however, they have a different

sound pattern within the word (i.e., the *ow* in "t*ow*n" has a gliding movement with the mouth, making it a diphthong).

5. Create an anchor chart for the particular vowel digraphs you are studying, noting the position of the mouth for each digraph. Use the Vowel Digraph and Diphthong Sorting Cards reproducible or objects that have the digraph sounds as anchor images for each digraph team. Students can use these sorting cards as category headings to identify various digraph and diphthong patterns within words and discuss from the word lists how these words relate phonically.

6. Add vowel digraph words to an interactive word wall list.

STEP 4: COLLABORATION

Have partners or teams reread the class poem and continue to find words that have vowel digraphs and demonstrate the sound that each digraph makes. Engage in conversational coaching by asking and answering the following questions:

- What vowel digraph is in the word ___?
- What other words have the same vowel digraph sound as the word ___?
- How do you position your mouth for the digraph in the word ___? Is it a diphthong? Why or why not?

STEP 5: APPLICATION

Have your students work alone or in groups to answer the vowel digraph riddles (see pp. 17–18). Students can sort the vowel digraph words to correspond with the vowel digraph teams and record their results for review as they sort the vowel digraphs for referencing. Remind them to use the class vowel digraph anchor charts as they reflect on the characteristics of each vowel digraph and the positioning of their mouth for the various sounds.

STEP 6: REFLECTION

Oral or Written Response

Have students keep word journals in which they record and categorize the vowel digraph words from the text they are reading. Students also can select three words with the same vowel digraph and use them in composing sentences, writing poetry, or creating their own riddles.

ADAPTATION AND EXTENSION

- Students can take words from the vowel digraph word list to create a poem or an acrostic. For example, selecting the word *flow*:

  Friends who work together
  Likely have more success
  Over those who don't
  When trying to keep the flow going!

- Display a collection of books featuring an array of vowel digraphs:
  - *Charlie Cooks Favorite Books* by Julia Donaldson and Axel Scheffler
  - *40 Wonderful Blend & Digraph Poems* by Dana Haddad and Shelley Grant
  - *Cloudy with a Chance of Meatballs* by Judi Barrett

- *English Language Learner Suggestion:* Set up a game-based technology station using programs (e.g., www.spellingcity.com) that have visual support, generated word lists, automated testing and grading to track students' progress, and generated student reports for monitoring goals while applying word analysis skills.
- *Struggling Reader Suggestion:* Apply intervention spelling strategies from *Words Their Way: Word Sorts for Within Word Pattern Spellers* by Marcia Invernizzi, Francine Johnston, Donald R. Bear, and Shane Templeton; or *Words Their Way with Struggling Readers: Word Study for Reading, Vocabulary, and Spelling Instruction, Grades 4–12* by Kevin Flanagan, Latisha Hayes, Shane Templeton, Donald B. Bear, Marcia Invernizzi, and Francine Johnston.

EVALUATION

"I can . . ." Statements

- I can use vowel digraph patterns to determine the most likely correct spelling of a word.
- I can identify the vowel digraph in a word.
- I can produce the corresponding sound for the vowel team in a word.

Behavior Indicators

- Decodes vowel digraphs in words and generates vowel team words.
- Isolates, identifies, and sorts vowel digraphs while distinguishing the positions of the mouth, lips, jaw, and tongue to correspond with the appropriate sounds.

Vowel Digraph Riddles

Here is a completed example of a vowel digraph riddle:

> I am the opposite of lost.
> I help things be discovered.
>
> Who am I? *found*

These individual riddles derived from "'Twas the Night Before School Starts" can be framed to make vowel digraph riddle cards. See below for answers to the riddles.

> I am the opposite of smile.
> I am an expression for being sad.
>
> Who am I? _____

> I am an outward sign of a good feeling.
> I show signs of excitement.
>
> Who am I? _____

> I am associated with quantity.
> I like overflow.
>
> Who am I? _____

> I am the opposite of indulge.
> I deliberately refrain from things.
>
> Who am I? _____

> I am a thought or image in one's mind.
> I can be a cherished desire.
>
> What am I? _____

> I am the opposite of decrease.
> I love to get something.
>
> What am I? _____

> I love to come together with others.
> I work toward a common goal.
>
> Who am I? _____

Answers for riddles: frown, aglow, abound, abstain, dream, gain, team

'Twas the Night Before School Starts

Twas the night before school starts

When all through the town,

The parents were smiling

Cause the children didn't frown!

This joy was abound

Based on a winning team,

As parents and teachers worked

Together…What a dream!

Good communication was needed

To keep the flow,

As steadfast and grit

We kept learning all aglow.

Without this partnership

Victory would abstain,

For when the brain is nurtured,

There is much to gain!

Together they work

To meet the students' needs

Setting these goals

Is the best way to succeed!

Vowel Digraph and Diphthong Sorting Cards

Students can use these cards as category headings to identify various digraph and diphthong patterns and sort other words or make lists of words.

Directly relating to demonstration poem:

ow	ea
frown	team

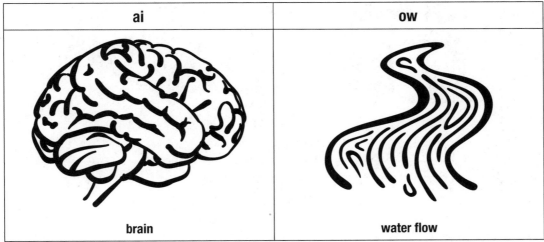

ai	ow
brain	water flow

continued

Other ideas for sorting cards:

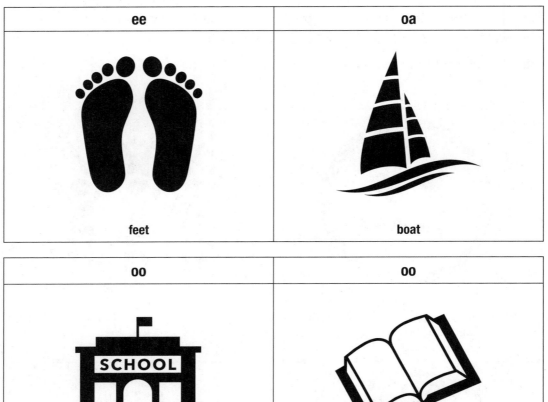

ee	oa
feet	boat

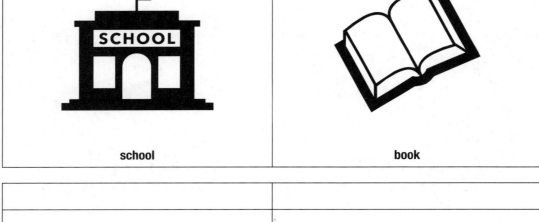

oo	oo
school	book

LESSON 2. VOCABULARY: GAMING WITH WORDS

Title WORD LADDERS

Trailer Think of all the games we play as adults when we get together with family and friends—Scrabble, Boggle, Balderdash, Taboo, Wheel of Fortune, and crossword puzzles. Isn't it interesting that so many of them are word games? If adults love playing games that are word-centric, wouldn't students? We think the answer is *yes!* In the process of playing with words, we actually increase our knowledge of them. We learn how words are pronounced and spelled, we learn new words and what they mean, we learn new meanings to words we already know, and we learn how to use the words in our daily language. We want to create an environment in our classrooms in which word study is fun and games. Word ladders are a simple method for helping intermediate grade students learn and explore words and word meanings.

Literacy Enhancer Word Study and Vocabulary—Analyzing Words & Spelling

Key Academic Vocabulary

Adjective: A word or phrase used to describe a noun

Noun: A word used to identify any of a class of people, places, or things

Spelling: The process of writing or naming the letters of a word

Syllables: Word that contains only one vowel sound; words can be made of one or more syllables

Verb: A word used to describe an action

Vocabulary: Words or phrases and the meanings they represent; collectively, they make up a language

Word Ladder: A game-like activity where one word is transformed into another by adding, subtracting, or changing one or more letters

Word Sort: A process used to categorize words according to features (*closed:* categories are provided and words are matched to them; *open:* categories are determined by the students as they discern the common features of the word groups)

Learning Objectives

- Increase students' corpus of words they know (vocabulary).
- Increase students' enjoyment in exploring words.
- Explore various features of words including multiple meanings, sound-symbols, and grammatical categories.

Essential Questions

- What can happen when a few letters in a word are added, subtracted, or changed?
- How do words change in meaning? How do they change in pronunciation?
- What are ways that a collection of words can be sorted?
- How can a set of words be integrated into a coherent sentence or text?

STEP 1: PREPARATION

Organize Materials

Use the *Word Ladder* reproducible (Figure 1.2) or create a word ladder that is appropriate for your students. The first and last words on the ladder should be related.

STEP 2: INITIATION

Stepping into New Words

Ask students to name any word games that they have played with their family or friends. Make a list of these games on a chart.

Now, put these words on display: chart, near, partner, capture, cat. Ask students to think of new words they could make by taking away, adding, or changing one or more letters (i.e., chart = chat; near = neat; partner = part, art; cat = cap, scat) in each word. Tell the students that they can use a word ladder to play a similar word game and make new words.

Provide each student with a *Word Ladder* reproducible that has the word *student* at the bottom of the ladder. Explain to the students that you will be working your way up the ladder by manipulating a few letters at a time, while also providing clues to the new words. We've given you an example of a word ladder that begins with *student* and ends with *pupil* that you can use at the beginning of the school year. See Figure 1.2 for a word ladder reproducible that you can customize.

Word Ladder

Pupil

Pup	Add two letters to make a word for "student"
Pun	Change one letter
Sun	Change one letter
Sunk	Take away one letter
Spunk	Take away one letter
Stunk	Change one letter
Stunt	Change one letter
Student	Take away two letters

FIGURE 1.2
Word Ladder Reproducible

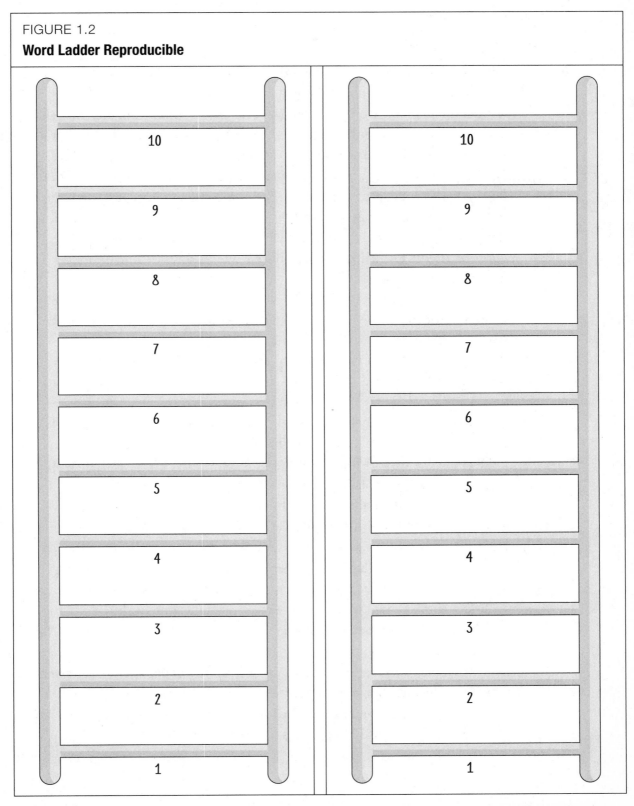

STEP 3: DEMONSTRATION

New Rung, New Word

1. Create a display version of the word ladder you will be doing so that students can see the words you are making.

2. Model the first new word *stunt* on the word ladder, indicating the letter change and providing the meaning clue you have devised for the new word. Think aloud the process you go through to come to the new word in the ladder.

3. Continue through the remaining words in the word ladder, providing the letter change and meaning clues. Before saying each new word, ask students if they know what the new word might be. Call on individual students for their hypotheses. When the correct word has been called, write it on the appropriate rung of the ladder and have students do the same on their own reproducible sheets.

4. When you come to the final word in the word ladder, point out that it is related to the first word in the ladder. Call on students to predict what the word might be.

5. When the word ladder is complete, display the words you have made with students on a word wall (chart) and discuss with students the meaning of the words and how they are constructed or spelled.

6. Look for ways to use the words in your oral and written interactions with students. In the days following the initial word ladder, create some new word ladders of your own or find them in published sources (e.g., search "word ladders" at www.scholastic.com).

7. Follow the same format in steps 1 through 4 above. As you make your own word ladders, share with students the process you go through to make them. Here are a few hints that we have found helpful:
    a. Find two words that go together in some way (e.g., *autumn* to *winter*).
    b. As you go from *autumn* to *winter*, try to winnow the longer word down to a shorter word. For example, *autumn* > Take away *u* and *m* and then rearrange the letters to make *tuna* > Change a letter to make *tuba* > Take away one letter to make *tub*.
    c. Then begin to expand to longer words until you get to your final word. From *tub*, rearrange the letters to make *but* > Change a letter to make *bit* > Change a letter to make *bin* > Change a letter to make *win* > Add a letter to make *wine* > Add two letters to make *winter*!

STEP 4: COLLABORATION

Word Sorting

Read and review the words from the word wall with students. In groups of two or three, have students find ways to sort or group the words from the word wall. Word sorts might be completed by putting the words in alphabetic order or sorting by grammatical category (nouns versus not nouns), spelling structure (words that contain a consonant blend versus words that don't), or meaning (words that have a positive connotation versus words that have a negative connotation). Students will have to explain their rationale for sorting in a specific category.

- When students have created their word sorts, they can share them with the class and have the whole class work together on a few of the word sorts. Engage in conversational coaching by asking and answering the following questions:
  - What can happen when a few letters in a word are added, subtracted, or changed?
  - How do the words change in meaning?
  - How do they change in pronunciation?
  - What are ways that a collection of words can be sorted?

STEP 5: APPLICATION

Personalized Word Ladders

Students can work alone or in groups to create their own word ladders using the procedures described above. After students have made their own word ladders, you can schedule them to present their results to other members of the class.

STEP 6: REFLECTION

Oral or Written Response

Have students keep word journals in which they record the words from each word ladder they complete. For example, if your students keep a daily journal, you could ask them to list two or more words from the daily word wall in their journal entry. In addition, ask students to write what they have learned from doing each word ladder. Their responses may range from learning new words to discovering that words often have words within them, that manipulating one or two letters can change a word into another word, or that word study can be fun.

ADAPTATION AND EXTENSION

- *Creating Word Ladders for Primary Grade Buddies:* Word ladders can also be easier to make with short words (*dog* to *cat*). Upper elementary grade students can be challenged to make easier word ladders for students in the primary grades where word length is generally shorter.
- *Three Target Word Challenge:* Challenge students to make word ladders that contain three target words (e.g., *read, write, math*). Students who take on the challenge can share the strategies they used to develop their word ladders.
- *English Language Learner Suggestion:* When doing a word ladder as a group, provide students with additional information about the meaning and use of the words they make.
- *Struggling Reader Suggestion: Random Word Choice Ladders:* If students experience difficulty with creating word ladders, you can make the activity easier by creating word ladders in which the first and last words *do not* relate to each other. The word ladder task is much easier if the developer of the ladder does not have to reach a targeted word.

EVALUATION

"I can . . ." Statements

- I can read the words we made in our word ladder.
- I can understand what the words in the word ladder mean.
- I can use the words in the word ladder in my own speech and writing.
- I can change (manipulate) one or two letters in a word to make a new word.
- I can see words and word patterns in other words and this helps me read and understand words.
- I can have fun playing with words with my classmates.

Behavior Indicators

- Creates and spells new words.
- Decodes (sounds out) words.
- Manipulates words by adding, subtracting, or rearranging individual letters.
- Increases vocabulary through exploration of various features of words including multiple meanings, sound-symbol, and grammatical category.

LESSON 3. VOCABULARY: ANALYZING WORDS—LATIN AND GREEK

Title **NUMERICAL PREFIX ROOTS** (*uni-, bi-, tri-, quad-/quar-*)

Trailer Did you know that most of the longer words in English, as well as most of the academic words, are derived from Latin and Greek word roots? Knowing Latin and Greek word roots can help with decoding, spelling, and knowing the meaning of many English words. Knowledge of one Latin or Greek word root can help with learning 10 or more English words! For example, if you know that the prefix root *re-* means "back" or "again," you can easily figure out the meaning to English words such as *revert, recede, return, replay, redo, reorganize, rearrange* and many more. Developing a consistent plan for teaching Latin and Greek word roots can go a long way to increasing students' knowledge of words, particularly academic words. One of the best places to start with word root instruction is with roots that indicate numbers.

Literacy Enhancer Vocabulary: Decoding—Spelling and Latin and Greek Roots

Key Academic Vocabulary

Bi-: A prefix meaning "two," derived from Latin

Greek: An ancient language whose words and word parts have influenced words in English

Latin: An ancient language whose words and word parts have influenced words in English

Quad-, Quar-: A prefix meaning "four," derived from Latin

Tri-: A prefix meaning "three," derived from Latin

Uni-: A prefix meaning "one," derived from Latin

Word Roots: Base words, prefixes, and suffixes in English words that are derived primarily from Latin and Greek

Learning Objectives

- Expand competency in parsing, or breaking down, words into base and affixes.
- Identify critical English word roots and affixes derived from Latin and Greek.
- Increase vocabulary by learning English words derived from Latin and Greek.

Essential Questions

- What are the meanings of critical numerical roots?
- How does knowledge of numerical roots help us understand words in which they are located?

STEP 1: PREPARATION

Organize Materials

- Word journals
- *Numeral Word List.* Make a list of words or display illustrations or pictures containing this root and put them on display for students to see. For example, here is a sample list of words with the prefix *uni-*:
    - *Unicycle*
    - *Uniform*
    - *Unicorn*
    - *Unison*
    - *United States*

STEP 2: INITIATION

The Root Matters

Explain to your students the concept of word roots and affixes—word patterns that have a particular meaning. Provide examples of word roots from compound words such as *cowboy, football, fireflies, grasshopper,* and *crosswalk.* Ask students to break the words down into roots and determine the meaning of the compound words by combining the meanings of the individual words. Examine how the root brings meaning to the word, making the root matter.

STEP 3: DEMONSTRATION

Parsing Roots

1. Draw the students' attention to the *uni-* words you have on display, or the illustration and picture cards containing the images to the words you will be modeling. Have them define the words as best they can. Ask them what is common in all the words: they contain the word pattern *uni-*. Now ask your students to determine what is common in the meaning of all the words. The answer, of course, is the concept of *one*.
2. Work through each of the words on the list and parse them into roots. Demonstrate to students that each word can be defined in this manner:

- *Uni* + *cycle* = one wheel
- *Uni* + *form* = one form or style
- *Uni* + *corn* = one horn
- *Uni* + *son* = one voice
- *Uni* + *ted* + States = many states made into one nation

STEP 4: COLLABORATION

Have students work in pairs and small groups. Ask if they can determine the meaning of the following words using a process similar to the one you demonstrated. Have students think and then discuss with their partners or in their groups.

- *Universe*
- *Unify*
- *University*
- *Unique*
- *Unilateral* (point out that *lateral* means "side")
- *Union*

Have groups share their thinking with the class and answer the essential question: How does knowledge of numerical roots help us understand words in which they are located?

Provide supportive and formative feedback as needed. Create a word wall that contains all the "uni-" words you have studied with your students. Read the words in unison and ask your students to use the words in their oral language whenever possible.

STEP 5: APPLICATION

Working and Writing *"Uni-"* Word Story Sentences

Create a short text or series of sentences that contain some of the *"uni-"* words from the word wall. Have students read these texts and respond to questions about the text.

> My friend Jacob and I were excited to learn that we were accepted for our school's unicycle show team. This means we will have to buy uniforms that match what the other members of the team wear. The practices for the team are challenging. But it's nice to know we work as a united team. In fact, at the end of each practice session, the entire team shouts out the team cheer in unison.
>
> *Question:* If there are eight members of the show team, how many wheels will be used when the team performs?
>
> *Question:* Do you think the author likes being part of a larger group? How do you know?

Have students write a short text like the one on unicycles that contains at least three words from the word wall, along with one question for their text. Have students share their texts in small groups and have classmates respond to the questions for each text.

STEP 6: REFLECTION

Oral or Written Response

Have students invent a word that contains the "uni-" word root (e.g., *uniglasses*). Then have them provide a definition for the word that they invented (glasses that have only one lens). Have students write and complete the following sentence in their Word Journals: I think it is important to know the "uni-" word root because ___

_____.

ADAPTATION AND EXTENSION

- Discuss with students that there are words that seem to have the "uni-" pattern but do not refer to "one" (e.g., uninterested, uninvited). Students need to understand that not all words that begin with "uni" (or other numerical prefixes) refer to "one."
- Have students invent new words that contain the "uni-" root. Students can challenge one another to define the new words.
- Teach word root lessons, using this same format, for other numerical word roots.
- *English Language Learner Suggestion:* Give students a set of "uni-" words and have them draw illustrations of the words that emphasize the concept of "one."
- *Struggling Reader Suggestion:* Give students additional practice with the words in the word ladder by playing other word games such as Wordo (see Chapter 4).

EVALUATION

"I can . . ." Statements

- I can understand what words mean that contain the word root we have studied.
- I can break longer words down into their root parts.
- I can better understand texts that contain words that have the word root we have studied.

Behavior Indicators

- Incorporates words and concepts that contain "uni-" into his or her working vocabulary.
- Locates words in texts that contain the "uni-" word roots.

- Defines and understands the meaning of words that contain the "uni-" word root.
- Comprehends texts that contain the "uni-" word roots.

Other Numerical Prefix Roots

Bi- = two

Bicycle

Biplane

Bicuspid

Biceps

Bifocals

Biannual

Bicentennial

Tri- = three

Tricycle

Trifocals

Triceratops

Tripod

Triceps

Triangle

Trident

Triplet

Quad-/Quar- = four

Quarter

Quart

Quarter

Quadruplet

Quadrangle

Quadrennial

Quad cities

LESSON 4. VOCABULARY: ASSOCIATING WORDS: SHADES OF MEANING AND COLORFUL WORDS

Title SHADES OF MEANING AND COLORFUL WORDS

Trailer The nuances of language surround us every day. Shades of meaning matter in life and in our literacy instruction. Choosing the word *upset* instead of *angry* or *furious* sends a specific message. Understanding synonyms and their varying degrees of meaning helps target comprehension while bolstering vocabulary. Think about the inferences that good readers make when an author states that a character scurried instead of sauntered into the room. When we teach students to look for these rich and varied words during reading and to use them in their writing, they experience literacy growth. Use the hands-on ideas in this lesson to inspire students to put their word detective skills to use to understand subtle shifts in meaning.

Literacy Enhancer Vocabulary: Associating Words—Adjectives, Synonyms, Verbs

Key Academic Vocabulary

Adjective: A word that describes a noun (a person, place, or thing)

Shades of Meaning: Words that are synonyms with varying degrees of different meanings

Synonym: A word that has a similar meaning to another word

Verb: An action word

Learning Objectives

- Identify and demonstrate the varying shades of meaning among commonly used verbs.
- Identify and demonstrate the varying shades of meaning among commonly used adjectives for emotions.
- Identify and demonstrate the varying shades of meaning among commonly used adjectives.

Essential Questions

- How do shades of meaning for common adjectives relate to one another?
- How do varying shades of meaning for common feeling words relate to one another?
- How do shades of meaning apply to different verbs?
- Why do authors use shades of meaning?
- How can we use shades of meaning when we read?
- How can we use shades of meaning when we write?

STEP 1: PREPARATION

Organize Materials

- Index cards or sticky notes
- Several different paint swatches with various shades of a color on each
- Multimodal text set for the topic of study
- Mentor texts or picture books that serve as models of shades of meaning and vibrant word choice
- *Shades of Meaning Word Cards for Emotions* reproducible (copies or enlarged for display)
- *Shades of Meaning Word Cards for Verbs* reproducible (copies or enlarged for display)
- *Shades of Meaning Word Cards for Adjectives* reproducible (copies or enlarged for display)
- Literacy Notebooks

STEP 2: INITIATION

Shades of Color

Show crayons or photos of a few different shades of crayons for a particular color such as red. Invite students to recall some jazzy names they have seen for crayon colors (e.g., midnight blue, cherry red). Read the names of the colors on the crayons or the paint swatches you've collected to your students. Discuss how one might use lighter or more intense darker shades of the same color for different purposes. Discuss how colors change artwork.

Ask students to think about how using different words with similar meanings is like using different crayons. Share an example using feeling words. Ask students to listen to the song "Happy" by Pharrell Williams or to sing the song "If You're Happy and You Know It." Write the word *happy* on the board and ask students to define it. Give partners or table teams two sticky notes, and ask students to work together to come up with two other words that also mean *happy*. Invite students to post the words on a chart or the board. As a class, sort the words in order of shades of happiness, such as from *joyful*, to *cheerful*, to *excited*. Explain to students that they are going to learn how using slightly different words for the same concept will help strengthen their reading and writing.

STEP 3: DEMONSTRATION

Shades of Emotions

1. Explain that the word *happy* is an adjective, or describing word, for a feeling or emotion. Ask students to discuss the synonyms collected in the initiation activity. Can they add a few others to the list? Invite students to make faces to demonstrate the intensity of each word. For example, "How happy is over-joyed, or elated? Show me with your face!" Using student names, make up a few sentences on the spot to show the difference in intensity of emotion for each word. The following examples show the change in intensity using synonyms of *happy*:

   • Sam was excited it was finally Saturday and he could sleep late.
   • Angelica felt joyful that her grandmother was coming to spend the weekend.
   • Juan was overjoyed that his birthday party was at the bowling alley.

2. Invite students to discuss the level of happiness inferred in each example.

3. Create a human word web (Roth, 2012). Write synonyms for *happy* (e.g., *excited, joyful, cheerful, overjoyed, ecstatic*) in large letters on 8.5" × 11" sheets of paper, one word per sheet. Invite one student to stand in front of the classroom and hold the word *happy*. Invite five more volunteers to hold the other words, and position them in a circle around the first student. Have the students in the circle stretch out their right arms and point to the student in the middle, and ask them to take turns holding up and reading their words. Then ask the same or a different group of students to hold up their cards for the word *happy*, and the class then directs them to stand in a line side-by-side in order of intensity from least to most, starting with the word *happy*. Do students agree or disagree with the order? Which words are the trickiest to order?

4. Begin to build a word wall or chart using paint swatches that have several shades of the same color on them. For example, using a strip of various shades of yellow, write words for *happy* on the strip. See Figure 1.3.

5. Repeat this lesson to demonstrate other emotion words and their synonyms. Repeat the human word web and paint swatch activities with new words for emotions and select different students to demonstrate in front of the class. Guide the class in discussing the words demonstrated. See Figure 1.4 for suggested paint colors corresponding to emotion words for building a word wall, chart, or bulletin board.

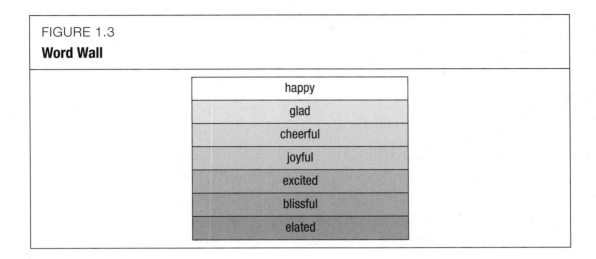

FIGURE 1.3
Word Wall

| happy |
| glad |
| cheerful |
| joyful |
| excited |
| blissful |
| elated |

FIGURE 1.4
Shades of Meaning for Emotions

Common Adjective for an Emotion	Synonyms in Order of Intensity	Suggested Base Color for Paint Swatches
mad	angry annoyed, irritated furious irate	red
sad	disappointed depressed sorrowful heartbroken	blue
scared	afraid nervous, worried frightened terrified petrified	purple
happy	satisfied pleased delighted ecstatic	yellow

Source: Literacy Strong All Year Long: Powerful Lessons for Grades 3-5 by Lori Oczkus, Valerie Ellery, and Timothy V. Rasinski. Copyright © 2018 ASCD. Readers may duplicate this figure for noncommercial use within their school.

6. Continue repeating this lesson over time using other types of words besides emotion words such as verbs, adjectives, and adverbs. Use the *Shades of Meaning Word Cards* in Figures 1.5, 1.6, and 1.7 for ideas.

FIGURE 1.5

Shades of Meaning Word Cards for Emotions

Directions: Cut out the cards, mix them up, sort them into emotion categories, and then put them in rank order from least to most by intensity of feeling.

happy	mad	sad	afraid
satisfied	angry	disappointed	scared
pleased	annoyed	melancholy	worried
delighted	irritated	depressed	nervous
excited	furious	gloomy	frightened
blissful	fuming	sorrowful	terrified
elated	livid	mournful	petrified
ecstatic	irate	heartbroken	panic-stricken

FIGURE 1.6
Shades of Meaning Word Cards for Verbs

Directions: Cut the words apart, mix them up, sort them in categories, and put them in order from least to most intense action.

say	walk	eat	see
whisper	stroll	nibble	peek
exclaim	march	gobble	look
shout	strut	chomp	stare
throw	jog	clean	whimper
toss	skip	rinse	sob
pitch	run	wash	weep
hurl	saunter	scrub	wail

Source: Literacy Strong All Year Long: Powerful Lessons for Grades 3-5 by Lori Oczkus, Valerie Ellery, and Timothy V. Rasinski. Copyright © 2018 ASCD. Readers may duplicate this figure for noncommercial use within their school.

FIGURE 1.7

Shades of Meaning Word Cards for Adjectives

Directions: Cut the cards apart, mix them up, sort them into categories, and then put them in order from least to most intense in size, feeling, or description.

big	small	nice	bad
huge	tiny	agreeable	inadequate
enormous	miniscule	pleasant	poor
mammoth	miniature	satisfactory	shoddy
monstrous	compact	gratifying	unacceptable
giant	little	delightful	awful
gargantuan	slight	marvelous	atrocious
humongous	teensy	amusing	deplorable

STEP 4: COLLABORATION

Rank the Words and Conversational Coaching

Give the words listed in the color word chart to different groups of students. Assign all groups the same emotion or different ones. Or, as another option, write the names of the emotions on papers and let groups draw one. Each group prepares to teach their example to the class. The students work together to write a list of synonyms that reflect shades of meaning for their emotion word and write each of their synonyms on separate large pieces of paper. Then students each hold up a word and stand in either a human word web or in an agreed-upon order. They might also act out the words or create sentences using the emotion words to demonstrate intensity. Students discuss their choices for ordering the words. For example, are the words in order from just a little bit upset to really mad or furious?

STEP 5: APPLICATION

Students work independently or in pairs or teams to sort words from the Shades of Meaning Cards for verbs or adjectives included in this lesson. Select any of the following ways for students to respond:

- *Word Dump and Sort.* Students cut out the words and put them in an envelope for storage. They dump the words and order them from least to most intense, either left to right or top to bottom, or order and glue the words into a notebook. Students explain the reasons for their choices.
- *Ring It.* Students write the words on paint strips, punch holes in them, and hook them together with a ring. They refer to them when writing.
- *Ring Race.* Using the cards from the *Ring It* activity, write the title categories for all of the words such as feeling words, color words for yellow, or adjectives for mad, and put them in a bag. One person reaches in and draws a word, and the partner or members of the team search on their rings for a word in that category to share. They use a sentence and tell a partner or the group.

STEP 6: REFLECTION

Oral or Written Response

Students record and illustrate their favorite shades of meaning words in their literacy notebooks. They can write about their day using as many of the words as possible or select one emotion and write a paragraph using a variety of words to show shades of feelings.

ADAPTATION AND EXTENSION

- Ask students to brainstorm other categories of words to rank the order of shades of meaning such as words for temperature (e.g., *hot, cold, warm, cool*); words for states of mind (e.g., *knew, believed, suspected, heard, trusted, wondered*); word for size (e.g., *thin, thick, tall, short*); or adverbs (e.g., *fast, slow*). Each week, allow students to select a category of words to study and brainstorm to add to their notebooks.

- Invite students to create their own poems with shades of meaning by using online resources such as ReadWriteThink's student interactive theme poems (see www.readwritethink.org/classroom-resources/student-interactives /theme-poems-30044.html).

- Have students create comic strips using shades of meaning verbs from the lesson by using an online cartoon generator such as the ReadWriteThink Comic Creator (see www.readwritethink.org/classroom-resources/student-interactives /comic-creator-30021.html).

- Read aloud to students from the following picture books that focus on rich word choice and shades of meaning. Add these rich words to their notebooks or vocabulary wall.
  - *I Love You the Purplest* by Barbara M. Joosse
  - *Halloween Hoots and Howls* by Joan Horton
  - *Hairy, Scary, Ordinary: What Is an Adjective?* by Brian P. Cleary
  - *The Boy Who Loved Words* by Ronnie Schotter
  - *Tulip Sees America* by Cynthia Rylant

- *English Language Learner Suggestion:* Introduce your students to word gradients by using resources available through Reading Rockets (see www.readingrockets .org/strategies/semantic gradients). This resource shows video clips and gives examples of students working in teams as they sort related word cards accord- ing to degree of meaning. Notice how students discuss and debate the order of their words as they learn the subtle differences in meanings.

- *Struggling Reader Suggestion:* Meet with struggling readers to brainstorm a list of shades of meaning using verbs. Encourage students to act out the words. Together, they can create a cartoon or comic strip using related words such as *toss, throw, pitch,* and *hurl*. Write a shared story using the words and then encourage students to act out the words.

EVALUATION

"I can . . ." Statements

- I can identify and demonstrate the shades of meaning of words that are synonyms for feeling or emotion words.
- I can identify and demonstrate the meanings of verb synonyms.
- I can identify and demonstrate the meanings of adjective synonyms.
- I can categorize and sort words that are synonyms.

Behavior Indicators

- Identifies, names, and categorizes synonyms for emotions.
- Orders emotion words according to level of intensity and explains choices.
- Identifies, names, and categorizes synonyms for common verbs.
- Orders common verbs according to meaning and explains choices.
- Identifies, names, and categorizes synonyms for common adjectives.
- Orders common adjectives according to meaning and explains choices.

LESSON 5. FLUENCY: PHRASING, PACING, EXPRESSING

Title KEEP A POEM IN YOUR POCKET AND A SONG IN YOUR HEART

Trailer The use of poetry and song in most upper elementary classrooms has been minimized over the past several years. Perhaps educators think of such activities as more appropriate for art and music teachers, or as "fluff" activities used primarily for enjoyment. Although we won't deny the enjoyment aspect of poetry and song, these types of texts offer wonderful opportunities to build students' reading fluency as well as other reading-related competencies. In this lesson we present how you might want to make poetry and song an integral part of your reading curriculum at the beginning of the school year and beyond.

Literacy Enhancer Reading Fluency: Word Recognition Automaticity, Expressive Reading

Key Academic Vocabulary

Performance: The act of presenting a play, concert, or other form of entertainment

Poetry: A genre of writing that emphasizes the expression of feelings and ideas by the use of distinctive style, rhyme, or rhythm

Rehearsal: The repeated practice reading of a text done in preparation of performing the text for an audience

Rhyme: Words that have the same or similar ending sounds

Rhythm: A regular, repeated pattern of movement, sound, or language

Song: A short poem set to music

Learning Objectives

- Recognize words automatically (word recognition automaticity).
- Read with appropriate expression and phrasing (prosody).
- Develop a great appreciation for poetry and song.
- Develop an ability to read poems and songs at a high degree of fluency and understanding.

Essential Questions

- Why is it that people love to read and sing poems and songs?
- What makes poems and songs easy to learn to read?
- What can I do to learn to read a poem or song fluently?

STEP 1: PREPARATION

Organize Materials

"Casey at the Bat" reproducible.

STEP 2: INITIATION

Baseball Background

The beginning of the school year usually comes at a time when baseball fans are looking forward to the playoffs and the World Series, so that would be a great time for students to learn one of the most beloved poems about baseball, "Casey at the Bat" by Ernest Thayer (1888). The poem is a long narrative about the failure of what should have been a triumphal moment in Casey's baseball career. See Figure 1.8 (p. 47) for a reproducible of the poem. Although most students are familiar with baseball, some may need basic background. Optional: Show a brief video of a game in action or provide these basic facts:

- There are nine players on a team. One team pitches the ball, and the other bats.
- The object is to score the most runs in nine innings. Batters try to hit the ball and run the four bases without being called "out" (i.e., the ball is caught in the air by an opposing player; a batter or runner doesn't reach a base before the ball). Teams get three outs per inning.
- Winners of the National and American Leagues play in a "best-of-seven" contest called the World Series.

Allow students to imagine playing in an important game where their team is losing, but there is one more chance to score runs to end the game. Ask students, "How would you feel if you were the last batter up? If you get a hit, your team could win; otherwise the game will be over and your team loses."

STEP 3: DEMONSTRATION

Fluent or Not

1. Rehearse the first verse of "Casey at the Bat" until you can read it smoothly and with appropriate expression.
2. Ask students to follow along silently as you read the first verse to them as expressively as possible.
3. After the initial reading, read it again, but in a less-than-fluent manner (e.g., word by word, with hesitations, mispronounced words, poor posture).

4. Discuss your readings of the passages. Ask, "Which reading was best and why?" What did they notice about your fluent reading? What did they notice about your not-so-fluent reading?

5. Discuss the content of the poem, noting the interesting words that the poet used in the first verse (i.e., *outlook, brilliant, patrons*). Put these words on the word wall as you talk with your students. Ask "What does *Mudville Nine* refer to? How do you know? Can you describe what the poet meant by the phrase *sickly silence?*"

STEP 4: COLLABORATION

Display a large copy of the poem in the classroom for students to read at their leisure and make a copy of the first verse for each student to rehearse. For each succeeding day of the lesson, make a copy of one or two more sections to be rehearsed, depending on how well students are reading with fluency. Have students work in small groups of two or three to rehearse the first verse for a few minutes. Partners can alternate between reading the verse and listening to provide support and positive feedback. Then students can read the first verse aloud together. Have them divide up and assign lines for each student to perform later to the entire class. Roam the classroom and visit each rehearsal group, listening to them read, providing formative feedback and support. Engage students in thinking deeply about how to make the reading a satisfying experience for the audience.

STEP 5: APPLICATION

Set a date for a grand performance by the students to an audience of other students, parents, school staff, and others. Here are some tips to help with planning:

1. Determine who will be invited and how invitations will be communicated.

2. Determine a location and consider the logistics, including sufficient seating and size of the stage area.

3. Choreograph the performance. Will each stanza be performed by a different student or groups of students? Will any stanzas be performed by all? How will students enter and leave the stage area?

4. Do a dress rehearsal with your students. Provide formative feedback during and after.

5. On the day of the performance:

   a. Introduce the audience to the performance and provide background on the poem.

b. Remind audience members of appropriate behavior during the performance and suggest ways they can show their appreciation.

c. Following the performance, allow audience members to share positive feedback with the performers and arrange a reception for performers and audience members.

d. Arrange for the performance area to be cleaned and returned to its original state.

STEP 6: REFLECTION

Oral or Written Response

Following the performance, ask audience members to write critiques focusing primarily on the positive aspects. Share selected critiques with your students. Have students write their own responses to the poetry experience. Ask, "What did you like best? How has practicing and performing a poem improved your reading? What will you do differently for future poetry performances?"

ADAPTATION AND EXTENSION

- Extend the poetry performance by making it a regular part of your English Language Arts curriculum throughout the first three months of the school year. Every two to four weeks, set the final day of the school week as Poetry Performance Day. Have students rehearse and perform new poems according to the protocol described in the lesson.

- The poems you select can be longer narrative poems such as "Casey at the Bat" or "The Cremation of Sam McGee" by Robert Service. Alternatively, as students become more comfortable with performing, you may assign them or ask them to select a shorter poem to rehearse and perform alone. You might want to focus each performance on the poetry of a particular poet who can also be a focus of research and study by your students. Poets you might want to consider include Robert Frost, Emily Dickinson, Langston Hughes, and Shel Silverstein. Most well-known poets have websites devoted to them where students can find poetry collections.

- *English Language Learner Suggestion:* With your students, identify, display, and discuss challenging words that appear in the poem (e.g., *spherical, melancholy*). Challenge yourself and your students to use the words in their oral and written language.

- *Struggling Reader Suggestion:* Use shorter poems that have a distinct rhythm and rhyming patterns that make them easier to learn. You may ask students to learn and then perform popular nursery rhymes for younger students.

EVALUATION

"I can . . ." Statements

- I can read a poem, or a portion of a poem, with ease.
- I can read a poem, or a portion of a poem, with appropriate expression.
- I can read a poem, or a portion of a poem, with good volume and confidence.
- I can read a poem, or a portion of a poem, aloud with good posture.
- I know the meaning of the words in the poem I read.
- I can understand the meaning of the poem that I and my classmates read.
- I can rehearse a poem to the point where I can read it well.
- I can listen to a poem being read and offer positive feedback to the reader.

Behavior Indicators

- Demonstrates excitement to rehearse and perform poetry.
- Collaborates with and provides good feedback to others in a rehearsal group.
- Exhibits positive mannerisms as an audience member.
- Locates poems to rehearse and perform for others.

FIGURE 1.8

Casey at the Bat Reproducible

Casey at the Bat
by Ernest Thayer

The outlook wasn't brilliant for the Mudville
Nine that day;
The score stood four to two, with but one
inning more to play.
And then when Cooney died at first, and
Barrows did the same,
A sickly silence fell upon the patrons of the
game.

A straggling few got up to go in deep despair.
The rest
Clung to that hope which springs eternal in
the human breast;
They thought, if only Casey could get but a
whack at that—
They'd put up even money, now, with Casey
at the bat.

But Flynn preceded Casey, as did also Jimmy
Blake,
And the former was a lulu and the latter was
a cake,
So upon that stricken multitude grim melan-
choly sat,
For there seemed but little chance of Casey's
getting to the bat.

But Flynn let drive a single, to the wonder-
ment of all,
And Blake, the much despised, tore the cover
off the ball;
And when the dust had lifted, and the men
saw what had occurred,
There was Jimmy safe at second and Flynn
a-hugging third.

Then from five thousand throats and more
there rose a lusty yell;
It rumbled through the valley, it rattled in the
dell;
It knocked upon the mountain and recoiled
upon the flat,
For Casey, mighty Casey, was advancing to
the bat.

There was ease in Casey's manner as he
stepped into his place;
There was pride in Casey's bearing and a
smile on Casey's face.
And when, responding to the cheers, he
lightly doffed his hat,
No stranger in the crowd could doubt 'twas
Casey at the bat.

Ten thousand eyes were on him as he rubbed
his hands with dirt;
Five thousand tongues applauded when he
wiped them on his shirt.
Then while the writhing pitcher ground the
ball into his hip,
Defiance gleamed in Casey's eye, a sneer
curled Casey's lip.

And now the leather-covered sphere came
hurtling through the air,
And Casey stood a-watching it in haughty
grandeur there.
Close by the sturdy batsman the ball
unheeded sped—
"That ain't my style," said Casey. "Strike one,"
the umpire said.

continued

FIGURE 1.8 (*continued*)

From the benches, black with people, there went up a muffled roar,
Like the beating of the storm-waves on a stern and distant shore.
"Kill him! Kill the umpire!" shouted someone on the stand;
And it's likely they'd have killed him had not Casey raised his hand.

With a smile of Christian charity great Casey's visage shone;
He stilled the rising tumult; he bade the game go on;
He signaled to the pitcher, and once more the spheroid flew;
But Casey still ignored it, and the umpire said: "Strike two."

"Fraud!" cried the maddened thousands, and echo answered fraud;
But one scornful look from Casey and the audience was awed.
They saw his face grow stern and cold, they saw his muscles strain,
And they knew that Casey wouldn't let that ball go by again.

The sneer is gone from Casey's lip, his teeth are clenched in hate;
He pounds with cruel violence his bat upon the plate.
And now the pitcher holds the ball, and now he lets it go,
And now the air is shattered by the force of Casey's blow.

Oh, somewhere in this favored land the sun is shining bright;
The band is playing somewhere, and somewhere hearts are light,
And somewhere men are laughing, and somewhere children shout;
But there is no joy in Mudville—mighty Casey has struck out.

LESSON 6. COMPREHENSION: PREVIEWING

Title SNEAK PREVIEW 1-2-3

Trailer Who doesn't love a sneak preview of a movie or upcoming television series? Doesn't it spark your interest and curiosity? A sneak preview of a text invites students to begin to figure out what it will be about and how it is put together. Many times our students glance at reading material and make bland, surface-level predictions such as "I think the article is about frogs." How can we guide students to move beyond simple predictions to more sophisticated ideas that help them begin to think about the author's purpose and text structure? A deeper prediction might sound like this: "I think I will learn that some frog species are endangered and what we can do to help because I got my clues from the headings." Intermediate students need to become like curious detectives gathering information about the organization, content, and purpose of texts before they read. Sneak previews of texts help students to deepen and expand their concept of making predictions.

Literacy Enhancer Comprehension: Craft and Structure; Previewing: Text Cover, Features, Organization

Key Academic Vocabulary

Author: Person who wrote the text

Author's Purpose: The reason the author wrote the text—usually to inform, entertain, or persuade the reader

Author's Point of View: In nonfiction, the opinion or feelings the author has toward the topic; in fiction, point of view also means who is telling the story

Illustrator: The person who draws or paints the artwork to accompany the text

Predict: To make an educated logical guess, or inference, about what will happen next in the text using clues from the text and one's own background knowledge

Prediction: An educated guess about what may happen in the future in a story or other text about to be read

Preview: To look over the text before reading to predict what it will be about and to see what text features the author has included

Text Features: The tools an author uses to support the reader to help navigate the text for locating and accessing meaning from the text; may contain a table of contents, headings, photographs, bold words, maps, graphs, charts, index, and glossary

Text Structure: The organizational structure of the information in the text. Fiction might consist of a problem and solution and a beginning, middle, and end; nonfiction may be organized around a main idea and details, a cause and effect, a problem and solution, a sequence of ideas, or a compare and contrast of ideas.

Learning Objectives

- Identify and describe the overall structure of an informational or fiction text.
- Preview a text to evaluate and integrate text features and clues to begin to predict what the text is about.
- Make predictions about the author's purpose.
- Consider the author's point of view during preview of text.

Essential Questions

- What predictions can be made by looking at the title of the text?
- What additional information can be gathered about the topic based on the cover art?
- Who wrote and illustrated the text, and what is the author's purpose?
- How is the text organized?
- What is the author's point of view? Whose voice is used? Does the author express an opinion or take a side on a topic?

STEP 1: PREPARATION

Organize Materials

- *Sneak Preview 1-2-3 Bookmark* reproducible
- Fiction or nonfiction texts
- "Point of View" mentor texts
- Literacy Notebooks
- Book order flyers

STEP 2: INITIATION

Movie Premiere

Ask students if they have ever seen a movie preview. Invite students to share with partners some of their favorite movies and previews. Share an appropriate movie trailer that sparked your interest. How do students feel when the movie trailer is a sequel to a movie they've enjoyed before, such as *Harry Potter* or *Finding Dory*? Are there certain production companies or directors that students are familiar with that help them predict what the movie will be like? Invite students to discuss the purposes of a movie or television show trailer. Why is a trailer important to the success of the movie or show? Invite table teams to come up with at least two or three reasons for a trailer. Share the following with students:

> Before you begin reading any text, whether it is in a book, magazine, or online, you are taking a sneak preview to begin thinking about what you will read. Good readers do this naturally! Sneaking a peek or previewing the text before you read is much like viewing a movie preview. In a way, you are creating your own book trailer in your head as you take a sneak preview of the book. It helps you to get excited and interested in the reading.

STEP 3: DEMONSTRATION

Sneak Preview 1-2-3

1. Select a fiction book or informational article to preview. Project the reading material on the screen using a smartboard or document camera so all students can see as you think aloud. Pass out copies for every student, if available; otherwise conduct the think-aloud using your displayed copy.

2. Explain to students that they are going to watch as you use a three-part sneak preview to help you predict what the text is going to be about. Have students repeat the name of the strategy: Sneak Preview 1-2-3. Invite partners to turn and talk to discuss what they think the three parts of the preview will entail. Tell students to observe as you demonstrate how to look for the three important pieces of information as you predict with a text.

3. Fiction Think-Aloud: Select a fiction text to use in your demonstration. Pass out copies of the bookmark so students can follow along while you demonstrate. Have students repeat the name of the strategy: Sneak Preview 1-2-3. Say, "The first place I look for clues to predict is the cover, so I call this first step **That Covers It!** The title says _____ so I think _____. The author or illustrator is ____. I may or may not be familiar with that person's work. Now, I am studying the cover art to see if it provides clues to what this might be about. I see _____ on the cover, so I think it might be about _____. I also look at the back cover to predict there as well." Next, show students how to flip through a text, skimming words and looking at visuals if there are any. Say, "I call this next step **Flip Through** because I flip through the pages hunting for clues as to what this could be about. So far, I think_____ because _____. The last part of Sneak Preview 1-2-3 is called **Puzzle, Purpose, and Point of View**. I need to think about how the author has organized the text and what kind of text it is.

I think this is a _____ (mystery, memoir, adventure) because _____. I also need to think about why the author wrote this: to inform, entertain, or persuade me. The fiction is told through the eyes of _____ (first person, a character, multiple characters, or a narrator)."

4. Informational Text Think-Aloud: Select an informational text to use in your demonstration or model from a fictional text one day and informational the next. Ask students to repeat the name of the strategy, Sneak Preview 1-2-3. Share, "This first step of a sneak preview is called **That Covers It!** because I focus on the front and back cover of the text to see what this may be about. I see the title _____ so I think I will learn about _____. I also look at the name of the author and illustrator to see if I am familiar with their work. Next, I study the cover art and any text on the front and back cover for more clues. Now I think I will learn _____ because I see _____. The next step is called **Flip Through** because I flip through the pages thinking about what I may learn. I read the headings, look at the visuals, and scan the text. So far, I think this is mostly about _____ because I see _____. The final step of Sneak Preview 1-2-3 is **Puzzle, Purpose, and Point of View.** I look through the text again and think about how it is organized and why the author wrote it. I am also thinking about what the author thinks about the topic or point of view. The text is organized _____ (in order, as compare and contrast, with a main idea and detail, as cause and effect). I think the author wrote this to _____ (inform, persuade, entertain). I can tell because _____. I think the author thinks _____ about the topic _____ because _____."

STEP 4: COLLABORATION

Ask students to turn and review the three main parts of the Sneak Preview 1-2-3 strategy with partners. Ask students to discuss how the strategy helps them to predict before reading. Why is this important for creating interest and motivation to read? Students may work in teams of three with each taking one part of a sneak preview. Students may refer to the text you modeled or select a new text to try out the strategy. Throughout the lesson, encourage students to talk to partners using the language from the lesson (e.g., title, art, author). Try discussing the Sneak Preview 1-2-3 with a fiction text and an informational text. Here is a summary of the main parts:

- **That Covers It:** title, author, illustrator, front and back covers, art
- **Flip Through:** art; skim text, headings, and titles

- **Puzzle, Purpose, and Point of View:** overall text type, what is the author's purpose (inform, entertain, persuade), what does the author appear to believe, point of view (who is talking: a character or narrator), and does the author express a point of view on a topic

STEP 5: APPLICATION

- **Book Study:** Distribute books on tables and ask students to work in pairs to apply the Sneak Preview 1-2-3 strategy to a text they select. Use the *Sneak Preview 1-2-3* reproducible in Figure 1.9 to try out the strategy on a few texts. Share findings with the class. After previewing all the texts, students select one to read.
- **Articles Study:** Apply the Sneak Preview 1-2-3 strategy to articles found online or in a weekly news leaflet. Encourage students to work in teams to apply the strategy to one of the articles of their choice and report their findings to the class.
- **Content-Area Textbooks:** Students work in teams to apply the Sneak Preview 1-2-3 strategy to an entire chapter or a few pages in a content-area textbook.

STEP 6: REFLECTION

Oral or Written Response

Invite students to make a list of at least two of their favorite authors for fiction or informational texts. Generate a list together if necessary so students can choose an author to write about. Ask students to reflect on the following prompts:

- I like the author_____ because _____ and also because_____.
- I especially enjoyed the book _____ written by _____ because_____. It was about _____. A part I remember was _____ _____.
- When I look at the books by _____ I want to read them because_____.
- I think other students should read books by _____ because_____.

Book Covers: Invite students to create book covers complete with jackets for a favorite book by a favorite author! Try a free online "Cover Maker" at ReadWriteThink (www.readwritethink.org/files/resources/interactives/bookcover/).

FIGURE 1.9

Sneak Preview 1-2-3 Bookmark

Sneak Preview/Fiction

#1. That covers it!
Preview the front and back covers.

_____ Title
_____ Author
_____ Cover art
_____ Back cover

I think _____ is about _____ because _____ .

#2 Flip through!
What do you think it's about?

_____ Chapter titles
_____ Visuals
_____ Other

I think _____ is about _____ because _____ .

#3. Puzzle, Purpose, POV!
What is the genre? Why did the author write this text? How is it organized?

Bonus: What is the point of view? Who is telling the story—a character or a narrator?

What genre of text is it? Adventure, mystery, comedy?

Why did the author write it?
_____ to entertain
_____ to persuade
_____ to explain

What is the point of view?
_____ 1st person / I
_____ 2nd person/ You
_____ 3rd person/ He or She

I think _____ is about _____ because _____ .

Sneak Preview 1-2-3 Bookmark

Sneak Preview/Nonfiction

#1. That covers it!
Preview the front and back covers.

_____ Title
_____ Author
_____ Cover art
_____ Back cover

I think _____ is about _____ because _____ .

#2 Page flip through!
What do you think it's about?

_____ Chapter titles
_____ Headings
_____ Visuals
_____ Other

I think _____ is about _____ because _____ .

#3. Puzzle, Purpose, POV!
What is the genre? Why did the author write this text? How is it organized?

Bonus: What is the point of view? Who is telling the story—a character or a narrator?

What genre of text is it? Adventure, mystery, comedy?

Why did the author write it?
_____ to entertain
_____ to persuade
_____ to explain

What is the point of view?
_____ 1st person / I
_____ 2nd person/ You
_____ 3rd person/ He or She

I think _____ is about _____ because _____ .

Stroll Line: After writing their reflections, students form two lines facing one another to share their written response with a partner. Decide on a signal for students to switch partners. One line moves while the other line remains stationary. Students move one step to the right, and the student at the end moves to the front of the line. Students share with their new partners. Students in the designated moving line continue shifting to the right to form new partners. Invite students to add to their writing after the stroll line discussion. Have them write blurbs to advertise books such as "You should read the book _____ because _____. _____ is such a great book because _____. On a scale of 1 to 10, I would give it a _____ because _____."

ADAPTATION AND EXTENSION

- As a class, view age-appropriate movie and television previews online or read print ads together. Discuss predictions about the shows. How do advertisers appeal to our natural curiosity as they promote their new shows? What clues do the viewers use to make predictions? What makes a good preview?
- Discuss and research authors who also illustrate their own books (e.g., J. R. R. Tolkien, Kadir Nelson, Chris Van Allsburg, Floyd Cooper). Ask students to consider why authors illustrate their own books. Do they illustrate books for other authors as well?
- Pass out book orders from companies such as Troll or Scholastic. Ask students to circle three books that they would like to read and then apply the Sneak Preview 1-2-3 strategy using the information presented in the flyer. Share at their tables with partners or teams. Is this enough information to make predictions? Why or why not?
- Read aloud and discuss picture book mentor texts that demonstrate point of view. Here is a list of titles to consider:

    First person
    - *The True Story of the Three Little Pigs* by Jon Scieszka
    - *Mirror, Mirror* by Marilyn Singer
    - *I Didn't Do It* by Patricia MacLachlan and Emily MacLachlan Charest
    - *Talkin' About Bessie: The Story of Aviator Elizabeth Coleman* by Nikki Grimes

    Second person
    - *If You Find a Rock* by Peggy Christian
    - *How to Babysit a Grandpa* by Jean Reagan

Third person
- *Can't You Make Them Behave, King George?* by Jean Fritz
- *Thank You, Mr. Falker* by Patricia Polacco
- *Boss Baby* by Marla Frazee

- *English Language Learner Suggestion:* Provide extra practice by filling a bag with several books. Select student volunteers to grab a book from the bag. Hold up the selected book and have the student and class apply the Sneak Preview 1-2-3 strategy.
- *Struggling Reader Suggestion:* Look for an informational article on a topic that students are interested in using by searching online resources such as Newsela (see https://newsela.com). Ask the class to work in pairs to apply the Sneak Preview 1-2-3 strategy. How does the strategy help them preview and predict articles? How does previewing help when reading multiple articles on the same topic?

EVALUATION

"I can . . ." Statements

- I can study the title and art on the covers of fiction or informational texts to make predictions about the text.
- I can use the information I know about the author and illustrator of a text to make predictions about what I will learn or what the text is about.
- I can look through an informational text at the headings, visuals, and other text features to make logical predictions about what I will learn.
- I can look through a fiction text and begin to figure out the genre (adventure, fairy tale, mystery).
- I can preview a text to figure out the author's purpose for writing the text (entertain, inform, persuade).
- I can preview an informational text and figure out how the author organized the material (cause and effect, problem and solution, main idea and detail, sequence, compare and contrast).
- I can preview a fiction text and begin to figure out what the author's point of view is by looking for pronouns to identify first-, second-, or third-person narration.

Behavior Indicators

- Identifies and uses key information on the cover of a fiction or nonfiction text including the author, illustrator, title, and cover art to make logical predictions about the text.
- Previews a fiction text by skimming the pages to gain an understanding and to identify the genre and author's purpose for the text.
- Describes the type of informational text or genre of fiction text.
- Identifies pronouns that indicate the narrator's (or author's) point of view.

LESSON 7. COMPREHENSION: INFERRING AND DRAWING CONCLUSIONS

Title MAKING PREDICTIONS

Trailer To be a good reader, you need to act like a scientist. One of the things scientists do when conducting an experiment is make a hypothesis about how they think the experiment will turn out. Good readers do the same thing. They are constantly making predictions about what they are about to read and then they engage in reading to determine if their predictions come true. In this lesson, you will explore and practice making predictions or hypotheses as you read.

Literacy Enhancer Comprehension: Making Inferences, Predicting

Key Academic Vocabulary

Background Knowledge (Schema): The existing knowledge a person has about a particular topic

Hypothesis: A prediction usually made prior to a scientific experiment that anticipates the outcome of the experiment; the experiment is then conducted to confirm or refute the hypothesis

Prediction: An educated guess about what may happen in a story or other text before reading

Learning Objectives

- Make reasonable predictions about the content and outcome of a text students are about to read.
- Provide appropriate reasons or rationale for making predictions about a text.

Essential Questions

- What is a prediction or hypothesis?
- What do I need to know to make a good prediction about what I am about to read?
- Am I able to justify the predictions I make about a text I am about to read?
- Am I able to confirm or refute the predictions I make?
- Am I able to revise my predictions based on new information I find as I read?

STEP 1: PREPARATION

Organize Materials

- Narrative texts for modeling and independent reading
- *Making Predictions Possible* reproducible

STEP 2: INITIATION

Describe to the students the notion of making predictions or hypotheses. Explain that good readers constantly anticipate or make predictions about what they are reading, and sometimes they are so good at making predictions that they don't even realize they have done it. Ask if they have ever read a book or watched a television program that had a surprise ending for them. The surprise ending is evidence that they had made a prediction about how the story or program was going to turn out and their prediction didn't come through. Thus, they were surprised.

Tell your students that predictions are usually based on what you observe about an event, and what you already know about it. For example, if you walk into a baseball stadium filled with people, your knowledge of such scenes means that a baseball game is to be played. If you see people walking around outdoors with umbrellas, your knowledge of umbrellas allows you to predict that rain will be falling soon. Tell the students that you are going to give them opportunities to make and share their predictions about their reading in the coming lesson.

STEP 3: DEMONSTRATION

1. Select a text that the students will read on their own and ensure that every student has a copy. Present the text you will read to the students and show them the cover illustration, if any. Then read the title of the story to the students. Think aloud by describing to the students what you think the story may be about from the information that has been shared and explain how you use your background knowledge to make a prediction or two.

2. Read the story aloud until you come to an appropriate stopping place where you can evaluate your predictions. Again, do a think-aloud to consider how well your predictions panned out.

3. *Think-Pair-Share.* Before continuing with the read-aloud, ask your students to consider what will occur next in the story. Have them share their predictions with a classmate and choose one prediction or consolidate each student's prediction into one that will be shared with the rest of the class. As students share their predictions, ask the critical question, "Why do you think so?" This question challenges students to justify their predictions based upon what they have encountered in the text so far and what they already know about the topic or event (background knowledge).

4. Continue the process in #3 above. Stop your reading at selected points and ask students to confirm or revise their predictions based upon new information provided in the next portion that you read to students.

5. When the read-aloud is complete, ask students to talk about how making predictions affected how they listened. Did they have to listen more closely to the story as it was read? Did they find themselves more actively thinking about how the story will play out?

STEP 4: COLLABORATION

Have students continue the same process described in the Demonstration section with the text(s) they will read on their own. Working in small groups, students should discuss and make predictions at logical stopping points throughout the text, come to consensus on agreed-upon predictions, and share with the class. Ask students to justify their predictions and display the predictions made by the group. As students move through the text, have them discuss how they confirmed, revised, or refined their predictions. Update revisions on the display board. At the end of the reading, use the predictions made by students as the basis for discussion of the story. Ask students to reflect on how actively making and revising predictions changed how they read the text.

STEP 5: APPLICATION

Over the next several texts that you read to and with your students, have them engage in the process of making, justifying, confirming, revising, and refining predictions. Create a Making Predictions chart for display that lists the process of making predictions. Here's a sample of the text you may want to use.

Good Readers Are Scientists: They Make Predictions as They Read

Predict:_____

_____

Justify predictions:_____

_____

Evaluate predictions:_____

_____

Confirm or revise predictions:_____

_____

If predictions are revised, justify revised predictions:_____

_____

Evaluate revised predictions:_____

_____

STEP 6: REFLECTION

Oral or Written Response

You may wish to create a Making Predictions chart like the one in Figure 1.10 for your students to use for each text they read. The final step for each reading requires students to reflect in writing on how making predictions affected their reading. At first students may indicate that repeatedly stopping to confirm or revise predictions is disruptive to their reading. However, with practice students should begin to habituate the activity and find themselves more engaged in making and anticipating meaning as they read.

ADAPTATION AND EXTENSION

Predictions made so far in this lesson have been based on the actual text read or on illustrations that accompany the text. Predictions, however, can be based on other pieces of information that are provided to students.

Pre-Voke (prediction based on vocabulary). Identify key words in the text to be read. Display the words in the order in which they appear in the text. Ask students to categorize words into those that suggest characters, those that suggest time and place, those that suggest the problem in the story, and those that suggest the outcome or resolution to the problem. Remind students that there are no correct answers, only good thinking by which they can explain their categorizing decisions. Have students discuss their decisions and make predictions about the nature and content of the text to be read based upon the words given, their order, and the ways students categorized the words. Display predictions and use the predictions as the basis for discussion after the story has been read.

Pre-Sent (prediction based on sentences). Identify key sentences and phrases in the text to be read. Put the sentences on display in the order in which they appear in the text. Discuss the possible meanings of each sentence with students. Then have students make predictions about the nature and content of the text to be read based upon the suggested meaning of the sentences and the order in which they appear. Display predictions and use them as the basis for discussion after the story has been read.

- *English Language Learner Suggestion:* Provide additional modeling of making predictions for students by
  - making your own predictions.
  - using a think-aloud process.
  - asking students to make comments and to pose questions about how you made your predictions.

- *Struggling Reader Suggestion:* Have students read a text a second time before making their predictions. Alternatively, have students listen to the text as it is read to them, and then have them read it on their own before making predictions.

EVALUATION

"I can . . ." Statements

- I can make good predictions about the text before and during my reading.
- I can justify my predictions based on what I know about the topic and what I have read.
- I can revise and refine my predictions based on new information presented in the text I am reading.
- I can work with my classmates to come to consensus about what we are reading.

Behavior Indicators

- Shares knowledge about a particular topic or event.
- Makes reasonable predictions about the reading.
- Makes good revisions to earlier predictions based on what he or she has read.

FIGURE 1.10
Making Predictions Reproducible

Name of Text: _____

Prediction 1: _____
Why I think so: _____

Revision: _____
Why I think so: _____

Revision: _____
Why I think so: _____

Prediction 2: _____
Why I think so: _____

Revision: _____
Why I think so: _____

Revision: _____
Why I think so: _____

Prediction 3: _____
Why I think so: _____

Revision: _____
Why I think so: _____

Revision: _____
Why I think so: _____

Reflection: How did making predictions throughout the text affect my reading? _____
_____
_____
_____

LESSON 8. COMPREHENSION: QUESTIONING FOR CLOSE READING

Title TOP FIVE INTERROGATIVE *W* WORDS FOR SPECULATIVE TALK

Trailer Lights. Camera. **Talk. TaLK. TALK!** Welcome to "Let's Get to *Really* Know the Character Talk Show," where the real action starts when you become the celebrity interviewer, like Oprah, and the characters in the story are your guests. We will be using the formula for developing speculative thinking using the Five Interrogative *W* Words as a springboard for character analysis and uncovering text-based evidence to support the answers our guests give today.

Key Academic Vocabulary

Close Read: Determine the purpose of the text and notice features and language used by the author to think thoughtfully and methodically about why they were used

Interrogate: To examine with questions and look for answers

Speculative Talk: Makes an inference by suggesting or hinting at connections and conclusions; element of imaginative thinking to support understanding

Text-Based Evidence: Evidence derived from key facts and details in the text

Text-Dependent Questions: Sentences in interrogative form that can only be answered by referring explicitly back to the text being read

Learning Objectives

- Ask and answer who, what, why, when, and where questions with supporting details to determine the main topic, concept, theme, and events.
- Ask and answer text-dependent questions to focus or set a purpose for speculative thinking and close rereading.
- Refer to details and examples from the text when asking and answering questions related to the text.

Essential Questions

- How do you ask and answer questions with text evidence?
- How can you use what is known to speculate on the evidence being examined?

STEP 1: PREPARATION

Organize Materials

- Paper, highlighters, pencils, sticky notes
- Microphone for role-play
- Sample text for modeling

- *Interrogating the Text Chart* reproducible
- Literacy Response Notebooks

STEP 2: INITIATION

Talk Show Q&A Style

Set up an area in the classroom for a talk show environment. Invite a student to be interviewed and supply predetermined questions that lead to getting to know him or her. Using a microphone, interview the student, emphasizing the question words (e.g., who, what, when, where, why, and how) to elicit information in an informal interrogative manner. After the interview, have students share with a partner what they learned about the student based on the interview. Explain that today's lesson will focus on asking questions using question words: who, what, when, where, why, and how based on a certain topic of study to elicit answers.

STEP 3: DEMONSTRATION

Informally Interrogating the Text

1. Make a chart with the question words (who, what, where and when, why). See Figure 1.11 for an example.

FIGURE 1.11

Interrogative *W* Words for Speculative Talk Chart

Text Sequence	Who?	What?	Where? When?	Why?
Beginning	Poppy	crept into open	under the bark and in the open	to show she was not a coward
Middle				
End				

2. Read aloud or display a portion of selected text and model how to categorize the information under each question category.
3. After carefully reading the text and pausing to react to main ideas and key details within the text, continue categorizing these details on the chart.
4. Model using the information charted to pretend to interview the characters in the text using the *W* words in an informal interrogative manner. For example,

if reading from *Poppy* by Avi (2005, p. 6), questions could be, "**Why** did you have to 'creep' into the open? **Who** were you showing that you were not cowardly? **What** happens next, after you 'creep' into the open? Did you think Ragwood was stupid? If so, **why**?"

5. Model how the answers to the questions can be discovered during reading—based on the evidence in the text.

6. Continue sampling the text for another sentence in the middle and toward the end of the story. Show students how to use text evidence when role-playing to answer questions about feelings, motives, and actions.

STEP 4: COLLABORATION

Pair up students. Role-play a character from a text and answer questions by using key ideas, details, and evidence in the text. Ask student pairs to read together and pause throughout the text to pose questions to the characters, taking turns role-playing as the character or the interviewer. *Optional:* Read the text multiple times, focusing on one character at a time and creating questions for that character. Reread and pose questions to a different character. Invite teams to engage in conversational coaching by verbally creating questions and posing them in an interview setting, and then analyzing text evidence gathered based on the words used to answer the questions.

- What did you learn about _____
  in the _____ paragraph based on the questions asked?
- What words did the author use to communicate the information?
- How can you speculate about _____ based on knowing _____?

STEP 5: APPLICATION

Using independently selected text, encourage students to use text-based evidence to complete the "ask and answer" questions for character analysis. Using the *Interrogating the Text Chart* reproducible in Figure 1.12, have students reread the text in sections (i.e., beginning, middle, and end), and record their answers for the *W* questions. They can then create three interview questions they would ask the character based on the information in the text.

FIGURE 1.12

Interrogating the Text Chart Reproducible

Text Sequence	Who?	What?	Where? When?	Why?
Beginning				
Middle				
End				

Interview Questions:

1._____

2._____

3._____

Source: Literacy Strong All Year Long: Powerful Lessons for Grades 3-5 by Lori Oczkus, Valerie Ellery, and Timothy V. Rasinski. Copyright © 2018 ASCD. Readers may duplicate this figure for noncommercial use within their school.

STEP 6: REFLECTION

Oral or Written Response

Have students respond to their completed chart by answering these questions in their Literacy Notebooks:

- How does each sequential section build on the one before it, based on the character's perspective to create a cohesive storyline?
- What is the relationship between the key details in the beginning, middle, and end? Include specific details from the text and how you used these details in your talk show questions.

ADAPTATION AND EXTENSION

- *English Language Learner Suggestion:* Read aloud biographies and model for your students how to ask questions of famous people throughout the reading. Take turns role-playing the interviewer and the famous person. This will allow the students to practice asking questions in an authentic language experience through role-playing.
- *Struggling Reader Suggestion:* As a class and in teams, invite students to create question-and-answer books about informational text topics they are studying. Create question stems to support students as they develop their ability to question the text for deeper meaning.

EVALUATION

"I can . . ." Statements

- I can ask questions to establish a purpose for reading.
- I can ask and answer questions about key ideas and details.
- I can ask and answer questions, using the text for support, to show my understanding.

Behavior Indicators

- Examines a text passage and searches for answers to the question stems Who? What? When? Where? Why?
- Draws on what a character thinks, feels, and does using text evidence to formulate an interrogative analysis.

LESSON 9. COMPREHENSION: DETERMINING IMPORTANCE AND SUMMARIZING

Title SIFTING WHAT MATTERS: DIGGING UP DETAILS

Trailer Details. Details. Details. Information OVERLOAD! There's so much information in the text, it can be overwhelming at times for readers. How can readers identify what is important in the text to determine the main idea? The answer can be found in the concept of a sieve. Readers learn how to sift through information to locate key details in a text to bring meaning to what they are reading. When you are finished with this lesson, you will say, "I can identify what matters!"

Literacy Enhancer Comprehension: Determining Importance: Key Details, Cause and Effect, Sequencing

Key Academic Vocabulary

Cause and Effect: A relationship between actions in which one event (the cause) makes another event happen (effect)

Contribute: To help achieve or provide something; to bring about the sequence of events

Text-Based Evidence: Evidence derived from key facts and details in the text

Learning Objectives

- Describe in depth the character(s), setting, events, or procedures using key details from the text.
- Analyze how characters' actions and reactions contribute to the sequence of events in a story.

Essential Questions

- How do authors convey cause-and-effect relationships through characters, setting, and events?
- What contributing factors determine the sequence of events in a text?

STEP 1: PREPARATION

Organize Materials

- Variety of sieves (i.e., sifters, colanders)
- Container, large rocks, small rocks, bucket of sand
- Multimodal text set of topic of study (mentor text *Thank You, Mr. Falker*)
- *Sifting the Details* reproducible (copy or enlarge for display)
- Literacy Notebooks

STEP 2: INITIATION

Determining the Big Rocks

Display a large container and sand, small rocks, and large rocks. Ask, "Do you think all this will fit into the container?" Elicit responses and reasonings. Begin with pouring in the sand, then add the small rocks. Next ask if there will be room for all the large rocks. Begin to place the large rocks in the container until it is full; you will have many left over. Discuss with the students how the ingredients do not fit, and ask, "What would happen if we reordered the sequence of items placed in the container. Would they all fit if they were placed in a different order?"

Pour all the items from the container into a large bowl. First begin to place in the container just the big rocks (those that fit in the first time, along with all the extras that would not fit) to fill it. Ask, "Is it full now, or is there room for any more?" Elicit responses and reasonings. Add in the smaller stones to fill in spaces and ask again, "Now, is it full?" Have students respond to a partner why they believe it is or is not full. Pour in the sand to demonstrate that there was still room for more. Ask, "What caused all of the items to fit, or not fit, into the container?"

Have the students explain to a partner the concept of what is happening (e.g., "We placed all of the large stones in first, so there is room for all the other elements"). We are going to take this same concept into our story, relating the rocks to the story elements and key details.

STEP 3: DEMONSTRATION

Sifting Details

1. Display a sieve or colander and ask students its purpose (e.g., cooking, building sandcastles, gem mining, filtering soil to recover artifacts). Highlight how this instrument has a mesh or a perforated bottom that helps to separate elements according to size.

2. Prior to meeting with students, select a few big stones and write characters, setting, or events from a selected text on them. Hold up these stones and explain how they represent the who, what, when, why, where, and how of the text. Place the stones in a bucket of sand. Have smaller stones ready so you can discuss the relationships of the large stones to one another and how the smaller stones can represent the character's traits, motivations, feelings, thoughts, words, or actions that contribute to events in the story. This relationship demonstrates how cause and effect throughout the text is determined, which establishes the sequence of events.

3. Hold up the bucket, saying that the contents represent an analogy to the text and the information found within it. Read aloud the selected text, noting along the way certain big rocks (i.e., characters, setting, events). In addition, use the smaller stones to represent traits, motivations, feelings, thoughts, words, or actions that contribute to the sequence of events. See Figure 1.13 for a sample analogy of Big Rocks, Small Rocks using the text *Thank You, Mr. Falker*.

FIGURE 1.13
Big Rocks, Small Rocks Analogy in *Thank You, Mr. Falker*

Story Elements	Big Rocks	Small Rocks
Character Who	Trisha	**Feelings:** felt alone, different, dumb; loved Mr. Falker **Traits:** insecure, hid from Eric; low self-esteem, could not read **Motivations:** changed school; hated school, realized she could not read; started to read; tasted the honey; death of grandparents
	Mr. Falker	**Feelings:** felt sorry for Trisha **Traits:** compassionate, made Trisha feel happy **Motivations:** realized Trisha could not read; taught Trisha to read; tutored Trisha
	Schoolchildren (Eric)	**Trait:** bullies **Motivations:** called her dumb and a toad; pulled her hair
	Gramma and Grampa	**Motivations:** encouraged Trisha; going to school and learning to read was as sweet as honey
Setting When & Where	Elementary School	**Feelings:** Trisha hated school **Motivations:** changed schools; moved from Michigan to California
	Playground	**Motivation:** Trisha hid to avoid being bullied
Events What & How	Learning to Read	**Feelings:** Trisha learned to love reading **Trait:** was difficult **Motivation:** Trisha realized she couldn't read; was teased by schoolchildren; Mr. Falker tutored Trisha in reading; Trisha learned to read

Source: Literacy Strong All Year Long: Powerful Lessons for Grades 3-5 by Lori Oczkus, Valerie Ellery, and Timothy V. Rasinski. Copyright © 2018 ASCD. Readers may duplicate this figure for noncommercial use within their school.

STEP 4: COLLABORATION

Have the students determine how the Big Rocks, Small Rocks experiment allows them to first think about the key details and be able to have text-based evidence to support these details. Have them discuss the details on the rocks and stones and how the details helped them to demonstrate the overall meaning of the text. Encourage students to engage in conversational coaching by discussing the following questions with diverse partners about the current text they are reading:

- In the text you are reading, what is the proper order for the sequence of events to make sense?
- How does the author show cause-and-effect relationships in the text to support your key details?

STEP 5: APPLICATION

Have students work in groups or individually to determine details from a text or topic by revisiting the text to analyze key details. Have them either use the *Sifting the Details* reproducible in Figure 1.14 or two different colors of highlighters to specify the big rock concepts and the smaller rock concepts that support the specific details.

STEP 6: REFLECTION

Oral or Written Response

Have students independently respond in their Literacy Notebooks to explain how using the rock demonstration analogy (i.e., large rocks representing character, setting, or events; small rocks representing details about characters) can help them process text as a reader and guide them as a writer.

ADAPTATION AND EXTENSION

- Adapt thinking from how characters' actions contribute to the events in a story to focusing on how an illustration contributes to the text's meaning.
- Create a song or rap that identifies the key details in the text, or view the free video from Flocabulary (www.flocabulary.com/fivethings/) that creatively covers the five main elements of a story.
- *English Language Learners Suggestion*: Formulate cause-and-effect relationships using an online or worksheet tool (Comic Creator or Make Beliefs Comix) to organize and create a comic strip (see ReadWriteThink: Engaging with Cause-and-Effect Relationships Through Creating Comic Strips at www .readwritethink.org/classroom-resources/lesson-plans/engaging-with-cause-effect-30678.html?tab=4.) ReadWriteThink, created by the National Council of Teachers of English and the International Literacy Association, provides free instructional practices and digital resources that support effective reading and language arts instruction for all learners.

- *Struggling Readers Suggestion:* Have students become reporters as they focus on oral language to formulate questions. Ask them to use the character's traits, feelings, and motivation as a basis or to use the text's features and structures (i.e., who, what, when, where, and why).

EVALUATION

"I can . . ." Statements

- I can describe a story's character, setting, or events using specific details from the text.
- I can explain how a character's actions contribute to the events in the story.
- I can describe steps in a procedure in the order they should happen.

Behavior Indicators

- Identifies the story's character(s), setting, events, or procedures for the key details (i.e., big rocks), and any actions, traits, feelings, or motivations for the supporting and causal details (i.e., smaller stones).
- Analyzes how characters' actions and reactions contribute to the sequence of events in a story.
- Describes the relationships of events, ideas, or concepts in a text.

FIGURE 1.14

Sifting the Details Reproducible

Name: _____ Title of text: _____

Directions: Use the sample rocks to label the key details of what you just read. Then, justify why you think these rocks are the BIG ideas of the text and should be discussed first.

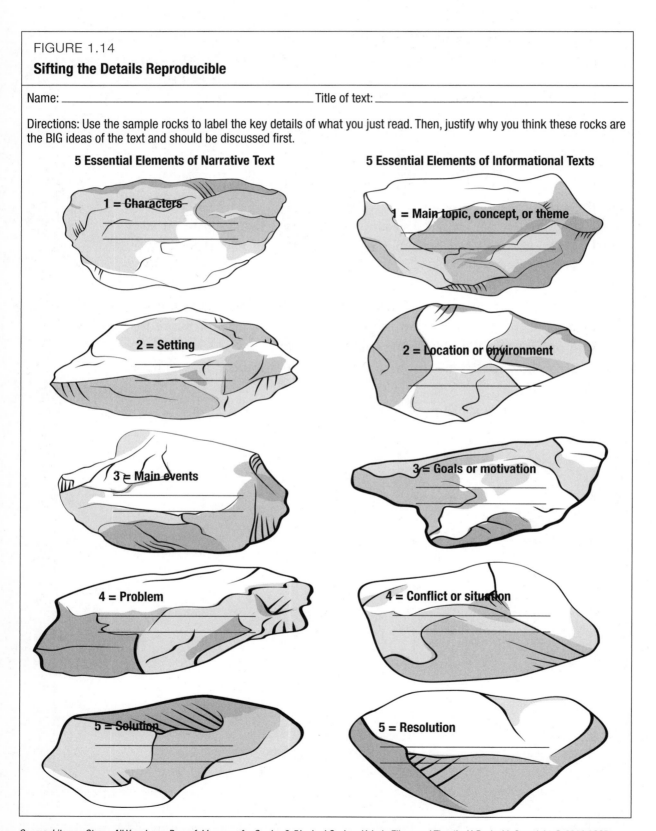

5 Essential Elements of Narrative Text

1 = Characters

2 = Setting

3 = Main events

4 = Problem

5 = Solution

5 Essential Elements of Informational Texts

1 = Main topic, concept, or theme

2 = Location or environment

3 = Goals or motivation

4 = Conflict or situation

5 = Resolution

LESSON 10. COMPREHENSION: MOTIVATING READERS

Title MOTIVATION WITH BOOK LOGS

Trailer Students in grades 3 to 5 especially enjoy participating in clubs for a sense of community and belonging. From scouting to sports and hobbies, this is the age of joining. The Class Book Club takes your usual teacher read-aloud time to the next level. Students become reviewers ready to provide evidence for savvy book choices when they use book logs. Logs can be used to record books that you read aloud to the class as well as books the class reads together. When you introduce individual book logs, students will be ready to increase their own reading.

Literacy Enhancer Motivation: Motivating Readers—Text features, Book logs, Predicting, Summarizing

Key Academic Vocabulary

Author: The person who wrote the book

Illustrator: The person who illustrated the book

Predict: To use information from a text to infer what the text will be about or what one might learn from it

Rating: A score assigned to reading material based on a scale from best to least

Reason: The rationale for an opinion or idea backed with text evidence

Summarize: To tell what has happened in the text by sharing important points and details

Title: The name of the text; tells what it is about or gives clues to the content

Learning Objectives

- Identify the title, author, and illustrator of books read by the teacher and the class.
- Evaluate and score books by providing reasons on the Class Book Log reproducible.
- Keep an individual book log.
- Participate in discussions about books using book logs.

Essential Questions

- What are the types of books the class has read?
- What makes you like or dislike a book?
- What are some different types of books you want to read next?
- How can you talk about books with others?

STEP 1: PREPARATION

Organize Materials

- Read-aloud books for the grade level
- *Class Book Club Log* reproducible
- *My Book Log* reproducible
- Independent reading books
- Literacy Journals
- Books to read to cross-age buddies

STEP 2: INITIATION

The Class Book Club: Invitation to Join

Ask students if they've ever belonged to a club. Remind them that clubs can focus on scouting, sports, religion, or hobbies. Sometimes children even create their own clubs with friends and neighbors. Tell the class about some clubs you belonged to as a child. Share that everyone in the class is automatically in the Room____ Class Book Club and that the purpose of the club is for them to enjoy and listen while you read aloud different titles. Hold up a few enticing grade-level chapter and picture books that you will read aloud and that the class will read together. The class will participate in keeping book logs and fun ways to advertise and rate books, for each other.

To grow more interest in reading and being a member of the book club, you can play popular song parodies about reading. Search the Internet for an appropriate song parody to share with your students about reading and books, including:

- "All About Those Books" by the Mountain Desert High School. Available: www .youtube.com/watch?v=g2pu8nsUtCQ, based on Megahn Trainor's song, "All About That Bass"
- "Gotta Keep Reading" by the Ocoee Middle School. Available: www.schooltube .com/video/e9bd79d29b4d0e6a2345/Gotta-Keep-!, based on The Black Eyed Peas' Song "I Gotta Feeling"

STEP 3: DEMONSTRATION

Read Aloud and Record on the Log

1. Select an exciting fiction or informational book to read aloud to the class. Show the cover and model how to preview it by discussing the title, art, author, and back cover information. Encourage students to turn and share their thoughts with partners after modeling.

2. Continue modeling how to preview the text by flipping through the pages and making more predictions about the story (fiction) or what you will learn (nonfiction). Invite students to turn and talk to share their thoughts.

3. Read aloud with much expression to generate excitement about the book and reading. Or you may wish to select a book that has an accompanying audio recording to play for students.

4. Pause at least once during a 15-minute read-aloud to discuss what has happened so far. Use the frame "So far, _____. Next I think _____ because _____" (Oczkus, 2009), and model a summary and prediction of what you think will happen next. Invite students to turn and talk to one another about their ideas as well. Finish reading and share your favorite part and your rationale. Explain, "My favorite part was _____. My reasons are _____ because _____." Tell students that when they share their favorite parts, they need to provide reasons and evidence from the text. Encourage partners to share.

5. Tell the class that the Class Book Club is going to keep track of the books that you read aloud to them by recording on a Class Book Club Reading Log. Make copies for every student of the reproducible in Figure 1.15 and enlarge one to display in the classroom or project on a screen. Fill in the title, author, illustrator, and rating, along with a reason for the rating. Have students each fill in their copies of the Class Book Log and store it in a construction paper folder, a file folder, or digital portfolio log.

6. When students share their ratings of the books, try using gestures as shown in Figure 1.16 and model for students. Students choose a rating from 1 through 4, and either vote as a class or individually. You may want to vary individual and class voting, or do both and code the class with one color and individual ratings with another.

FIGURE 1.15

Class Book Club Reading Log Reproducible

Rating   4 = Great   3 = Good   2 = OK   1 = Poor

Reader's Name _____ Classroom _____

Date	Title	Author or Illustrator	Rating and Reason(s)
			I gave it a ____ (rating) because
			I gave it a____ (rating) because
			I gave it a____ (rating) because
			I gave it a____ (rating) because

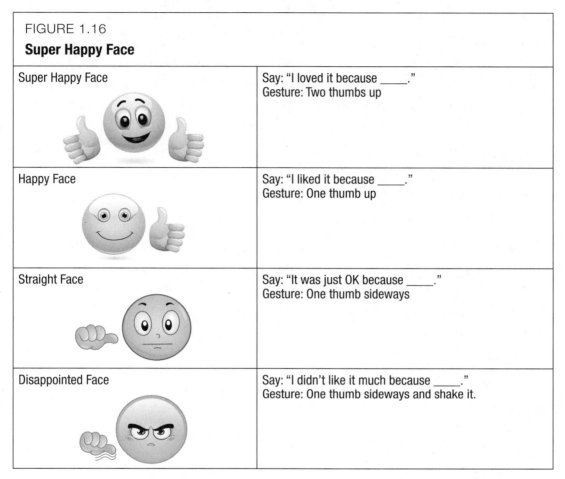

FIGURE 1.16
Super Happy Face

Super Happy Face	Say: "I loved it because _____." Gesture: Two thumbs up
Happy Face	Say: "I liked it because _____." Gesture: One thumb up
Straight Face	Say: "It was just OK because _____." Gesture: One thumb sideways
Disappointed Face	Say: "I didn't like it much because _____." Gesture: One thumb sideways and shake it.

Source: Literacy Strong All Year Long: Powerful Lessons for Grades 3-5 by Lori Oczkus, Valerie Ellery, and Timothy V. Rasinski. Copyright © 2018 ASCD. Readers may duplicate this figure for noncommercial use within their school.

STEP 4: COLLABORATION

After reading another book to the class and following the same pattern of previewing the text, pausing for predictions, and discussing favorite parts, encourage partners and teams to use full sentences and the academic language in the lesson such as author, illustrator, preview, and reasons as they discuss their thoughts about the text. Next invite students to fill in their *Class Book Club Reading Logs* for the title. Ask students to rate the book individually and as a class and provide text examples and reasons for the rating. Discuss responses.

Show a stack of books to the class that are possibilities for the Class Book Club. Include poetry, nonfiction, short stories, and chapter books. Tell students where you find your read-aloud book title ideas (e.g., librarian, other teachers, online sources).

Invite students to share their suggestions for the teacher read-alouds and to add to the book club list. Encourage students to give strong reasons for their choices.

STEP 5: APPLICATION

Pass out the *My Reading Book Log* reproducible to each student (see Figure 1.17). Invite them to fill in the log with a book they've read recently or are reading now. Ask students to share their reading log with a partner and to use full sentences and academic language. You can help them start by offering sentence starters. Be sure that they include reasons for their ratings of the books.

- The title of my book is_____.
- The author is_____.
- I (loved it, liked it, thought it was just OK, or I didn't like it much) because _____.

Rotate and Rate Around. Ask students to take their book and completed personal book log on a quick Rotate and Rate Around. Play music and allow students to quietly walk around the room. When the music stops, they must freeze and share their book log information with a partner who is standing near them. Play the music again so students can rotate to new partners.

STEP 6: REFLECTION

Oral or Written Response

Explain to students that using a book log helps readers keep track of the number and types of books they are reading over time. That way readers can think about what they've enjoyed and also try to stretch to read new types of texts. Discuss as a class how keeping a reading log is helpful both for the Class Book Club and for individuals. What are the benefits? How does it motivate you to read more or to vary your reading material? After discussing the value of the *Class Book Club Reading Log*, ask students to write in their literacy journals. Some possible prompts:

- The class book club log selection I like the most so far is _____, because _____ .
- I think having a class book club log is helpful because_____.
- Keeping my own reading log is helpful because_____.
- I can't wait to read the book _____ because_____.

ADAPTATION AND EXTENSION

- *Big Buddies.* Pair students with buddies from a lower grade level to read to all year long in weekly 20-minute sessions. Show the big and little buddies how to fill out the *My Reading Book Log* reproducible in Figure 1.17 to record the books they read together during their buddy sessions.

- *Online Rating.* Use a social media platform such as Ning (see www.ning.com) where students can rate books and create reviews to share with one another. You can create your own secure message board for your class.
- *English Language Learners Suggestion*: Work with ELLs in a small group to assist and guide them as they share their reading logs with one another. Encourage them to use full sentences and academic language. Make sure they include reasons for their rating of the books.
- *Struggling Readers Suggestion:* Meet in a small group and invite students to share one book log entry. Encourage them to act out a favorite scene from the book and tell why they selected that scene. Work together to create an "I want to read next" list of books. Invite students to share reasons for the books they add to the list.

EVALUATION

"I can . . ." Statements

- I can fill out the Class Book Club Log and provide a rating for books complete with reasons for my rating.
- I can share information about my independent reading on My Book Log complete with reasons for my ratings.
- I can participate in class, partner, and team discussions about the books our teacher reads aloud to us.

Behavior Indicators

- Identifies the author, illustrator, and title of books the teacher and class has read.
- Rates books and gives at least one reason for the rating.
- Shares class book summaries and ratings verbally with others in discussions.
- Keeps the Class Book Club reproducible updated.
- Identifies the author, illustrator, and title of independent reading books.
- Rates independent reading books and provides one reason for the rating.
- Participates in discussions about independent reading choices and gives brief summaries and ratings.

FIGURE 1.17

My Reading Book Log Reproducible

Rating   **4 = Great**   **3 = Good**   **2 = OK**   **1 = Poor**

Reader's Name _____ **Classroom** _____

Date	Title	Author or Illustrator	Rating and Reason(s)
			I gave it a ____ [rating] because
			I gave it a____ [rating] because
			I gave it a____ [rating] because
			I gave it a____ [rating] because

Beating the Midyear Blahs

A book is a dream you hold in your hand.
—Neil Gaiman

I owe everything I am and everything I will ever be to books.
—Gary Paulsen

Staying motivated and literacy strong is especially important during the middle months of the academic calendar. Just like a marathon runner passing the halfway mark in a race, when we hit the middle of the school year, we can view our position in two ways. There's a sense of satisfaction from reaching the halfway point, but then stark reality sets in with the realization of the enormous effort needed to reach the finish line. Sometimes, depending on where you live and teach, the weather dramatically affects the classroom mood with a seemingly endless string of rainy, snowy, cold days. The good news about the middle of the school year is that there is still plenty of time for your students to grow academically. In addition, this is the time we often notice spikes in student maturity levels, and sometimes reading and writing jump to new heights as well. The need to assess progress and target the ongoing needs of students, especially struggling readers, becomes a priority at this critical juncture in the school year (Hiebert & Taylor, 1994; Torgesen, 2005).

So, how do we maintain momentum, stay focused, and remain literacy strong in the middle of the school year? Here are some great ways to beat the midyear blahs, energize your students, yield positive results, and bring joy to the classroom.

Literacy-Strong Classroom Scenarios

What does a literacy-strong classroom look like in the middle of the school year? Here are some short classroom stories for inspiration.

Motivation: Take Off and Partner Talk Bookmarks

"Talking to one another about our reading improves our understanding and comprehension," explains Mr. Lowe to the 4th graders. The class is reading an article together about sharks and using their *Take Off and Partner Talk* bookmarks. The students refer to their bookmarks and the before-reading prompt and turn to their partners to respond. Brendan tells George, "I think I will learn about shark measurements because the title says *Shark Specs*. And I see a chart with measurements in it at the end." George adds, "I think we will learn about the size of the Great White shark because I saw it when I skimmed the article." The boys sketch a quick "thinking" bubble on a sticky note and put it near the title of the text to remember their predictions. They read a paragraph and pause as Mr. Lowe signals the class to stop and sketch what they've learned so far. Brendan sketches a shark and writes the number 350 under it as he uses the bookmark prompt to respond, "So far I've learned that there are 350 species of sharks." Mr. Lowe circulates to the pairs around the room and encourages students to refer to their bookmark as they make their way through the article. At the end of the lesson students sketch a star on a sticky note and share favorite facts that they learned. The students are practicing using the bookmarks, which they will use again when they read the social studies chapter later in the week. The students enjoy using the sticky notes, talking to their partners, and learning about sharks!

Comprehension: Informational Text Features Tour!

Mrs. Ko leads the 5th grade students in a lively discussion about tours they've experienced that were conducted by a tour guide at places like museums and zoos and even a haunted house. Then Mrs. Ko asks the students about the kinds of comments tour guides make. She records on a chart "tour talk" such as "Over here we have . . ." and "on the right you will find an example of . . ." and "Watch closely as we pass by the . . . ." She then explains that to understand informational texts and their text features, such as the headings and table of contents, students are going to become expert tour guides. They will give tours of informational books rather than museums or the zoo. Mrs. Ko demonstrates a tour using an informational picture book about volcanoes. She holds up the text and shows the cover and says, "Welcome to the tour of this book." She continues as students giggle when she reaches for a plastic echo microphone to ham it up even further. "So, as you can see from this table of contents, we will learn about . . ." and Mrs. Ko continues turning the pages using her best tour guide manner to discuss each of the text features. She invites students to turn and talk to partners to discuss what they think they will learn and to review the name of the text feature. Mrs. Ko puts copies of a variety of informational texts on their desks and invites pairs to choose a text to "tour" together. The students take turns previewing and touring the features using the tour guide language from the chart. Mrs. Ko circulates and offers assistance. She invites students to demonstrate their best tour guide personas in front of the class. Tomorrow the class will break into four teams and serve as guides for one of the following text features: table of contents, headings, maps and charts, and photos and captions. The memorable lesson has made an impression as students go to recess talking in "tour guide speak"!

Vocabulary: Like What? Similes and Metaphors Galore

Giggles abound as the students in Miss Brown's 3rd grade class work in teams to create their own similes and metaphors as they play the game Bag It. Jaime shakes the brown bag and draws the first card, the word *car*. He shakes the bag again and draws the word *enemy.* His team of four other students gasp at the word *enemy* and wait to see how Jaime responds. Using the hand gesture Miss Brown has taught the class, Jaime holds the word *car* in his left hand and says, "The car is like a _____." He places the *enemy* card in the other hand and completes the metaphor, "The car is like an enemy because the engine roars red-hot and mad!" The team writes the simile and sketches a red car racing down the road on their chart. Jaime passes the bag to the next team member to give it a shake. The students have experienced lots of metaphors and similes in the past week as Miss Brown has read aloud books with those elements, including *My Dog Is as Smelly as Dirty Socks* by Hanovich Piven (2007). Miss Brown also plays Disney songs with similes and metaphors, including a student favorite— "Let It Go" from the movie *Frozen.* The class is building a similes and metaphors chart and adding examples they find in their reading as well as in songs, on television, and in everyday conversations.

Addressing Midyear Challenges

Educators face many competing challenges in the middle of the school year. In this section are some suggestions for facing these challenges head-on to set the stage for maximum literacy growth.

Questions Teachers Ask to Address Midyear Challenges

- What are some ways to continue to inspire my students to read more and to read more rigorous texts?
- What are some strategies that will encourage my students to work collaboratively?
- How do I help students become more independent readers?
- What are some formative assessment strategies that I can use to show growth and adjust instruction to meet students' needs?
- What can I do to ensure that all my students learn the expected literacy standards?
- How can I actively engage students in lessons?
- How can I continue to maintain a strong rapport with each of my students and their parents?

Must-Have Moments for Maintaining Momentum

1. Inspire Students to Read with Funny Books

A whopping 70 percent of students ages 6–17 say they enjoy and prefer reading books that make them laugh (Scholastic, 2017). What does this mean for the classroom? If we read aloud from humorous texts, our students will be inspired to read them on their own. Host a read-aloud and laugh-around and invite students each to share a funny poem, story, or joke book while sitting in a circle. Videotape students sharing their titles and post it on the class or school website. Take what Miller (2009) calls "shelfies" (i.e., photos of students with their funny books) and compile them into a class album. Stock up on silly and outrageous books for read-alouds and the classroom library. Of course, you can rely on kid favorites, such as the easy readers Junie B. Jones series by Barbara Park, anything by Dr. Seuss, and the Captain Underpants series by Dav Pilkey. Try some of these to see if they tickle your students' funny bones:

Picture Books
- *I Wanna Iguana* by Karen Kaufman Orloff
- *How I Became a Pirate* by Melinda Long
- *Never Ride Your Elephant to School* by Doug Johnson
- *Monkey and Duck Quack Up!* by Jennifer Hamburg
- *Polar Bear's Underwear* by Tupera
- *Don't Let the Pigeon Drive the Bus!* by Mo Willems
- *Honest Abe's Funny Money Book* by Jack Silbert

Chapter Books
- *Potterwookiee Creature from My Closet* by Obert Skye
- *Boys Only: How to Survive Anything* by Martin Oliver
- *Girls Only: How to Survive Anything* by Martin Oliver
- *The Summer Camp from the Black Lagoon* by Mike Thaler

2. Focus on Fluency

Fluency is a bridge to comprehension. When you help students become more fluent readers, they grow dramatically in their reading. One way to help students with fluency is to conduct minilessons as you model reading aloud and discuss how you embedded fluency. Help students recognize that you changed your voice when becoming a different character in the reading by using prosodic functions, such as pitch, tone, and stresses (Ellery, 2014). Help students notice where you became louder or softer, or faster or slower, in your reading. Then, discuss how your fluency made the reading more interesting and understandable. Point out that you rehearsed the book so you were able to read with fluency. This is an important message for students as they reread to gain momentum: whenever they are to read something orally for an audience, they should rehearse the text in advance (repeated readings). As you work with students throughout the year, coach them in three areas of fluency—rate, accuracy, and prosody (Rasinski & Griffith, 2011). Here are a few samples of prompts:

- Rate: The student reads at a natural rate. *Coaching Prompt: Nice slowing down to show the emotions of the character.*
- Accuracy: The student decodes words effortlessly and accurately. *Coaching Prompt: Great rereading! You read the sentence to check it.*
- Prosody: The student reads with expression, phrasing, and intonation. *Coaching Prompt: Read it again and group the words the way you would talk.*

3. Teach Close Reading with Poems

Invite students to reread poems to partners or chorally as a class for fluency and understanding. Keep a notebook of poems so students can access them to reread many times. Make copies of poems for students to mark up with crayons or highlighters as they reread for close reading lessons. Reread to ask questions, circle interesting words, underline main ideas and details, and put stars or smiley faces next to favorite words or parts (Rasinski & Oczkus, 2015a, 2015b, 2015c).

4. Try Short, One-Minute Assessments

Use informal, quick-check assessments at least once a month for all students and every two weeks for struggling readers. The assessments will give ongoing information about the reading strategies that your students are using, their comprehension, and their fluency. Then use the information you've gathered to guide your conferences with students and to help you decide what to focus on in your lessons. You can also use the information to help you with flexibly grouping students. For example, you can group students together who are having trouble with fluency or summarizing.

Have individual students read for one minute while you mark the substitutions and omissions that each student makes. Also, note how many words the student reads and how fluently in just one minute. Reread the text aloud to the student. After this, remove the passage and ask the student to retell what is remembered. Mark the student's responses. Did the student tell what was read in order, including main ideas and details? To find more tips, try *3-Minute Reading Assessments: Word Recognition, Fluency, and Comprehension: Grades 1–4* (Rasinski & Padak, 2005).

5. Boost Reading with Big Buddies and Beam Reading

When younger and older children read together, they both benefit (Topping, 2005). Have your students read once a week with a buddy class of lower-grade students. For a 20- to 30-minute period, follow a simple protocol in which the older student reads aloud to the younger one first. A flashlight or laser pen can be used for beam reading to allow tracking and to demonstrate reading rate (Ellery, 2014). The older buddy should select a title that the younger buddy will enjoy and practice reading it fluently before reading it to the younger partner. If there is time, the younger student may select a brief text to read aloud to the older student.

6. Book Clubs Based on Choice

Midyear is a great time to begin, if you have not done so already, student-led book clubs. By now students are well grounded in the classroom rules and procedures and they've been introduced to discussion protocol. Discussion protocol includes listening actively, taking turns, encouraging others to contribute, agreeing or disagreeing respectfully, and adding or "piggybacking" comments onto the discussion. If you have not taught these basics of discussion, then do so by creating a class chart and demonstrating each behavior. Introduce the concept of book clubs by discussing what students already know about them. What do they read and what is the purpose of a book club? Then choose some high-interest titles that students will enjoy reading together.

You can select books for book clubs in many ways, including books about the same topic, different titles by the same author, or books at a variety of reading levels. As long as you have three to six copies of each title, you can host a book club. Once you've selected the texts, give a quick book commercial about each choice and allow students to sign up for their number one or two choices. Let students determine how long a chunk of text for reading in a given class period should be (e.g., a chapter, a few pages) so that they have time to read some material and then discuss it. Or students may read a portion of text ahead of time and use group time to discuss the pages.

Use some of the tools in this book as guides for students to follow for discussions. Try using the *Take Off and Partner Talk* bookmark (Figure 2.19) to help guide students in their discussions. Or use the *Informational Text Features Tour Guide* in Figure 2.9 or the *Sneak Preview 1-2-3* in Figure 1.9. Also, students may fill in *Text Trip Maps* (Figure 3.12, to be introduced in Chapter 3).

Begin the book club reading sessions with a quick minilesson where you spend only five minutes demonstrating an aspect of reading or the discussion that you want students to cover. Determine if teams will meet at tables or on the floor. Knee to knee works well and improves eye contact and listening skills. Then students read the text in their teams, silently or in pairs. For longer chapter books, students read the text ahead of time so when they meet with the group, they've marked their books with sticky notes and can discuss their ideas. Continue to model social skills when necessary. Join in with the groups and circulate to help facilitate the discussions.

7. Teach Informational Text Features with a Text Feature Wall

Informational text features serve as road markers that guide readers through nonfiction texts. Over a few weeks, teach your students about these features by building a text feature wall or chart. Divide a large chart or chart paper into sections and label them with text features, such as headings, table of contents, visuals, maps, bold words, captions, and glossary. As you read informational texts with students, teach lessons on each of the features. Make copies of texts and cut out text features to glue or tape onto the text feature wall or cut text features from weekly newspapers or magazines as examples (Kelley & Clausen-Grace, 2008; Oczkus, 2014). Also, using weekly news magazines and printouts of articles, students can make text feature booklets and cut and paste examples of each feature.

8. Cover and Retell with a Partner

Many students in intermediate grades experience challenges when retelling and summarizing. They need to practice without the stress of having to write, too. Try the strategy "Read, Cover, Remember, Retell" (Hoyt, 2002, p. 58). Students work in pairs and take turns reading a page at a time. After reading, the student covers the text with a hand, tries to remember the material, and summarizes or retells without looking. The student may peek just once. Partners continue taking turns reading, covering, and retelling the material. When you use this strategy in a center or workstation, model and coach often so students continue to improve in their retellings.

9. Celebrate Wonderful Words Everywhere!

Vocabulary is a strong predictor of reading success. Teaching vocabulary improves reading comprehension for native speakers as well as second-language students (Beck, Perfetti, & McKeown, 1982; Carlo et al., 2004). Students can study words by sorting, illustrating, and playing games such as Concentration. Continue to add to word walls in the classroom. Here are some word walls and charts to display:

- An alphabetical word wall that features a square space (at least 8.5″ × 11″) for each letter for adding student names and high-frequency words
- Charts of synonyms for the word *said*
- Charts of synonyms for the feeling words *happy* and *sad*
- Charts of words for common adjectives and verbs
- Charts for similes and metaphors

10. Lucky Listeners

Ask students to practice reading a book, a poem, or other reading material at school. Then have them take the text home to read again to at least three "Lucky Listeners" (Rasinski & Griffith, 2011). Reading to the dog, a baby, and Grandma all count!

11. Share Home Reading Ideas with Parents

Conduct a midyear workshop for parents to demonstrate some of the ideas found in this book. Share the bookmarks, reproducibles, and games of your choice. Or run a series of workshops and introduce only two of the lessons and practice materials at a time. Provide materials such as books and sticky notes for parents to try out the ideas. If students attend with their parents, make the workshop interactive and brief. See the parent letters in Chapter 4 for more ideas on sharing lessons with parents.

Here is a list of midyear read-alouds to entertain and motivate your students to love to read.

- *The Tale of Despereaux* by Kate DiCamillo
- *The Witches* by Roald Dahl
- *The Lion, the Witch, and the Wardrobe* by C. S. Lewis
- *Bridge to Terabithia* by Katherine Paterson
- *The One and Only Ivan* by Katherine Applegate

12. Midyear Word Ladder

Start with a word that means "to continue a certain action."

Keep	Change one letter to make another word for crying.
Weep	Add one letter to make what you do with a broom.
Sweep	Change one letter to make an animal that makes the sound *baa*.
Sheep	Take away the two vowels and replace with one to make a large boat.
Ship	Change one letter to make what might happen if you step on a banana peel.
Slip	Change one letter to make another word that describes someone who is slender or thin.
Slim	Change one letter to make what you can do in the water.
Swim	Change one letter to take a large drink or gulp of a liquid.
Swig	Add one letter to make a piece of playground equipment.
Swing	Take away one letter to make a part of a bird or airplane.
Wing	Add two letters to the beginning to describe what you should be doing when in a rowboat.
Rowing	Add one letter to describe what we want to keep doing in the middle of the year.
Growing	Keep growing!

Overview of Chapter 2 Lessons

Lesson 1. Word Study: Decoding—Syllable Segmentation
Lesson 2. Vocabulary: Gaming with Words—Making and Writing Words
Lesson 3. Vocabulary: Analyzing Words—Functional Roots
Lesson 4. Vocabulary: Associating Words—Like What? Similes and Metaphors Galore
Lesson 5. Fluency: Phrasing, Pacing, Expressing—Honoring President John F. Kennedy Through Oratory
Lesson 6. Comprehension: Previewing—Informational Text Feature Tour!
Lesson 7. Comprehension: Inferring and Drawing Conclusions—A Text with a View
Lesson 8. Comprehension: Questioning for Close Reading—Inference Dance Moves: Reading Between the Lines
Lesson 9. Comprehension: Determining Importance and Summarizing—Recount Recipe
Lesson 10. Comprehension: Motivating Readers—Take Off and Partner Talk Bookmarks

LESSON 1. WORD STUDY: DECODING

Title SYLLABLE SEGMENTATION: HAIKU STYLE

Trailer Karate and haiku poetry have something in common. They both come from Asia and require slicing and dicing. You see, haiku makes the reader think of a rhythmic pattern flow as it slices through the syllables to segment them into a succinct pattern. In this lesson, you will be creating a mental image of the words you will need to craft the perfect art form of haiku.

Literacy Enhancer Word Study: Decoding—Syllables; Writing: Haiku Poetry

Key Academic Vocabulary

(Terms spiraled from previous lessons)

Decoding: The process of translating a printed word into its oral representation. Readers use a variety of strategies in word decoding, including phonics (sound-symbol relationships), structural analysis (prefix, base word, suffix), and context.

Diphthong: A unit of sound gliding the vowel sound by the combination of a vowel digraph allowing the tongue to move and change

Vowel Digraph: A pair of vowel letters coming together to form a vowel team representing one sound

(New terms in this lesson)

Closed Syllable: A syllable that has only one vowel followed by a consonant, with the vowel usually pronounced as a short vowel sound

Haiku: A form of Japanese poetry used mainly to describe nature and the seasons in a restricted syllable format

Multisyllabic: A word having more than one syllable

Open Syllable: A syllable ending in only one vowel, with the vowel usually pronounced as a long vowel sound

Segmenting: Breaking a word by phoneme (sound) or syllables

Syllable: A part of a word that contains only one vowel sound; words can be made of one or more syllables

Learning Objectives

- Examine word-analysis skills in decoding words through multisyllabic awareness.
- Identify syllable guidelines.
- Investigate elements of haiku poetry and how syllables play a key role.

Essential Questions

- How does separating words into syllables help the reader decode (read) and encode (spell)?
- How are syllables segmented?
- How do you write a haiku poem?

STEP 1: PREPARATION

Organize Materials

- Multimodal text sets with samples of haiku
- Book: *The Year Comes Round: Haiku Through the Seasons* (optional)
- Supplies to create a class Anchor Chart (e.g., chart paper, markers). Most of the time teachers and students create anchor charts together. See Step 3, number 4, where it appears that the anchor chart is part of the Syllable Segmenting Guidelines.
- *Haiku Writing* reproducible
- Word Work Journals or Writing Notebooks
- *Syllable Segmenting Guidelines* reproducible
- *Syllable Structure and Vowel Jingle*

STEP 2: INITIATION

Go on a nature walk or display photographs of the current season and discuss observations with the class. Then select and display these two haiku poems written by Janie Hull that relate to the present season and read them to the students aloud.

Transitions
Cold winter snow melts
White snowmen have disappeared
Notice bright crocus!

Freshness
Hear lawn mowers hum
Drifting scent of fresh-mown grass
Spring season brings life.

Have students figure out the season the haikus are referencing. Remind them this is like the *Who Am I?* vowel digraph riddles from Chapter 1, Lesson 1 on decoding. Student partners can share what they notice about the two poems (e.g., short, winter and spring seasons, three lines, similar rhythm). Reread and clap out the rhythmic syllable pattern in each line and identify the pattern they both have (i.e., five syllables on the first line, seven on the second line, and five on the third line). Remind students that words can have more than one syllable, and that each syllable has one vowel sound. Explain that haiku poetry originated in Japan and is mainly used to describe nature and the seasons. It has a combination of two seemingly unrelated parts that come together to suggest a surprise, and it rarely rhymes like most poetry.

STEP 3: DEMONSTRATION

Syllable Segmenting

1. Pronounce the words *snowmen, notice,* and *mowers* from the haiku poems. Have the students listen for the number of syllables they hear in these words.
2. Count syllables and vowel placements:
    a. Model by placing your hand under your chin to feel how many times your chin touches your hand and demonstrate that each word has two syllables.
    b. Say each word slowly and identify the point of sound where your chin drops and touches your hand (i.e., right after the first vowel sound in each word).
    c. Count and analyze the vowels in each word: *snowmen* (two) *ow* and *e; notice* (two) *o* and *i*, with silent *e; mowers* (two) *ow* and *er, r*-controlled vowel.
    d. Isolate the first syllable in each word and think about the vowel sound in it. Isolate the first vowel sound in the word *snowmen* (-*ow*). Review how the -*ow* forms a vowel team called a vowel digraph (see Chapter 1, Decoding: Lesson 1) and the two letters make the long /o/ sound, as in the first syllable of the word *notice*. Identify the first syllable in the word *notice* is *no*, and because it ends with a vowel, it is considered an open syllable and the vowel sound usually makes the long sound. Continue to isolate the first vowel sound in *mowers* (-*ow*).
    e. Compare the first vowels in the three demonstrated words. Highlight that they all make the long /o/ sound, but that *mowers* and *snowmen* have the –*ow* vowel digraph.
3. Model dividing syllables by analyzing the letter and sound structure and vowel placements in the words. You can use a slash mark, a raised dot, or even a hyphen to demonstrate the syllable segmentation. *Snowmen* is a compound word; you will place a marker after the first separate word *snow/men*. For *no/tice* and *mow/ers,* divide after the first vowel.

4. Create a class Syllable Segmentation anchor chart or use the *Syllable Segmenting Guidelines* reproducible to guide students as they read and write throughout the day. Continue adding to this chart as you analyze words by syllables. Revisit words describing nature and explain that partners or groups will have an opportunity to write a haiku reflecting on the 5-7-5 syllable pattern.

STEP 4: COLLABORATION

To begin creating their own haikus, students study words or phrases that pertain to the season and examine the syllable segmentation. Remind them to be descriptive, using 17 total syllables in only three lines. They can record their writing process on the *Haiku Writing* reproducible in Figure 2.1. Engage in conversational coaching by asking students to discuss the following questions with diverse partners:

- How many syllables do you hear in the word _____? How do you know?
- Does our haiku "paint a mental" image of _____? Explain it.
- Is there a combination of two seemingly unrelated parts suggesting a surprising relationship?

STEP 5: APPLICATION

After the prewriting stages and conversational coaching, have the students record their published work on the bottom of the *Haiku Writing* reproducible in Figure 2.1. Have students keep word journals in which they record and categorize the vowel-digraph words from text they are reading or their writing pieces (e.g., interpretation or response to literature, argumentative or persuasive). Students can also select words to analyze by syllable mapping, and then record their syllable analysis in their Word Work Journals. These words can have the same vowel digraph. Have students use selected words in sentences for creating their own riddles or haiku poems to describe a selected topic.

STEP 6: REFLECTION

Oral or Written Response

Students may respond to the essential questions through written or oral response: How many syllable segments are in the word _____? Describe how the word is segmented by syllables. How do you write a haiku?

ADAPTATION AND EXTENSION

- Create individual charts to illustrate the identified guidelines in the *Syllable Segmenting Guidelines* reproducible, Figure 2.2. It should consist of the guideline, a cartoon image or illustration, and at least two example words mapped out to demonstrate how they meet the guideline that is being highlighted.
- To verify the syllable count in words and how to pronounce a word, use online tools such as American Heritage Dictionary (www.yourdictionary.com); Syllable Dictionary (www.howmanysyllables.com); Syllable Counter (syllablecounter.net); Syllable Counter and Word Count (www.wordcalc.com); Dictionary.com (dictionary.reference.com); and OneLook (www.onelook.com).
- Explore the online detailed lesson plan from the Haiku Poem Interactive Lesson located on the ReadWriteThink website (see www.readwritethink.org /classroom-resources/student-interactives/haiku-poem-interactive-31074.html).
- Use the Haiku Poem App for tablets (see www.readwritethink.org/classroom -resources/mobile-apps/haiku-poem-31073.htm).
- View the haiku animal riddles called "What Am I?" as a guide for students to write their own haikus and create their own class video version (see www .youtube.com/watch?v=RUy2bQc5DFc).
- Display a collection of books featuring an array of haikus:
  - *The Year Comes Round: Haiku Through the Seasons* by Sid Farrar and Ilse Plune
  - *Hound Dog's Haiku and Other Poems for Dog Lovers* by Michael J. Rosen and Mary Azarian
  - *Haiku Baby* by Betsy Snyder (or see www.haikubaby.com)

- *English Language Learner Suggestion*: Explore online game-based programs for word-analysis skills (e.g., www.spellingcity.com/syllables-segmenting.html).
- *Struggling Readers Suggestion*: Have students practice sorting words by syllables. Use Figure 2.3, *Syllable Structure and Vowel Jingles,* as a scaffold to check for understanding. Additional syllable support strategies can be found in the resource *Words Their Way: Word Sorts for Syllables and Affixes Spellers* by Johnston, Invernizzi, Bear, and Templeton (2018).

EVALUATION

"I can . . ." Statements

- I can decode multisyllabic words.
- I can examine a syllable and determine the vowel sound in each syllable.
- I can write a haiku poem.

Behavior Indicators

- Identifies the number of syllables in a word.
- Determines the vowel sound and vowel-letter correspondence in each syllable.
- Sorts words by syllable patterns.

FIGURE 2.1

Haiku Writing Reproducible

Author(s):_____ Date_____

Elements of Haiku

___Content = clear purpose, relative parts, surprise   ___Mechanics = spelling, grammar, punctuation

___Imagery = sensory descriptive word   ___Syllabic format = 17 syllables (5-7-5)

Prewriting: Select a topic of interest. List word or phrases associated with the topic. Map out the syllables in each word.

Draft 1: Begin to collect thoughts and form a short message to convey the theme. At this time, don't be concerned with counting syllables; just capture the purpose of your topic along with sensory and descriptive words for clear imagery.

Draft 2: Revisit the message and your thoughts and begin to follow syllabic guidelines for haiku. Edit as needed.

1st Line:

2nd Line:

3rd Line:

Write Your Published Haiku Here:

FIGURE 2.2

Syllable Segmenting Guidelines Reproducible

Counting Vowels to Equal Syllables

- Say the word and listen for the syllabic rhythmic beat (drum it, clap it, mouth it).
- Count how many vowels are in the word, not sounds.
- Add them together for a total vowel letter count.
- Subtract any silent vowel letters (e.g., silent *e* at the end of a word; one of the vowels in a vowel digraph, counted as one sound, like *ea*).
- Total the number of vowels left and it should equal the number of syllables in the word.

Segmenting Syllables

- Divide between two words in a compound word (*touch/down*).
- Divide between two middle consonants unless they form a digraph (*mid/dle*, *sen/tence*).
- Divide between two vowels if they have different sounds (*po/em*), but not if they make only one sound together to form a vowel digraph (*mow/er*).
- Divide when a consonant comes between two vowels (*mu/sic*).
- Divide before the consonant that precedes an *le* (*fum/ble*), unless it is a consonant digraph like *ck* (*tick/le*) or comes before a vowel (*file* = 1 syllable).
- Divide between a prefix (*re/write*) or suffix (*hope/less*) and the base or root word.

Syllable Placement for Vowel Sounds

- **Open Syllable:** For a syllable ending in only one vowel, the vowel is usually pronounced as a long vowel (*to/tal; no*). The vowel is long when the syllable ends in a vowel (*ba/by*).
- **Closed Syllable:** For a syllable that has only one vowel followed by a consonant, the vowel is usually pronounced as a short vowel sound (*rab/bit, cat*). The vowel is short when the syllable ends in a consonant.

FIGURE 2.3

Syllable Structure and Vowel Jingles

Syllable Name and Description	Examples	Vowel Generalization Jingles
Closed: A single vowel that follows one or more consonants (typically a short vowel)	cat camp	**Closed-Vowel Pattern** One lovely vowel squished in the middle says its special sound—just a little.
Open: The syllable ends with a single vowel (typically a long vowel sound).	n**o** fl**y**	**Open-Vowel Pattern** If one vowel at the end is free, It pops way up and says its name to me.
Silent *e:* A single vowel is followed by a consonant, which is then followed by a silent *e* (typically, the first vowel says its long vowel sound).	bike n**o**tebook	**Silent *e*** When the *e* is at the end, the sound is gone. It makes the other vowel in the syllable say its name long.
Two Vowel Team: A syllable that has two adjacent vowels Long: The first vowel says its long vowel sound, while the second vowel is silent.	sp**ee**d container	**Long Two-Vowel Team** When two vowels go walking, the first one does the talking (and says its name).
Whiny (variant): The two vowels together make neither long nor short sound, but its own whiny sound (diphthong).	coles**law** enj**oy**ment b**oo** dr**ew**	**Whiny Two-Vowel Team—Diphthong** Sometimes when two vowels are together, they make a whiny sound; like when you fall down and want to be found (ow, aw, oy, boo-hoo).
R Controlled: When one or two vowels are followed by the letter *r*, the vowel is neither long nor short but is influenced by the *r* and makes an *r* sound.	star **tur**moil **four**	**Bossy *R* Pattern** When the vowel is followed by the letter *r*, the vowel has to let the *r* be the star.
Vowel with *l:* (al, el, le, il): A consonant is followed by the letters *le*, *al*, *il*, or *el*. The *le*, *al*, *il*, or *el* grabs the consonant just before it to make a clean syllable break.	pur**ple** med**al** reb**el**	**Consonant *l* with a Vowel** The *le*, *al*, *il*, or *el* grabs the consonant right before it, and makes a clean syllable break to form the split.

LESSON 2. VOCABULARY: GAMING WITH WORDS

Title MAKING WORDS / MAKING AND WRITING WORDS

Trailer Gaming. Masterminds. The thrill of the hunt. Some like it, some do not! Remember back when you were in school and your teacher put a relatively long target word on the chalkboard (e.g., blizzard) and then asked the class to make as many words as possible from the letters of the word. We loved this anagram activity in which new words are made from rearranging words; we were good readers, spellers, and writers. When counting the number of words, we were always close to the top of our class. The students who were not good readers neither enjoyed nor appreciated this word game. They were likely to be struggling readers, spellers, and writers with limited vocabularies. They had no one to help them, as the teacher often used the activity to keep her class busy for a few minutes. *Making and Writing Words* are anagram activities that engage all students, especially those who may otherwise struggle with words. Although they are game-like activities, because they are teacher-led they also involve students in considering the meaning and construction of words.

Literacy Enhancer Vocabulary. Gaming with Words: Decoding, Spelling

Key Academic Vocabulary
(Terms spiraled from previous lessons)

Adjective: A word or phrase used to describe a noun

Decoding: The process of translating a printed word into sounds by using knowledge of the conventions of letter-sound relationships and knowledge about pronunciations of words to derive written words

Noun: A word used to identify any of a class of people, places, or things

Spelling: The process of writing or naming the letters of a word

Syllables: A part of a word that contains only one vowel sound; words can be made of one or more syllables

Verb: A word used to describe an action

Vocabulary: A collection of words or phrases, and the meanings they represent, that make up a language.

Word Ladder: A game-like activity where one word is transformed into another by adding, subtracting, or changing letters

Word Sort: A process used to categorize words according to features (closed: categories are provided and words are matched to them; open: categories are determined by the students as they discern the common features of the word groups)
(New terms in this lesson)

Anagram: A word formed from another word by using or rearranging its letters (e.g., *angel–angle*)

Consonant: Language sounds and letters that are represented by all letters of the alphabet except *a, e, i, o, u,* and sometimes *y* and *w;* letters that represent consonant sounds usually appear at the beginning of words and syllables

Vowel: Language sounds and letters represented by the letters *a, e, i, o, u,* and sometimes *y* and *w*

Learning Objectives

- Increase students' corpus of words they know (vocabulary).
- Explore various features of words including multiple meanings, sound-symbol, and grammatical category.
- Improve students' abilities to encode (spell) and decode (sound out) written words.
- Increase students' enjoyment in exploring and learning words.

Essential Questions

- What new words can be made from a given set of letters?
- What one word can be made from *all* of a given set of letters?
- What are ways that a collection of words can be sorted?
- How can a set of words be integrated into a coherent sentence or text?

STEP 1: PREPARATION

Organize Material

- 6–10 target words related to a time of year (e.g., *winter, valentines*) or area of study (e.g., *rectangle, independence, coniferous*)
- List of words developed from target words, from shortest to longest
- Online resource: www.wordsmith.org/anagram to find anagrams
- Provided clues for derived words
- *Making Words with Letter Cards* reproducible
- Copied set of letters, divided into vowels and consonants
- Scissors
- *Making and Writing Words* reproducible

STEP 2: INITIATION

Put the word *reading* on display for all students to see and say, "Get out a sheet of paper. I am going to give you one minute. Write all the words you can make from the letters of *reading*." At the end of one minute, have students share the words that they have made. There are 100 possible words that can be made from the letters. Here are a few: *rained, anger, grain, range, grand, drain, grind, grade, diner, raid, dear, dine, ride, rage, grin, rand, ring, gear, arid, rain, aged, nerd, dire, gain, drag, rig, rid,* and *age.*

For a quick way to determine possible words, go to the website www.wordsmith .org/anagram. Click on "advanced" setting; click "yes" to the prompt "Show candidate words only." Then type in the target word and click "Find Anagrams." Within seconds all the words that can be made from the target words are presented in order from shortest to longest. Select 10 to 15 words that you want to use for your lesson. The last word in the lesson will be the target word.

Think of clues you can give students to make each of the words in the lesson. Tell them you are going to do a similar activity in which you give them a set of letters and guide them to make a set of words using only those letters. The last word they will make in the lesson will include all the letters. You will not give them any clues for the last word, though, so they can be challenged to think of a word that uses all the letters.

Pass out to each student the set of letters that you have copied for the *winter* Making Words lesson. Have students cut the letters into individual letter cards and separate them into vowels and consonants. Have a larger set of letter cards on display for yourself so you can demonstrate how they can make the words you have selected.

STEP 3: DEMONSTRATION

Making Words

Since *Making Words* is a lesson that you will be doing regularly with students, you will want to demonstrate how the lesson is implemented (Cunningham & Cunningham, 1992; Rasinski, 1999).

1. Put the large set of letters for the *winter* lesson on display for all your students to see. Separate vowels and consonants. Write the letters of the target word on Figure 2.4. Put the letters in alphabetical order and circle or mark the vowels in some way. Make a copy of the figures that contain the target letters for each student in your class or who will be participating in the lesson. As an example, we have chosen *winter* as our target word and have written the letters on the figure. Although more than 40 words can be made from the letters, we chose only a few for our demonstration lesson.

FIGURE 2.4

Making Words with Letter Cards Reproducible

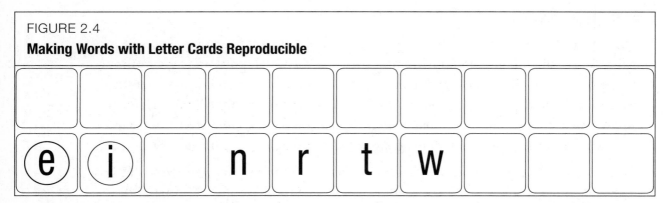

2. Have your students place their own letter cards in front of themselves, again separating vowels and consonants. Go through each of the words you will make in the lessons, providing the clues that you have created. You may also offer other clues (e.g., number of letters, vowels, how the word is pronounced). Then, by thinking aloud, show how you solved each new word.

Ten	The answer to the problem: 6 × 3 – 8 =
Net	What a basketball goal is sometimes called
Wet	The opposite of dry
Wit	The ability to use words in clever and interesting ways
Win	The opposite of lose
Twin	One of two children born at the same time
Twine	A kind of string or rope
Tine	The prong or sharp part of a fork
Wine	An alcoholic drink generally made from grapes
Wire	A metal thread
Write	What happens when you place a pen to paper
Winter	(Provide no clues unless needed—uses all the letters.) The coldest season of the year

1. Arrange the large letters so that each word is displayed for students, and have them do the same at their desks. The lesson ends as you make the word that uses all the letters—*winter*.

2. Display all the words you have made on the classroom word wall so students have easy access to them.

STEP 4: COLLABORATION

Read and review the words from the word wall with students. In groups of two or three, have students find ways to sort or group the words. For example, they can put the words in alphabetic order, sort by grammatical category (nouns versus not nouns), spelling structure (words that contain a consonant blend and words that do not), or words that have a positive connotation and words with a negative connotation. Students should be able to explain their rationale for choosing their sorting category. After creating their word sorts, they can share them with the class. For another option, have the whole class engage in doing a few of the word sorts. Have the students respond to the *Making Words* experience using a Think-Pair-Share format answering these questions: Did they enjoy doing the making words? Why or why not? Did they learn any new words? If so, which ones?

STEP 5: APPLICATION

Now that students are familiar with *Making Words*, do a lesson with them several times per week. It is beneficial to choose a target word related to something you may be studying in class, a time of the year, or some other connection that can be used as a segue into further discussion and study. You can control the difficulty of the lesson based on the length of the target word; shorter target words generally lead to easier lessons. Choose words that you feel match the appropriate level of difficulty for your students. After several weeks of doing *Making Words* lessons that you have developed, have the students work alone or in groups to create their own lessons to present to the class.

STEP 6: REFLECTION

Oral or Written Response

Students can use their word journals to record the words from each *Making Word* lesson and to write what they have learned from doing it. Responses may include learning new words or learning that words often have words within them, that manipulating one or two letters can change a word into another word, or that word study can be fun.

ADAPTATION AND EXTENSION

- As a set of words is made, you can guide students to transfer their knowledge of some of the word patterns to new words that contain the same word pattern. For example, the *-ine* word pattern from the *Making Words* lesson above can be transferred to *dine, fine, line, mine, nine, pine, swine, shine, and vine.*

- Have students write the words they have made in the *Making Words* lesson (including any transfer words) on word cards and use them for word sorts or word games like "Concentration."
- Cutting and manipulating individual letters for each *Making Words* lesson can be a bit time consuming. An alternative would be to have students write the words on a *Making and Writing Words* reproducible (see Figure 2.5) as you guide them to make words. Provide a copy of the sheet for each student. When the lesson is completed, students can cut the words into individual word cards for word sorting and games.
- Have students write sentences that contain at least two words that were part of the *Making Words* lesson.
- After completing several *Making Words with Letter Cards* or *Making and Writing Words* lessons with students, ask them to develop their own lessons in which they guide classmates in making words. Schedule the lessons so that every student gets a chance to lead a lesson.
- *English Language Learner Suggestion*: When doing a *Making Words* or *Making and Writing Words* lesson, provide additional elaboration on the meaning and use of the various words that students will make in the lesson.
- *Struggling Reader Suggestion*: The length of the final or target word for each lesson dictates the difficulty of the lesson. For struggling readers, choose a shorter final or target word—instead of a nine-letter final word like *fireplace,* choose a seven-letter word such as *snowman.* Fewer letters mean less complexity and difficulty for students.

"I can . . ." Statements

- I can read the words we made in our *Making Words* lesson.
- I can understand what the words in the lesson mean.
- I can use the words in the lesson in my own speech.
- I can use the words in my own writing.
- I can make words from a given set of letters.
- I can see words and word patterns in other words, and this helps me read and understand words.
- I can have fun playing with words with my classmates.

Behavior Indicators

- Adds words to a growing vocabulary list.
- Increases ability to accurately spell words.
- Increases ability to decode (sound out) words.
- Manipulates words by adding, subtracting, or rearranging individual letters.

FIGURE 2.5

Making and Writing Words Reproducible

Vowels		Consonants	
1	6	11	
2	7	12	
3	8	13	
4	9	14	
5	10	15	

Transfer Words

T-1	T-2	T-3
T-4	T-5	T-6

LESSON 3. VOCABULARY: ANALYZING WORDS

Title **FUNCTIONAL ROOTS** (*com-, col-, co-, con-, pro-, ex-*)

Trailer *Onward together!* In the previous lesson, students learned that many English words relating to numbers contain word roots or patterns from Latin and Greek. But the influence of Latin and Greek into English goes far beyond numbers. Many basic function concepts are used continually in English; the most common are "with, together," "for, forward, outward," and "out of." In this lesson we help students see that when they encounter a word that contains one of these word roots (prefixes), the essential meaning of the word has something to do with these concepts. More than that, however, we want students to develop a propensity (notice the *pro-* word root in this word that means "an ability going forward") to find word roots in words and use that knowledge to determine and remember the meanings of many English words.

Literacy Enhancer Vocabulary: Analyzing Words, Decoding, Spelling

Key Academic Vocabulary

(Terms spiraled from previous lessons)

Greek: An ancient language whose words and word parts have influenced words in English

Latin: An ancient language whose words and word parts have influenced words in English

Word Roots: Base words, prefixes, and suffixes in English words that are derived primarily from Latin and Greek

(New terms in this lesson)

Com-: A prefix meaning with or together

Col-: A prefix meaning with or together

Co-: A prefix meaning with or together

Con-: A prefix meaning with or together

Pro-: A prefix meaning forward or outward

Ex-: A prefix meaning out of

Learning Objectives

- Expand competency in parsing words into base and affixes.
- Learn critical English word roots and affixes derived from Latin and Greek.
- Expand vocabulary by learning English words derived from Latin and Greek.

Essential Questions

- What are the meanings of English words containing *com-*, *col-* word roots?
- What are the meanings of English words containing *co-*, *con-* word roots?
- What are the meanings of English words containing *pro-* word roots?
- What are the meanings of English words containing *ex-* word roots?
- How does knowledge of Latin and Greek roots help students understand words in which they are located?

STEP 1: PREPARATION

Organize Materials

- List of *com-*, *col-* words
- Texts that correspond with root words being studied
- Word Journals

STEP 2: INITIATION

Explain to your students the concept of word roots and affixes—word patterns that have a particular meaning. Provide examples of word roots from compound words (e.g., *cowboy, football, fireflies*) as well as from words from the previous set of lessons on numerical roots (e.g., *unicycle, biplane, tripod, quadruplets*). Ask students to break the words down into roots and determine the meaning of the compound words by combining the meanings of the individual words.

Make a list of words several *com-*, *col-* words and put them on display for students to see. Have them define the words as best they can and ask what is common in all the words (i.e., they contain the word pattern *com,* or *col*). Now ask the students to determine what is common in the meaning of all the words. The answer, of course, is the concept of "with" or "together." Here is a partial list of *com-*, *col-* words you can display:

Communicate	Collide
Committee	Collection
Community	Collage
Compatible	Collegial
Companion	Colleague

STEP 3: DEMONSTRATION

Work through each of the words on the list and define them so that the concept of "with" is highlighted. Demonstrate to students that each word can be defined in this manner.

- Communicate: To speak with another person or persons
- Committee: A group of people who work with one another on a task
- Community: A group of people who live with one another
- Compatible: When two or more people get along with one another
- Compete: To be in a competition or battle with another
- Companion: A person who enjoys being with another person
- Collide: To crash with (or into) another person or object
- Collection: A group of objects with common characteristics (e.g., marbles or books)
- Collage: Artwork that is made by putting different forms together with one another
- Collegial: Friendly

STEP 4: COLLABORATION

Have students work in pairs and small groups. Ask if they can determine the meaning of the following words using a similar process of employing the concept of "with": *compare, combine, company, colleague, collaborate,* and *college.* Have students think and discuss with their partner or in their groups, and then share their thinking with the class. Provide supportive and formative feedback as needed. Create a word wall that contains all the *com-, col-* words you have studied with your students up to this point. Read the words in unison and ask the students to use the words in their oral language whenever possible.

STEP 5: APPLICATION

Create a short text like the one below or a series of sentences that contain some of the *com-, col-* words from the word wall. Have students read the texts and respond to questions.

> After high school I plan to go to college, where I hope to learn from and collaborate with experts in the field of chemistry. I will have to compare colleges to find the one with which I am most compatible. Because I am interested in living things, my mother thinks I should combine my interests and study chemistry and biology. I know that whatever I study I will be in the company of very smart colleagues.

> *Question:* What are some things that the writer should think about in deciding on a college that would be most compatible?
>
> *Question:* Who are the colleagues that the writer of this essay refers to?

Have students write a short text that contains at least three words from the word wall, along with one question for their text. While sharing their texts in small groups, have classmates respond to the questions for each text and discuss possible answers to the essential question: "How does knowledge of Latin and Greek roots help you understand the words in which they are located?"

STEP 6: REFLECTION

Have students invent a word that contains the *com, col* word root (e.g., *comclass, collimp*) and a definition for it (e.g., two classrooms that are connected; two people walking together who have injured legs). New ideas and concepts in science and technology are often given names that are derived from Latin and Greek roots. For example, *aquarium* contains the roots *aqua-* which means water and *-arium* which means place. Have students reflect on why scientists may want to use word roots when inventing new ideas. Have students write and complete the following sentence in their word journals: "I think it is important to know the *com, col* word root because _____."

ADAPTATION AND EXTENSION

- Not all words that appear to contain a particular root have meanings related to the root. Discuss with students some words that have the *com-, col-* patterns but do not refer to the concept of *with* (e.g., *comb, comedy, cold, color*).
- Students can invent new words that contain the *com-, col-* root, draw pictures of the words, and challenge one another to define them.
- Teach word root lessons using this same format for the other word roots in this chapter (*co-, con-; pro-, ex-*):
- *English Language Learner Suggestion*: Give students a set of *com-, col-* words from the word wall and have them work in small groups to draw images of the words that emphasize the concept of "with" or "together."
- *Struggling Reader Suggestion*: Provide additional practice with the words from the *com-, col-* word wall by having students play word games such as Wordo (see Chapter 4, Lesson 2).
  - Co-, con- (with, together): *cooperate, cohesive* (note similar root *adhesive*), *coexist, coauthor, copilot, copay, construct, conjoined, concoct, confer, conference, congregate, conductor, contract*

○ *Pro-* (forward, outward): *proceed, procession, prominent, profess, propel, proclaim, produce, propose, provoke*

○ *Ex-* (out of): *exit, exhale, expel, extract, excavate, exclude, expire, exception*

EVALUATION

"I can . . ." Statements

- I can understand what words mean that contain the word root we have studied.
- I can break longer words down into their root parts.
- I can better understand texts that contain words that have the word root we have studied.

Behavior Indicators

- Adds words and concepts that contain *com-, col-* to a growing vocabulary list.
- Finds words in texts that contain the *com-, col-* word roots.
- Defines and understands words that contain the *com-, col-* word root.
- Understands texts that contain the *com-, col-* word roots.

LESSON 4. VOCABULARY: ASSOCIATING WORDS

Title LIKE WHAT? SIMILES AND METAPHORS GALORE

Trailer Life without similes and metaphors would be pretty dull. Imagine songs without metaphors and similes in the lyrics. If the beginning of Elvis Presley's 1956 hit "Hound Dog" were "You keep bothering me all the time," we probably wouldn't be singing it today! Similes and metaphors add pizzazz to songs, literature, and even conversations, making them memorable and more interesting. When students clarify and pay attention to these figures of speech during reading, their comprehension improves. Let your students experience metaphors and similes firsthand as they learn the beauty and magic of comparisons.

Literacy Enhancer Vocabulary: Associating—Similes, Metaphors

Key Academic Vocabulary

(Terms spiraled from previous lessons)

Adjective: A word that describes a noun (a person, place, or thing)

Shades of Meaning: Words that are synonyms with varying degrees of meanings

Synonym: A word that has a similar meaning to another word

Verb: An action word

(New terms in this lesson)

Metaphor: Comparison of two unlike entities; does not use the words *like* or *as*; often implies meaning and uses a form of the verb "to be"

Simile: Comparison of two unlike entities using the words *like* or *as* to connect the ideas

Learning Objectives

- Identify similes or comparisons using *like* or *as* in song lyrics, literature, and poetry.
- Identify metaphors or comparisons using a form of the verb "to be" in song lyrics, literature, and poetry.
- Tell the difference between a simile and a metaphor.
- Create similes and metaphors individually and in teams.
- Provide reasons why clarifying similes and metaphors in reading is important to comprehension.
- Provide reasons why using similes and metaphors in writing is a useful craft tool.

Essential Questions

- What is a simile?
- What is a metaphor?
- What is the difference between a simile and metaphor?
- Why do authors use similes and metaphors in their texts?
- How can using similes and metaphors help improve one's own writing?

STEP 1: PREPARATION

Organize Materials

- Fiction, informational texts, or poetry to read aloud that contain similes and metaphors
- Chart paper, document camera, or smartboard for recording examples on a T-chart
- Sticky notes or strips of paper
- Smartphone, computer, a device to play music
- *Bag It! Simile and Metaphor Maker* reproducible
- *Simile Maker* reproducible
- *Metaphor Maker* reproducible

STEP 2: INITIATION

Musical Metaphors

Tell students that sometimes authors of books, poetry, and songs use comparisons, called metaphors and similes, to make stories or songs more interesting. Ask students what they already know about metaphors and similes. Briefly mention that a simile is a comparison of two things that are different that use the words *like* or *as*. Give an example and write it on the board underlining the word *as*: "She was as hungry as a lion!" Then explain that a metaphor is also a comparison of two different things, but it does not use the words *like* or *as*: "The dog is a joyful bright light in their lives."

Play the beginning portions of age-appropriate songs for students and point out the lyrics that feature metaphors and similes—usually in the first line or verse. Consider writing a line of lyrics on the board or a chart. Ask students to discuss why they think so many love songs and poems include such comparisons. Invite students to listen for the words *like* or *as* to identify which are similes and which are metaphors.

Popular songs are filled with great examples of similes and metaphors. Most of your students are familiar with Rihanna comparing people to diamonds in the song of that title, and Taylor Swift comparing words to knives in the song "Mean." In the

Michael Bublé song "Everything," he refers to someone being a falling star, and Katy Perry boosts everyone's self-esteem by saying each person is a "Firework." Favorite Disney movies also contain catchy song lyrics, such as a thought being compared to an icy blast in the song "Let It Go," and comparing a man's strength to a raging fire in the movie *Mulan*.

STEP 3: DEMONSTRATION

Like What? Charting Similes and Metaphors

1. Ask students to brainstorm what they know already or realize now about similes and metaphors. Tell students that authors and songwriters use these comparisons in their writing to convey messages to the listener. The comparisons include varied nouns and verbs as well.

2. Return to the examples in the songs mentioned above to discuss the author's word choice, and sketch a T-chart on the board with similes and metaphors (see Figure 2.6). Tell students that you are going to demonstrate how to spot these figures of speech in texts and how to categorize them.

3. Read aloud from a picture book that includes rich examples of metaphors and similes. Pause for partners to turn to talk about each metaphor or simile and let them identify on which side of the chart to place the comparison. Chart together examples of similes and metaphors with sticky notes or by writing on the chart. Discuss what students liked and noticed about each example. You can repeat this lesson many times using different texts. Here are a few suggestions:

   - *Skin Like Milk, Hair of Silk* by Brian P. Cleary
   - *Fireflies* by Julie Brinckloe
   - *Owl Moon* by Jane Yolen
   - *My Friend Is as Sharp as a Pencil* by Hanovich Piven
   - *My Dog Is as Smelly as Dirty Socks* by Hanovich Piven
   - *Crazy Like a Fox* by Loreen Leedy
   - *The Ocean Is . . .* by Kathleen Kranking
   - *You're Toast and Other Metaphors We Adore* by Nancy Loewen

4. Add a simple two-step gesture while asking "Like, what?" to help students understand similes. Hold one hand palm facing up and open and pretend you have something resting on it. Say, "A simile is like . . . " and then hold the other palm facing up and complete the question, "what?" Put either a word card, object, or picture of something in one hand and say "A _____ is like what?" Select another word card or picture to hold. Now complete the simile.

FIGURE 2.6

Similes and Metaphors T-Chart

Similes (Use the words *like* or *as*)	**Metaphors** (Use a form of the verb *to be*)
• It was as cold as ice in that doctor's office. • You are as sharp as a tack. • Ben's room smells like a gymnasium because he leaves his stinky workout clothes on the floor. • The horse was as fast as lightning. • The roses smelled like her mom's perfume. • The fireworks sounded like a sonic boom.	• Whew, it is an oven outside today. • You are one sharp cookie. • This test is a piece of cake! • The toddler is a pig when she eats with her bad manners at the formal dinner. • He is the rock of our family. • The moon was a giant red ornament decorating the sky.

Source: Literacy Strong All Year Long: Powerful Lessons for Grades 3-5 by Lori Oczkus, Valerie Ellery, and Timothy V. Rasinski. Copyright © 2018 ASCD. Readers may duplicate this figure for noncommercial use within their school.

"A _____ is like _____ because ____." For example, hold a photo of a cat in one hand and say, "A cat is like what?" Then hold the photo of a car in the other hand and say, "A cat is like a car because it purrs like a motor." For fun, you can ask students to repeat the "Like what?" question in a teenage "Valley girl or guy" voice!

5. Hold up a series of objects or photos in one hand and repeat the activity and language frame. Invite a couple students in front of the class to help create some "like what?" similes. Chart the examples so students can refer to them. Discuss the role of adjectives in making the simile sentence longer, more detailed, and ultimately more interesting.

STEP 4: COLLABORATION

Bring in two small, brown paper bags or other containers. Have students cut up the noun word cards in the *Bag It! Simile and Metaphor Maker* reproducible (see Figure 2.7) and place half in each bag. Working in pairs, students will take turns drawing a card from each bag to practice creating metaphors and similes. For example, a student draws out of Bag #1 the word *car* and Bag #2 the word *apple*. The student holds the car card in one hand and says, "The car is like" and then holds the other card in the other hand and finishes the simile by adding a comparison: "The car is like a bright red shiny apple." Encourage elaboration with adjectives and vivid verbs such as, "The new sports car gleams in the sun like a bright red shiny apple." Circulate and assist students with the language of metaphors and similes as they work in pairs and teams to create them.

Next, have students cut out the *Simile Maker* and *Metaphor Maker* reproducible cards in Figures 2.8 and 2.9. After a few practice rounds, students can write down their best ideas or draw new words from the bags and record the words on the sheets. First, they will write a basic simile or metaphor in simple terms, and then an elaborated version of that comparison with more words relating to color or size and other adjectives that describe the nouns.

STEP 5: APPLICATION

Ask students to keep track of the metaphors and similes they encounter in their reading in their literacy notebooks. Tell students to look for comparisons in all kinds of texts, including informational. They can record their findings in a T-chart like the one you created for the class with one side for metaphors and one for similes. They can use sticky notes in their texts to mark them as well. Continue adding to the class chart. Type up the metaphors and similes that the class has collected. Have students cut them apart and glue them into the proper columns for similes and metaphors to see if they recall them.

STEP 6: REFLECTION

Oral or Written Response

Lead students in a discussion about the value of similes and metaphors. Why do authors use them? Why is it important to pause during reading and make sure you understand metaphors and similes? Which is easier to spot in a text? Which is harder to write, a simile or metaphor? Which do students prefer? Have students write in their literacy notebooks to reflect on using comparisons in their reading and writing:

- One of my favorite metaphors or similes that I've found in my reading is

  _____.
- I like it because it makes me think _____.
- Authors use metaphors and similes to_____.
- When I write, I would like to try making a comparison for the topic_____
  _____ because _____.

ADAPTATION AND EXTENSION

- Invite students to pay attention to radio and television advertising to see how metaphors and similes are used to market goods. Have them collect examples to share with the class. Students can create advertisements with metaphors and similes for use on the school website or morning announcements, or to promote school products (e.g., spirit wear) or a schoolwide event.

- *English Language Learner Suggestion*: Play charades with metaphors and similes. Work with students to fill in the *Metaphor Maker* and *Simile Maker* reproducibles. Write the metaphors the group has created on cards. Turn them over or put the cards in a container. Students take turns acting out the cards they've selected while the rest of the group guesses the simile or metaphor.
- *Struggling Reader Suggestion*: Second language learners often enjoy reading and listening to poetry because it provides practice for repeated readings and exposure to vocabulary as well as opportunities to learn about comparisons. Poetry is filled with metaphors and similes. Place stacks of poetry books on tables for students to share as they go on a "comparison hunt." Ask students to mark the similes with one color sticky note and metaphors with another color.

EVALUATION

"I can . . ." Statements

- I can identify similes in song lyrics, texts, and poetry.
- I can identify metaphors in song lyrics, texts, and poetry.
- I can sort similes and metaphors and record examples on a chart.
- I can write a simile creating a comparison using *like* or *as*.
- I can write a metaphor comparison.
- I can elaborate on a basic metaphor or simile by adding adjectives to make it more interesting.
- I can provide reasons why authors might use metaphors and similes in their writing.

Behavior Indicators

- Identifies similes in song lyrics, texts, and poetry.
- Identifies metaphors in song lyrics, texts, and poetry.
- Finds examples of similes and metaphors in texts and other materials.
- Sorts similes and metaphors and records examples on a chart.
- Writes a basic simile comparison using *like* or *as*.
- Elaborates using adjectives to create a more interesting simile.
- Writes a basic metaphor comparison.
- Elaborates using adjectives to create a more interesting metaphor.
- Provides reasons why authors might use metaphors and similes in their writing.

FIGURE 2.7

Bag It! Simile and Metaphor Maker Cards Reproducible

Directions: Cut out the noun word cards and divide them into two paper bags. With a partner, draw one card from each bag and use the words to create a simile or metaphor. Use the blank cards to add nouns.

girl	boy	dog	car	house
friend	enemy	cat	flowers	bus
clouds	tree	hair	bird	ocean
mountain	snake	apple	music	pizza
snow	thoughts	hands	song	heart
rain	voices	smile	jewels	sun
wind	pebbles	diamonds	lightning	razor
leaves	chimes	frost	breeze	heat

FIGURE 2.7

FIGURE 2.8

Simile Maker Reproducible

Simile Maker	**Simile Maker**
1. Choose a word from Bag #1 and Bag #2.	1. Choose a word from Bag #1 and Bag #2.

Word #1	Word #2

Word #1	Word #2

2. Write a basic simile using words #1 and #2.

_____ (*is like* or *as*) _____
_____ .

Write an elaborated improved version by adding descriptive words.

_____ (*is like* or *as*) _____
_____ .

Sketch a drawing of your simile.

2. Write a basic simile using words #1 and #2.

_____ (*is like* or *as*) _____
_____ .

Write an elaborated improved version by adding descriptive words.

_____ (*is like* or *as*) _____
_____ .

Sketch a drawing of your simile.

Source: Literacy Strong All Year Long: Powerful Lessons for Grades 3-5 by Lori Oczkus, Valerie Ellery, and Timothy V. Rasinski. Copyright © 2018 ASCD.
Readers may duplicate this figure for noncommercial use within their school.

FIGURE 2.9

Metaphor Maker Reproducible

Metaphor Maker	**Metaphor Maker**
1. Choose a word from Bag #1 and Bag #2.	1. Choose a word from Bag #1 and Bag #2.

Word #1	Word #2

Word #1	Word #2

2. Write a basic metaphor.

_____ (*is* or *are*) _____

_____ .

2. Write a basic metaphor.

_____ (*is* or *are*) _____

_____ .

3. Write an elaborated improved version by adding descriptive words.

_____ (*is* or *are*) _____

_____ .

3. Write an elaborated improved version by adding descriptive words.

_____ (*is* or *are*) _____

_____ .

4. Sketch a drawing of your metaphor.

4. Sketch a drawing of your metaphor.

LESSON 5. FLUENCY: PHRASING, PACING, EXPRESSING

Title HONORING PRESIDENT JOHN F. KENNEDY THROUGH ORATORY

Trailer Something is missing from the school literacy curriculum: the study of speeches or oratory. Our history can be traced through significant speeches that were made by various political leaders at different milestones in time. Rehearsal was necessary, precision was important, and delivery was everything, because the speaker had only one opportunity to address a crowd and convey a persuasive message. Some time ago, the rehearsal and performance of speeches or oratory was a staple of school curricula, but it is now a scarce element in the English language arts curricula. Today's young students are missing out, because rehearsing and performing historic speeches can be an effective way to make history come alive and provide critical connections between language arts and social studies.

Literacy Enhancer Reading Fluency: Word Recognition Automaticity, Expressive (Prosodic) Reading

Key Academic Vocabulary
(Terms spiraled from previous lessons)

Performance: The act of presenting a play, concert, or other form of entertainment

Poetry: A genre of writing that emphasizes the expression of feelings and ideas by the use of distinctive style, rhyme, or rhythm

Rehearsal: The repeated practice reading of a text in preparation of performing the text for an audience

Rhyme: Words that have the same or similar ending sounds

Rhythm: A regular, repeated, pattern of movement, sound, or language
(New terms in this lesson)

Inauguration: A ceremony to mark a formal induction into office

Oratory: The art or practice of formal speaking in public

Speech: A formal address or discourse delivered to an audience

Learning Objectives

- Increase ability to recognize words automatically.
- Improve ability to read with appropriate expression and phrasing (prosody).
- Develop a greater appreciation for the role of oratory and language to motivate and inspire.

- Develop a greater appreciation for the significance of President John F. Kennedy.

Essential Questions

- What is the purpose of speeches such as Kennedy's inaugural address?
- How does fluent and expressive reading add to the nature of the speech?
- What do I need to do to read a speech fluently?
- What speech might I like to write, rehearse, and give?

STEP 1: PREPARATION

Organize Materials

- Copy of President John F. Kennedy's inaugural address
- A recording of Kennedy reading his inaugural address
  Note: Both of these items can be found at www.jfklibrary.org/Research /Research-Aids/Ready-Reference/JFK-Quotations/Inaugural-Address.aspx.

STEP 2: INITIATION

Each year in early February, students in the United States celebrate Presidents' Day to honor those who have served the United States as president. One way to honor presidents is to study and perform notable speeches they have made. In one widely known speech—the 1961 inauguration of the youngest U.S. president elected to office—President John F. Kennedy laid out his vision for the United States and the world. Although most students should have some familiarity with President Kennedy, you may wish to provide them with some background on him and the tumultuous times in which he lived (1917–1963). You can find a brief video about Kennedy online to share with students.

Make a copy of the first section of President John F. Kennedy's inaugural address for each student in your class. For each succeeding day of the lesson, you will need to make a copy of the section to be rehearsed. You may also wish to make a large copy of the entire speech and put it on display for students to read at their leisure. If the students are familiar with President Kennedy, allow them to brainstorm what they know about him and list the facts on a display board. Next have students group the facts into categories and supply labels for each group. Then ask the students to put themselves into the audience of U.S. citizens listening to President Kennedy. What do you hope he will say to inspire you to become a better U.S. and world citizen?

STEP 3: DEMONSTRATION

1. Play a recording of Kennedy's inaugural address. Have students follow along with their copy of the speech, reading silently as they listen to the recording.

2. Discuss the content of the full speech with your students, noting the interesting words that he used, and place those words on the word wall. Also take note of various oratorical devices that Kennedy used to emphasize his message, such as repetition of key phrases. Four common oratorical devices are (1) asking rhetorical questions, (2) repeating an idea in the same words, (3) repeating the use of the same words or pattern to begin or end a series of sentences, and (4) exclamations, or the use of highly emotional or provocative statements.

3. Ask students to select what they feel is the key line in the speech and to provide valid reasons why they feel it is important.

STEP 4: COLLABORATION

Have students work in small groups of two or three to rehearse the first section of Kennedy's inaugural address for a few minutes. One student should read as others follow along and provide support and positive feedback, taking turns so each student has a chance to read. Students can then chorally read the first section together. Students can divide up and assign lines for each student to perform later to the entire class. Roam the classroom and visit each rehearsal group, listening to them read and providing formative feedback and support. Engage students in thinking deeply about how to make the reading of Kennedy's inaugural address a satisfying experience for the audience. Engage in conversational coaching by asking students to discuss the following questions with diverse partners:

- What is the purpose of speeches such as Kennedy's inaugural address?
- How does fluent and expressive reading add to the nature of the speech?
- What do I need to do to read a speech fluently?

STEP 5: APPLICATION

When the full speech (or what you determine is the full speech for your students) has been mastered, arrange for individuals or small groups of students to read and perform the speech to various audiences such as classmates, parents, or other classrooms, or to record it for the classroom website. Set a date for a performance—around President's Day would be ideal. Here are some steps for a successful performance:

1. Determine who will be invited and how invitations will be communicated.

2. Determine a location and consider the logistics including sufficient seating and size of the stage area.

3. Choreograph the performance. Will each section be performed by a different student or groups of students? Will any sections or important lines be performed by all? How will students enter and leave the stage area?

4. Do a dress rehearsal with your students. Provide formative feedback during and after.

5. On the day of the performance, do the following:

   a. Introduce the audience to the performance.

   b. Have one or more students provide background on President Kennedy and his speech. This background should also be rehearsed in advance of the performance.

   c. Remind audience members of appropriate behavior during the performance and suggest ways they can show their appreciation.

   d. Arrange a reception for performers and audience members; allow audience members to share positive feedback with the performers. Arrange for the performance area to be cleaned and returned to its original state.

STEP 6: REFLECTION

Oral or Written Response

Following the performance, ask audience members to write critiques focusing on the positive aspects. Share selected critiques with your students. Have students write responses to the oratorical experience. What did they like best? Why? How has practicing and performing the speech improved their reading? What will they do differently for future performances?

ADAPTATION AND EXTENSION

- Extend the oratory performance by making it a regular part of your English language arts curriculum throughout the middle months of the school year. Approximately once a month, set the final day of the school week as a speech performance day. Have students rehearse and perform new speeches in a manner similar to the protocol described.

- You can find famous speeches from U.S. history online (e.g., www.american-rhetoric.com). We recommend these speeches:

   o The Gettysburg Address by President Abraham Lincoln

   o "I Have a Dream" by Dr. Martin Luther King Jr.

   o "The Only Thing We Have to Fear" by President Franklin Roosevelt

   o "We Shall Overcome" by President Lyndon Baines Johnson

- o "Ain't I a Woman" by Sojourner Truth
- o "A Time for Choosing" by Ronald Reagan
- o "The Duty, Honor, Country" by General Douglas MacArthur

- After your class has read, analyzed, and performed several notable speeches, you may challenge your students to write and perform their own speeches. The topics selected can range from school-related issues to broader national or world-related topics. Students should keep in mind that the purpose of a speech is generally to convince or inspire the listeners to the importance of the issue at hand. Encourage students to use oratorical devices in their own speeches.

- *English Language Learner Suggestion*: Have students work in small groups as they rehearse the speech. Encourage groups to engage in additional rehearsal with formative feedback provided by other members of the small group.

- *Struggling Reader Suggestion*: Break the speech into shorter segments so that students have the opportunity to work with suitable parts.

EVALUATION

"I can . . ." Statements

- I can read a speech or portion of a speech with ease.
- I can read a speech or portion of a speech with expression that reflects and amplifies the meaning of the speech.
- I can read a speech or portion of a speech with good volume and confidence.
- I can read a speech or portion of a speech aloud with good posture.
- I know the meaning of the words within the speech I read.
- I can understand the purpose of the speech that I read.
- I can rehearse a speech to the point where I can read it well.
- I can listen to a speech being read and offer positive feedback to the reader.

Behavior Indicators

- Demonstrates excitement about being able to rehearse and perform speeches.
- Collaborates with others in a rehearsal group and provides good feedback to others.
- Exhibits appropriate behavior and is positive as an audience member.
- Finds interesting speeches or portions of speeches to rehearse and perform for others.

LESSON 6. COMPREHENSION: PREVIEWING

Title INFORMATIONAL TEXT FEATURE TOUR!

Trailer In this lesson, students "hop on" a tour bus, not to explore ancient structures, museums, or elaborate houses of the rich and famous, but to preview informational text features for strong comprehension. Informational texts differ from fiction because they are loaded with a variety of features such as headings, charts, and graphs that serve as guides and signposts along the way for readers. Yet many of our students are unfamiliar with these signposts. If students don't understand how text features can help them read, they miss valuable information and their comprehension suffers. Learning to preview informational text by using text features is essential for building good comprehension. Taking a "pretend tour" of a text is a fun analogy to help students remember text features and their purposes (Ellery, 2014; Wood, Lapp, & Flood, 1992).

Literacy Enhancer Comprehension: Previewing—Craft and Structure of Text Features

Key Academic Vocabulary

(Terms spiraled from previous lessons)

Author: Person who wrote the text

Author's Point of View: In nonfiction, the opinion or feelings the author has toward the topic; in fiction, point of view also influences who is telling the story

Author's Purpose: The reason the author wrote the text, usually to inform, entertain, or persuade the reader

Illustrator: The person who draws or paints the artwork to accompany the text

Predict: To make an educated guess, or inference, about what will happen next in the text using clues from the text and one's own background knowledge

Prediction: An educated guess about what may happen in a story or other text about to be read

Preview: To look over the text before reading to predict what it will be about and to see what text features the author has included

Text Features: The tools an author uses to help the reader navigate the text to locate and access meaning; may include a table of contents, headings, photographs, bold words, maps, graphs, charts, index, and glossary

Text Structure: The organizational structure of the information in the text; fiction might consist of a problem and solution, and a beginning, middle, and end; nonfiction may be organized around a main idea and details, a cause and effect, a problem and solution, a sequence of ideas, or a compare and contrast of ideas
(New terms in this lesson)

Heading: Divides the text into sections and tells the main idea of each section; often in larger or bold type, it helps the reader locate information in the text

Table of Contents: A list of the text's topics, chapter titles, and page numbers so the reader can locate information and see how the text is organized

Learning Objectives

- Preview informational text using text features.
- Identify key text features in an informational text.
- Share how text features aid in understanding the text.

Essential Questions

- What text features appear in the text students are reading?
- How can each text feature help in predicting what the text will be about?
- How is the text organized?
- What clues from each of the text features help you determine what the text is about?
- Which text feature is most helpful in a particular text during the preview?
- How does previewing text features help with comprehension?

STEP 1: PREPARATION

Organize Materials

- *Informational Text Tours* reproducible
- Informational texts with a variety of text features
- Construction paper and markers for table team charts
- Informational text to read to younger buddies
- Pretend microphone (optional)
- Video equipment (optional)

STEP 2: INITIATION

Tour Talk

Invite students to briefly discuss tours they've taken or watched on television such as a museum walking tour, bus tour, or open house tour, and tell them about some of the tours you've experienced. Ask students to reflect on the purpose of various tours: to inform (museum), entertain (haunted house), or persuade (open house for sale). Remind them of the language that tour guides use when leading a tour, such as "Over here we have_____. On the right you will see _____. Look now as we pass _____." Brainstorm how touring or browsing through an informational text before reading might help with comprehension. Tell students they are going to take a pretend tour of a text instead of a building or place.

Team Text Feature Hunt and Race

Put students in teams and provide them with one or more informational texts that contain different text features you wish to highlight this school year. Give teams around three to five minutes to look through the books and quickly list as many text features as they can identify on a team chart (Harvey, 1998). Allow teams to share and add to their lists after discussion. Assist students with vocabulary for some of the text features if they aren't familiar with the terms (Oczkus, 2014).

STEP 3: DEMONSTRATION

1. Select an informational text to project for all to view and provide students with a copy. Explain to students that good readers use text features throughout the reading process to help guide their way through the reading material.

2. Demonstrate how to take a text tour by conducting a think-aloud using the following features and "tour talk." Ham it up if you wish, using gestures as you point to the text features throughout the text. Students follow along in their copies. Optional: use a pretend microphone. (The idea of a text tour is adapted from Ellery, 2014; Oczkus, 2014; Wood, Lapp, & Flood, 1992.)

    a. **Cover:** "Welcome to the text tour of _____ [title] by ___ [author] [or name the content area chapter in a textbook or article]. I think this is about_____ because I see _____ on the cover."

    b. **Table of Contents:** "As you can see inside, we have a grand table of contents that tells us the major topics that are in this text. I can use the table of contents to find pages about _____. I think I will learn _____ from this chapter. Tell your partner what you think you will learn from one of the chapters."

    c. **Headings:** "This fabulous text is loaded with headings to guide me so I know what each page is about. Look on your right on page _____. There is a spectacular heading that says _____. So I think I will learn _____. Watch me as I read aloud from these headings on every page. (Encourage students to chime in and orally read headings with you.) On these pages all these incredible headings are about_____ so I think I will learn_____."

   d. **Photos, Sketches, Visuals, Maps, and Charts:** "On page ___, today's tour includes a walk-through of some helpful _____ [photos, visuals, maps, charts] that are sprinkled on pages ____ and ___. As we pass by more of these _____ [photos, charts, visuals, maps], we notice how they tell us about _____. Focus your attention on the ____ on page ____. It helps me understand more about _____. Tell a partner which visual you are most interested in learning about."

   e. **Glossary and Index:** "Please note that at the very end of the book we have two important features: the glossary and the index." Continue modeling and touring by showing students specific information found in the glossary and index. Invite students to choose two or three interesting words they want to learn more about.

STEP 4: COLLABORATION

Ask students to turn and talk and share the "tour" language they've heard so far. Chart some of the tour phrases such as "Over here we have _____. I see a _____ on this page, and it is helpful because _____. We are passing by several_____ which are great for_____. Coming up, you will see_____." Discuss and act out using body language, such as pointing with fingers and sweeping motions with the arms.

Invite students to work with partners or in teams to practice taking each other on nonfiction text tours, previewing the same text you just modeled or another text. Use the *Informational Text Tours* reproducible (see Figure 2.10) to provide a framework. Circulate to assist students in their efforts. After students work in pairs or teams, discuss their predictions for the text. Ask how the text features assist in predicting what the text is about. Have students read the text to see how the text features help them stay on track.

STEP 5: APPLICATION

Students work independently or in pairs or teams to fill in the *Informational Text Tours* reproducible in Figure 2.10 as they preview a new text. They select a text feature to be "in charge" of as they lead the tour. For example, one student leads the group through the table of contents, another shares headings, and one more leads the tour of the visuals in the text. Pass out the *Nonfiction Road Signs* reproducible (see Figure 2.11) for students to use as they work their way through a text. Students may put the cards in a pile and take turns drawing the cards and previewing that particular text feature.

FIGURE 2.10

Informational Text Tours Reproducible

Date: _____   Tour Guide Name: _____

Title of Informational Text: _____   Author_____

Directions: ☑ **Check off each item after you "tour" it. Take turns being the tour guide.**

Tour Guide 🚩 Table of Contents

☐ Read each chapter title.
☐ Flip through or look over the text.
☐ Write or sketch what you think you will learn.

Tour Guide 🚩 Headings

☐ Read each heading in the text.
☐ Talk about what you think you will learn.
☐ Choose two headings.
☐ Write or sketch what you think you will learn.

Tour Guide 🚩 Maps & Charts & Graphs

☐ Tour the text maps, charts, and graphs.
☐ Study each one you find.
☐ Choose one map, chart, or graph to predict what you will learn.

Tour Guide 🚩 Photos & Drawings

☐ Tour the text photos, drawings, and captions.
☐ Study each one you find.
☐ Choose one photo or drawing to predict what you will learn. Sketch it!

Tour Guide 🚩 Index & Glossary

Does the text have an index? ☐Yes ☐No
☐ Look over the words and page numbers.
Does the text have a glossary? ☐Yes ☐No
☐ Look over the words and definitions.

🎤 Tour Guide Talk

Try it with a partner or team!
☐ Over here we have . . .
☐ On the (right/left) you will see…
☐ As you can see…
☐ Look now as we pass…
☐ Coming up you will see…
☐ Notice as we pass…
☐ Focus your attention on…

FIGURE 2.11

Nonfiction Road Signs Reproducible

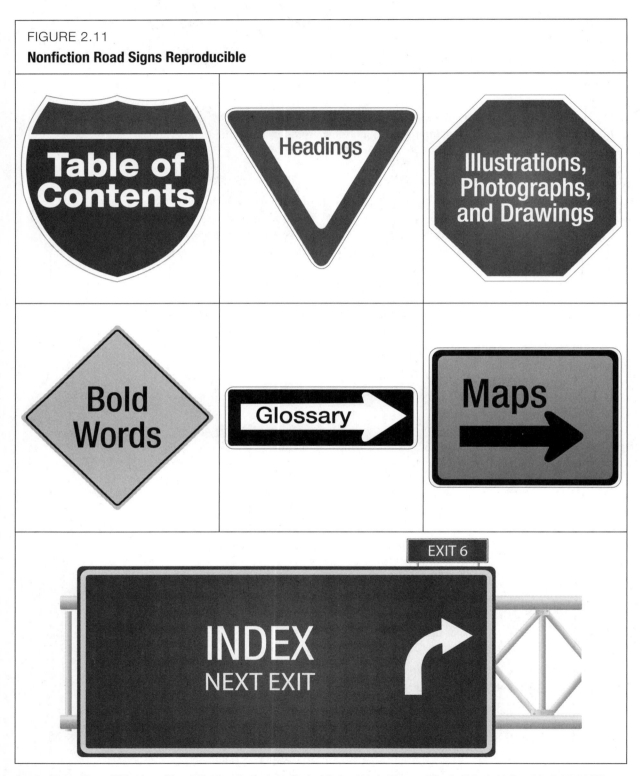

Try using many different types of informational texts for informational text tours including weekly newspapers, online news articles, content area textbooks, and picture books. Discuss the differences. Ask students to discuss how text features help them comprehend. Which text features do they prefer? Which are not as important?

STEP: 6 REFLECTION

Oral or Written Response

Invite students to reflect upon text features using the following discussion points and writing in their literacy notebooks:

- Name the text features we often see in informational texts.
- Make a three-column chart to discuss each text feature by defining it and tell why it helps us understand the content. Use a chart like the one in Figure 2.12.

FIGURE 2.12

Three-Column Chart

Informational Text Feature	What is it?	How does it help us?

- Discuss why authors include text features.
- Think about why taking a tour of the text helps us comprehend better.

ADAPTATION AND EXTENSION

- *Videotape*: Record students as they role-play as tour guides giving text tours before reading. Post on the classroom or school website.
- *English Language Learner Suggestion*: Choose a text to use with a small group of ELLs. Brainstorm a list of tour guide phrases and record them on a chart for students to refer to during the lesson. Go around the group and ask students to take turns being the "tour guide." Scaffold language as needed to support students.

- *Struggling Reader Suggestion*: Cross-age buddies. Have students select an informational text to read aloud to a little buddy or partner in the classroom. The text should be on a topic the little buddy is interested in such as trains, insects, or soccer. The older student practices the before-reading "text tour" at least three times with classmates before sharing it with the younger child or the classmate partner. Research supports cross-age tutoring, as both students grow from the experience (Topping, 2005).

EVALUATION

"I can . . ." Statements

- I can preview the table of contents in an informational text to help me predict what it will be about.
- I can preview the visuals including maps, charts, graphs, photos, and drawings in an informational text to help me predict what I will learn.
- I can give a pretend "tour" of the text features in a given informational text.
- I can define text features and tell why they are important (i.e., table of contents, headings, visuals, glossary, index).

Behavior Indicators

- Identifies main text features in an informational text during a text preview or tour.
- Identifies the visuals (i.e., maps, charts, graphs, photos) in an informational text during a text preview.
- Uses informational text features to make logical predictions about the text and what can be learned by reading it.

LESSON 7. COMPREHENSION: INFERRING AND DRAWING CONCLUSIONS

Title A Text with a View: Imagery in Reading

Trailer Have you ever seen a movie based on a book that you read? Is the movie ever as good as the book? Probably not. The movie that you created in your mind's eye while reading is always better because the movie that you saw at the theater was someone else's "vision" of the book. Good readers constantly imagine the visual scenes in a book, as well as all the senses of the reading—what was seen, heard, felt, and smelled. Indeed, often emotions are imagined as one reads. The images that we create usually contain inferences or guesses about what we read. In this lesson you will explore ways to encourage students to create and share images as they read texts.

Literacy Enhancer Reading Comprehension: Making Inferences; Imagery

Key Academic Vocabulary

(Terms spiraled from previous lessons)

Background Knowledge (Schema): The existing knowledge a person has about a topic

Hypothesis: A prediction usually made prior to a scientific experiment that anticipates the outcome; the experiment confirms or disconfirms the hypothesis

Prediction: An educated guess about what may happen in a story or other text about to be read

(New terms in this lesson)

Imagery: The creation of an internal representation of meaning based on something that is read; consists of the sight, sound, smells, movements, and feelings associated with a scene in a text

Inference: An educated guess or prediction about some aspect of the content of a text that is not specifically mentioned; a sophisticated form of reading comprehension

Learning Objectives

- Make, describe, share, and revise elaborate images based on texts students read.
- Provide appropriate rationales for their images.

Essential Questions

- What is an inference?
- What do I need to know to make appropriate images about the texts I read?
- Am I able to explain the nature of the images I create while reading?
- Am I able to appreciate and understand the images created by my classmates?

STEP 1: PREPARATION

Organize Materials

- Narrative texts that contain rich sensory descriptions that lend themselves to the development of rich images
- *Image Maker* reproducible
- *How to Use Imagery to Enhance Comprehension* reproducible

STEP 2: INITIATION

Describe to your students the notion of making images from words. Say the following words and ask students to create a mental image that comes to mind: *family, picnic, Thanksgiving, blizzard, automobile,* and *dessert.* Share with students the image that comes to you with these words (e.g., the concept of *blizzard* might evoke a snowstorm cutting across a country road, a person slipping and sliding while trying to walk down a snowy sidewalk, or a time to cozy up at home on a snow day from school). Have students share their own images in small groups and discuss how the images could be different from one another. Most often, the images or inferences we make are based on our own background knowledge and experience—even though we may be processing the same word.

Indicate to students that the same process of making images from a word or words is true when reading a text. Good readers will create images that we feel reflect the meaning of the passage we are reading. Those images are shaped by our own background, so we may add details to our image that are not mentioned in the passage. Adding details that are not directly mentioned in the text is a form of inferencing.

STEP 3: DEMONSTRATION

1. Choose the text you will read to your students. Do not show them any illustrations that may be part of the text. Then read the title of the story.
2. Think aloud and describe to your students the images that come to mind from simply reading the title. If the title does not lend itself to the development of an image, read the actual text until you reach a natural stopping point. Describe how you use your background knowledge to make your images. Try to include other senses besides vision in your images—what you hear, smell, feel.
3. Continue this process of reading and sharing images that you develop with your students. You may wish to do simple drawings of your images to show concrete examples.

4. When the read-aloud is complete, ask students to discuss how making images while reading influenced your reading and understanding of the text.

STEP 4: COLLABORATION

Have students continue the same process described in the Demonstration section with the texts that you will have them read on their own. Working in small groups, students can make, share, and discuss text-based images at logical stopping points throughout the text. Groups should come to consensus images that reflect the meaning of the text and share them with the class, justifying choices images. Display the groups' images using a document camera or other device. As students move through the text, have them discuss how they confirmed, revised, or refined their images. At the end of the reading, use the various images made by students as the basis for sequencing and discussing the story. Ask students to reflect on how actively making, sharing, and discussing their images changed how they read the text.

STEP 5: APPLICATION

Throughout the next several texts that you read to and with your students, have them engage in making, sharing, discussing, and refining or revising their images. Display a chart that lists the process of using imagery to enhance reading comprehension (see Figure 2.13).

FIGURE 2.13

How to Use Imagery to Enhance Comprehension Reproducible

1. Read the text.
2. Sketch an image that reflects the meaning of what you read.
3. Share and discuss your image with classmates.
4. Refine or revise your image based on feedback from classmates.

Source: Literacy Strong All Year Long: Powerful Lessons for Grades 3-5 by Lori Oczkus, Valerie Ellery, and Timothy V. Rasinski. Copyright © 2018 ASCD. Readers may duplicate this figure for noncommercial use within their school.

STEP 6: REFLECTION

Oral or Written Response

You may wish to create an *Image Maker* sheet for students to use for each text they read (see Figure 2.14). The final step for each reading requires students to reflect in writing on how making images affected their reading. Students' responses may indicate that, in the process of making and discussing their images, they had to add things that were not actually reflected in the text. In adding to their images, they are making inferences that are derived both from the text and from the background information that students bring to the reading.

ADAPTATION AND EXTENSION

- Create displays of the various images made by students while reading a text. The images could be a few images that represent one episode in the text, or various images arranged sequentially to provide a visual summary of the text.
- In addition to having students make and share visual images of texts they encounter, you can also have them create "images" using other senses. For example, as you read a text, ask students to share the emotions that are present in the text or various characters that display in the text. Are there any sounds that might be reflected in the text (e.g., traffic, a noisy crowd, chirping birds)? Perhaps students think of smells that could be shared as part of a text. Developing and sharing these other "imagery" forms encourages students to think beyond the literal level of the text and make inferences.
- *English Language Learner Suggestion*: In addition to making images, students can write captions or titles. If necessary, students could dictate their captions to a scribe who may be more proficient in writing.
- *Struggling Reader Suggestion*: Before reading, provide students with a graphic organizer that provides a sequential summary of the text and the stopping points at which they will be asked to make images.

EVALUATION

"I can . . ." Statements

- I can make images that reflect my understanding of a text.
- I can justify my images based on what I know about the topic and what I have read.
- I can revise and refine my images based on feedback from others or new information presented in the text.

- I can work with classmates to share our images with one another and provide meaningful feedback on my classmates' images.

Behavior Indicators

- Shares what she knows about a topic or event.
- Makes images that provide a reasonable reflection of the meaning of a text.
- Makes good revisions and refinements on images based on feedback from others and new information in the text.

FIGURE 2.14

Image Maker Reproducible

Name of Text: _____

[ ]

Description: _____

[ ]

Description: _____

[ ]

Description: _____

Reflection: How did making images throughout the text affect my reading? _____

_____

_____

LESSON 8. COMPREHENSION: QUESTIONING FOR CLOSE READING

Title INFERENCE DANCE MOVES: READING BETWEEN THE LINES

Trailer Triple "I" Dancing = Step–Infer! Twirl–Imply! Dip–Interpret! What is *really* going on here? Stepping, twirling, dipping. Do you ever feel like you have to dance around and figure out what the author is trying to say? You might feel like you need to read as if you were a detective, speculating about clues for understanding left by the author but not directly stated in the text. You find yourself doing the Triple "I" Dance to derive meaning from what you are reading. Let's learn this new dance move called "reading between the lines" to do the Triple "I" Dance smoothly through the pages of text.

Literacy Enhancer Comprehension—Questioning, Inference

Key Academic Vocabulary
(Terms spiraled from previous lessons)

Close Read: Determine purpose and notice features and language used by the author; to think thoughtfully and methodically about the details and why they were used

Interrogate: To examine with questions; to look for answers

Speculative Talk: Making an inference by suggesting or hinting at connections and conclusions; element of imaginative thinking to support understanding; expression based on assumption rather than factual knowledge

Text-Based Evidence: Evidence derived from key facts and details in the text

Text-Dependent Questions: Sentences in interrogative form that can only be answered by referring explicitly back to the text being read
(New terms in this lesson)

Inference: An educated guess or prediction about some aspect of the content of a text that is not specifically mentioned; a sophisticated form of reading comprehension based on a conclusion (i.e., may involve interpretation, judgment, opinion, prediction) or based on text evidence and reasoning merged with personal background knowledge

Interpretation: A person's explanation of the meaning of something

Judgment: The ability to make decisions or come to logical conclusions

Opinion: A view or judgment formed about something not necessarily based on facts

Reasoning: Thinking and processing information in a logical way

Learning Objectives

- Confirm or modify questions, inferences, and predictions by referring to details and examples from the text when asking and answering questions related to the text.
- Merge background knowledge and textual clues to construct interpretations of text.

Essential Questions

- How can you use what is known to develop speculative views on evidence being examined?
- How do you use the author's clues to make inferences?

STEP 1: PREPARATION

Organize Materials

- *Talk Show Cue Cards* reproducible
- Microphone for talk show (optional)
- Book: *The Invisible Boy* by Trudy Ludwig (optional)
- *Inference Dance Moves: I Question, It Says, I Say, So I Infer* reproducible
- Supplies to create a class anchor chart (e.g., chart paper, markers)

STEP 2: INITIATION

Revisit the Talk Show concept from Chapter 1, Lesson 8. Set up a talk show environment, with student camera crews filming using phones or other devices to post as a podcast show. Choose a student to be the talk show host and you can be the author of a book the class is currently reading to help model the art of inferring based on evidence provided by the author. Have predetermined questions on cards for the student host to navigate the interview. The host opens the interview by looking at the title and cover of a book, and makes an inference based on what he or she sees and reads. Using *The Invisible Boy* by Trudy Ludwig (2013) as an example text, the host begins with his or her questions:

> **Host (1)**: *Based on the title and cover, I believe this boy feels like no one sees him. Can you **explain** to us **what** you, as the author, really want us to know here on the cover before we even begin to dive into reading this book?*
> **Author (1)**: *Well, I wanted you, the readers, to wonder about this little boy and why he is all alone on the cover. I wanted you to use what you know about the key words and vocabulary (invisible) in the title.*

Host (2): *So I hear you saying that you wanted to lead us into asking questions like,* What would make this boy invisible? Is he all alone? Does he really want to even be noticed?

Author (2): *Absolutely—that is what proficient readers do. They use what they know to make a guess about what they don't know.*

Host (3): *After I read the opening part in the text, it made me want to ask you* **why** *you chose to begin the story that way.* **Why** *did you tell us that?*

Author (3): *I wanted you to begin to infer what the boy was feeling and for you to begin to recall times you might have felt that way. I think it is very important to think beyond what I have said directly in the text.*

Host (4): *I see—you wanted us to interact with the text and illustrations to provoke us to think and respond* by drawing a conclusion on our own.

Author (4): *Exactly. I want you to not just read the lines I have in print for you, but for you to* **read between the** *lines so you can derive meaning based on what you know from your past experiences and key ideas and details that I gave in the text.*

Host: Wow! Thank you, Trudy, for giving us insight on how to go deeper in your book for meaning. *We will need to read closely for your details and connect them with our own experiences to process what is really going on in the text.*

The italic words above are posted on the *Talk Show Cue Cards* reproducible (see Figure 2.15) and are generic to place into any talk show model to expand on the concept of questioning and inferring.

STEP 3: DEMONSTRATION

Inference Dance Moves: I Question, It Says, I Say, So I Infer

1. Revisit the points from the *Talk Show Cue Cards* and create with the students a purpose for a "Reading Between the Lines" anchor chart. Ideas might include the following:

   - Helps you fill in the blanks the author didn't provide outright in the text
   - Dives deeper in the text than what is actually there

FIGURE 2.15

Talk Show Cue Cards Reproducible

Host Card 1: Based on the title and cover, I believe . . .

Can you **explain** to us **what** you, as the author, really want us to know here on the cover before we even begin to dive into reading this book?

Author Card 1: Well, I wanted you, the readers, to wonder about . . .

Host Card 2: So I hear you saying that you wanted to lead us into asking questions like . . .

Author Card 2: Absolutely—that is what proficient readers do. They use what they know to make a guess about what they don't know.

Host Card 3: After I read the opening part in the text, it made me want to ask you **why** you chose to begin the story that way?

Why did you tell us that?

Author Card 3: I wanted you to begin to infer . . .

I think it is very important to think beyond what I have said directly in the text.

Host Card 4: I see—you wanted us to interact with the text and illustrations to provoke us to think and respond. We will need to read closely for your details and connect them with our own experiences to process what is really going on in the text.

Author Card 4: I want you to not just read the lines I have in print for you, but for you to read between the lines so you can derive meaning based on what you know from your past experiences and key ideas and details that I gave in the text.

- Makes predictions to figure out motives and author's purpose
- Uses common sense and activates prior knowledge
- Analyzes the thought process and draws a conclusion
- Requires close reading of key details and the ability to connect these details to own thoughts, opinions, and claims

2. Share how these points can be applied into steps that can create an "Inference Dance." Make a graphic organizer chart with four columns (adapted from Beers, 2003) as a visual form of processing text (see Figure 2.16). Identify the four steps needed for this particular "dance" that will help navigate a smooth read.

- **Step 1 Dance Move.** Title the first column "I Question." Hold up a text you are studying and think of questions you want to know about the information in the text. Pose a few questions. Read and continue to pose some inferential questions (who, what, when, where, how, or why). *What do you need to know or clarify from the text?*
- **Step 2 Dance Move.** Title the second column "It Says." Reread and begin to search for information from the text that will help answer the question. Record explicit textual key details that support what could be part of the answers to the questions. *What are the key details (words, phrases, ideas, or images)?*
- **Step 3 Dance Move.** Title the third column "I Say." Think about the information presented and explain what you already know about it or what you are thinking would make sense as you "read between the lines" based on your own life experience. Read beyond what has been literally expressed. *What do you already know about . . . ? What is between the lines that is not stated but you think needs to be noted?*
- **Step 4 Dance Move.** Title the fourth column "So I Infer." Draw a conclusion by combining what the text says and what you say and state the claim. *What do you conclude? What is the best answer to your question?*

STEP 4: COLLABORATION

Have partners or teams analyze the "Read Between the Lines" anchor chart that they generated and the modeled "dance moves." Have them engage in conversational coaching by asking and answering the following questions:

- Why is it important to use information from the text to support my inference?
- How does interaction with text provoke thinking and response?

FIGURE 2.16

Inference Dance Moves: I Question, It Says, I Say, So I Infer

I Question Elicit Information	It Says Text Evidence	I Say Interpretation	So I Infer Inference or Answer
Step 1 Formulate a question and write it down. *What do you need to know or clarify from the text?*	Step 2 Search for evidence from the text that will help answer the question. *What are the key details (words, phrases, ideas, or images)?*	Step 3 Explain what you already know about the information. *What do you already know about . . .? What is between the lines you need to know?*	Step 4 Combine what the text says with what you say to draw a conclusion for an answer. *What do you conclude? What is the best answer to your question?*

STEP 5: APPLICATION

Have your students work alone or in groups to process the text they are reading using Figure 2.16 *Inference Dance Moves: I Question, It Says, I Say, So I Infer* reproducible. They can either answer predetermined inferential questions or write their own questions in column 1. When the chart is completed, students can present their claims to their partners to articulate their reasoning and justification for their conclusions to the questions. Partners can cross-examine with some of these sample questions:

- What details, facts, or evidence led you to believe _____?
- What clues led you to believe _____?
- What can the reader conclude after reading _____?
- Why do you think _____?
- What information from the text supports the conclusion that _____?

STEP 6: REFLECTION

Oral or Written Response

Have students independently respond in their literacy notebooks to evaluate their reasoning processes and how the steps to making an inference can help them read and process text. Use the essential question as a possible prompt for response: "How can you use what is known to develop speculative views on evidence being examined?"

ADAPTATION AND EXTENSION

- Show bumper stickers or signs and have students state the author's implied meaning as opposed to the actual meaning.
- *English Language Learner Suggestion*: Display cartoons and have partners make inferences based on the visual clues in the cartoons.
- *Struggling Reader Suggestion*: Play a guessing game to scaffold vocabulary acquisition and inferring opportunities in a collaborative environment. Step 1: Think of a word based on a current unit of study. Step 2: Have a player in the group ask a yes or no question to try to guess what the mystery word might be. Step 3: Players in the group can infer based on the questions and answers. Step 4: Continue asking yes or no questions until the correct word is figured out. Step 5: Optional: Create a yes or no T-chart to record and collect information that will help players infer or guess the word.

EVALUATION

"I can . . ." Statements

- I can infer a character's feelings, motives, thoughts, and actions by using text evidence and connections to my life, other books, and the world around me.
- I can infer meanings of an informational text from the title page, table of contents, and chapter headings to answer questions about what I read.

Behavior Indicators

- Infers what a character thinks, feels, and does by using text evidence and connections to her own life, other books, and the world.
- Explains inferences, conclusions, and generalizations by citing appropriate details and examples from the text by connecting to her personal life and activating her background schema as she determines meaning from what is being read.
- Incorporates the combination of explicitly stated information, background knowledge, and connections to the text to answer questions she has as she reads.

LESSON 9. COMPREHENSION: DETERMINING IMPORTANCE AND SUMMARIZING

Title RECOUNT RECIPE

Trailer How good of a cook are you? What kind of ingredients do you think it would take to recount the delicious details in a text? Some recipes have secret ingredients that can bring all the flavors together to serve up a special dish. A top chef learns to identify which ingredients are key to a recipe. Just like a cook, it can be overwhelming for readers to identify the individual flavors (i.e., story elements) that contribute to the overall meaning of what they are reading. Readers describe how specific details are essential in a literary recipe for determining importance and recounting what they read!

Literacy Enhancer Comprehension: Determining Importance and Summarizing: Recount, Fables, Morals

Key Academic Vocabulary
(Terms spiraled from previous lessons)

Cause and Effect: A relationship between actions in which one event (the cause) makes another event happen (effect)

Contribute: To help achieve something; bring about the sequence of events

Essential: Absolutely necessary for the meaning and purpose

Key Detail: Important feature, fact, or item that supports the overall meaning

Information: Gathered knowledge; facts and ideas

Retelling: Recalling in a sequential order what is happening in a text

Sequencing: Placing information in a certain order

Sift: To filter and examine which detail is most important

Story Elements: Parts (ingredients) of a story (i.e., character, setting, event, plot, problem, solution)

Text-Based Evidence: Evidence derived from key facts and details in the text
(New terms in this lesson)

Chronological: Organized within a sequential order of time

Compare and Contrast: A method of analyzing similarities and differences of two or more objects

Fable: A story passed down among generations to teach morals and valuable lessons using animals that personify people, plants, or forces of nature

Moral: The teaching of a practical lesson contained in a story

Recount: To give detailed descriptions of information from a text in chronological order and past tense to convey the message of the text

Learning Objectives

- Identify similarities and differences between characters, settings, and events.
- Sequence story elements through a detailed recount of what was read.

Essential Questions

- What are the story elements needed to determine the main idea of the text?
- How does comparing and contrasting elements of a story provide deeper insight?
- Why is it important to be able to recount a text in chronological order?

STEP 1: PREPARATION

Organize Materials

- Cooking accessories (e.g., pizza box, apron, chef hat) (optional)
- "The Fox and the Stork" fable
- Multimodal text set of topic: Fables
- *Recount Recipe* reproducible (copy or enlarge for display)
- *Student Detailed Recount Checklist* reproducible
- Literacy Notebooks

STEP 2: INITIATION

Chronological Cooking

Think about how a pizza is made. Make a class list of everything that is needed to make a pepperoni pizza, and chart the steps needed to make it. Ask the students, "Does it really matter which step you take first when cooking?" Present what-if scenario analysis emphasizing time connective (transitional) words: "What if the sauce went down *first, then* the crust was laid on top of the sauce, and *finally* the toppings are added. Would the finished pizza be properly made?" Discuss the process of making a pizza incorporating transitional words (i.e., *first, then, next*) in order.

STEP 3: DEMONSTRATION

Recount Recipe

1. Think aloud about making the pizza again and how you used transition words to help you sequence the process. Share how the relationship of ingredients in a recipe interact to make a delicious dish for sharing!

2. Make the connection that there are certain ingredients in a text that help bring meaningful flavor to it, also. Read the fable or any text you are studying as an example.

The Fox and the Stork
Aesop for Children (translator not identified), 1919

The Fox one day thought of a plan to amuse himself at the expense of the Stork, at whose odd appearance he was always laughing. "You must come and dine with me today," he said to the Stork, smiling to himself at the trick he was going to play. The Stork gladly accepted the invitation and arrived in good time and with a very hearty appetite. For dinner the Fox served soup. But it was set out in a very shallow dish, and all the Stork could do was to wet the very tip of his bill. Not a drop of soup could he get. But the Fox lapped it up easily, and, to increase the disappointment of the Stork, made a great show of enjoyment.

The hungry Stork was much displeased at the trick, but he was a calm, even-tempered fellow and saw no good in flying into a rage. Instead, not long afterward, he invited the Fox to dine with him in turn. The Fox arrived promptly at the time that had been set, and the Stork served a fish dinner that had a very appetizing smell. But it was served in a tall jar with a very narrow neck. The Stork could easily get at the food with his long bill, but all the Fox could do was to lick the outside of the jar, and sniff at the delicious odor. And when the Fox lost his temper, the Stork said calmly: *Do not play tricks on your neighbors unless you can stand the same treatment yourself.*

3. Compare how the ingredients and procedural steps in a recipe can relate to the flavorful ingredients found in story elements (i.e., characters, setting, events, problem, solution) and to chronological order for bringing meaning to the text.

4. Put on an apron and begin to interactively read aloud the *Recount Recipe* in Figure 2.17. Point out that a recount is a detailed retelling that describes in past tense an account of an event or experience in chronological order, using precise word choice to convey the main idea.

5. Insert the specific story elements from the text you read aloud into the recipe to model a recount. The *Recount Recipe* reproducible can also be used as an anchor chart for future referencing.

FIGURE 2.17

Recount Recipe Reproducible

Literacy Recipes

From the Kitchen of Literacy Strong

Ingredients

- Orientation: who, when, where, why
- Main Events: what—detailed descriptions, time connectives
- Conclusion: personal comments, reactions (i.e., moral, lessons)

Directions

1. Gather the main character(s): who.

2. Place the character into a specific time and place to describe the setting: when, where.

3. Sprinkle in a motivation or goal the character may have: why.

4. Measure in something the character is doing that is important: what.

5. Add a dash of detailed descriptions that are happening with the character(s).

6. Whisk in time connectives to demonstrate chronological order.

7. Simmer in a grueling problem and how it is solved.

8. Garnish with a conclusion that can include personal reflections, comments, reactions, moral, or lesson.

6. Demonstrate how to interpret information presented visually and explain how the information contributes to an understanding of the text in which it appears.

STEP 4: COLLABORATION

Engage in conversational coaching by asking students to dialogue the following various questions with diverse partners: "What are story elements? What makes a good retell? Why is it important to be able to retell a text? What makes a good recount? Why is it important to be able to recount a text? Compare and contrast a retell and a recount."

Here is a sample retelling of "The Fox and the Stork" fable:

> The sly Fox invites the hungry Stork for lunch. He serves soup on a shallow dish. Stork tries to eat but can't get to his food because of his long beak. Fox tricks Stork. So, Stork devises a way to get the last laugh by tricking Fox with his own trick of inviting him for lunch. Stork serves fish in a tall jar to Fox to get him back.

Now compare that sample retell to a sample recount for the same fable:

> First, Fox invited Stork for lunch. Fox thought he was very smart when he played a trick on Stork. Fox served soup on a shallow dish to Stork, but Stork could only get the tip of his bill into the soup. Later, Stork retaliated by serving Fox a delicious fish dinner in a tall jar with a narrow neck so that he could only smell the nice aroma and lick the outside of the jar. At last, Stork outsmarted Fox.

Discuss the lesson in the fable: *Treat others the way you want to be treated, and a friend who tricks another is no friend at all.* Have the students collaborate and discuss the Retell Versus Recount Feature Chart in Figure 2.18.

FIGURE 2.18
Retell Versus Recount Feature Chart

Retell	Recount
3rd person Present tense Simple details Sequential order	1st and 3rd person Past tense Detailed descriptions of information Chronological order Connective time words (*first, next, later*)

Source: Literacy Strong All Year Long: Powerful Lessons for Grades 3–5 by Lori Oczkus, Valerie Ellery, and Timothy V. Rasinski. Copyright © 2018 ASCD. Readers may duplicate this figure for noncommercial use within their school.

STEP 5: APPLICATION

Using the *Recount Recipe* reproducible (Figure 2.17), have students work in groups or individually to practice cooking up a good recount of what they read. They can use the *Student Detailed Recount Checklist* reproducible (see Figure 2.19) as a taste tester.

STEP 6: REFLECTION

Oral or Written Response

Have students use their Literacy Notebooks to independently create a recount from a text they read. Remind students to think about the story elements (ingredients) and the chronological order of the text to "cook up" their recounts. Have them use the *Recount Recipe* and *Student Detailed Recount Checklist* to evaluate their writing.

ADAPTATION AND EXTENSION

- Read two or more versions of "The Fox and the Stork" from *Aesop's Fables* and compare and contrast the story ingredients (e.g., characters, settings, events), drawing on specific details in the text.
- Have students place sentence strips in order as they recount a text.
- Use an informational text and model using the text features and text elements (e.g., concept, historical figure, location, motivation, goal, conflict, resolution) in place of the story elements (e.g., character, setting, problem, solution) for class and student recount.
- *English Language Learner Suggestion*: Have students use the Explain Everything app that allows them to describe and visually represent what they want to explain. Have them take pictures or create a sequential list to "explain" or retell what is happening.
- *Struggling Reader Suggestion*: Have students interpret information presented visually, orally, or quantitatively (e.g., in charts, graphs, diagrams, timelines, animations, interactive elements on web pages) and explain how the information contributes to an understanding of the text in which it appears.

EVALUATION

"I can . . ." Statements

- I can recount a fable using key details from the text.
- I can convey how information presented helps me interpret the text around it.
- I can compare and contrast important relationships between information presented using specific details based on the text.

FIGURE 2.19

Student Detailed Recount Checklist Reproducible

Yes	No	
___	___	Identifies and elaborates on main characters using names
___	___	Identifies an orientation with key details answering *who? when? where? why?*
___	___	Identifies and describes events in chronological order
___	___	Uses precise and concise word choices (e.g., verbs, adverbs, adjectives) to clearly state key details
___	___	Delivers recounting in past tense
___	___	Presents in 1st or 3rd person point of view
___	___	Applies connective time words that link events (e.g., *next, later, when, then, after, before, first, finally*)
___	___	Concludes with comments that express a personal reflection regarding the events

Indicators	Retell	Recount
Oral		
Written		
Told in 1st person		
Told in 3rd person		
Delivered in past tense		
Delivered in present tense		
Specific details about characters		
Chronological order using connective time words		
Beginning, middle, and end		

Source: Literacy Strong All Year Long: Powerful Lessons for Grades 3–5 by Lori Oczkus, Valerie Ellery, and Timothy V. Rasinski. Copyright © 2018 ASCD. Readers may duplicate this figure for noncommercial use within their school.

Behavior Indicators

- Identifies similarities and differences of the important relationships between information presented using specific details based on the text.
- Sequences story elements through a detailed recount of what was read.

LESSON 10. COMPREHENSION: MOTIVATING READERS

Title Take Off and Partner Talk Bookmarks

Trailer Many clubs create a special secret handshake, song, or rituals and routines reserved for their special community. Membership in the Class Book Club means students talk about books as part of the club's routines or rituals. Talking about books and reading helps promote deeper comprehension and helps students become more excited about reading. Using the bookmark tools in this lesson, partners discuss reading as their comprehension grows. Since many classrooms already incorporate partnerships during reading lessons, the engaging suggestions in this lesson help make discussions even more productive.

Literacy Enhancer Motivation: Motivating Readers—Text Features, Book Talks, Predicting, Summarizing

Key Academic Vocabulary

(Terms spiraled from previous lessons)

Author: The person who wrote the book

Illustrator: The person who illustrated the book

Predict: To use information from a text to infer what the text will be about or what one might learn from it

Summarize: To tell what has happened in the text by sharing important points and details

Title: The name of the text; tells what it is about or gives clues to the content

Rating: A score assigned to reading material; includes a scale from best to least

Reason: The rationale for an opinion or idea backed with text evidence
(New terms in this lesson)

Fiction: The genre that consists of stories that are make-believe; also poetry

Nonfiction: The genre that consists of factual information that is portrayed to answer, explain, or describe

Learning Objectives

- Discuss fiction and nonfiction with diverse partners using a variety of sentence stems before, during, and after reading that promote comprehension.
- Follow rules for discussion that consists of taking turns, making eye contact, and elaborating or adding onto the comments of others.

Essential Questions

- What are the rules, or the protocols, for discussing a book with a partner or in a group?
- What are some prompts to discuss before, during, and after reading?

STEP 1: PREPARATION

Organize Materials

- *Take Off and Partner Talk Bookmarks* (fiction and nonfiction) reproducibles
- *Partner Talk Symbols and Gestures* (fiction and nonfiction) reproducibles
- *Take Off and Partner Talk Guidelines* reproducible
- Read-aloud books (teacher read-aloud)
- Class books (books the whole class will read: novels, picture books, basal reader)
- Leveled texts for guided reading groups

STEP 2: INITIATION

Club Member Chats

Invite students to share some special codes, rules, and rituals that clubs often use to communicate (e.g., song, handshake, greeting). Some clubs even use a secret language for members to communicate. Tell students that they are going to learn some engaging ways to talk to partners about books in the Class Book Club. Ask them to brainstorm a list of possible discussion topics that the club might use in the guidelines.

STEP 3: DEMONSTRATION

Take Off and Partner Talk Bookmarks

For Fiction

1. Explain to students that when good readers talk to one another about reading, their comprehension improves. Demonstrating with a fiction book, display the *Take Off and Partner Talk Bookmark for Fiction* reproducible (see Figure 2.20) and provide a copy for each student.
2. Before reading the text, lead the class in a preview of the text by looking at the title, visuals, and cover art. Make predictions using the language on the bookmark by saying, "I think this is about ____ because____." Add in what it may remind you of—possibly an experience or event from your life, another book, a television program, or something on the world stage. Say, "This reminds me of____ because_____." Back your predictions with evidence from the text. Invite students to turn to a partner and repeat the prompts on the bookmark.

FIGURE 2.20

Take Off and Partner Talk Bookmark for Fiction

Before Reading

- I think this is about_____

because _____.

- This reminds me of_____ because_____.

During Reading

- So far,_____.

- Next, I think_____

will happen because_____.

- I want to know the word _____.

- I think the author chose the word _____

because _____.

?

- I am wondering_____.

After Reading

- In the beginning, _____.

- During the middle,_____.

- At the end,_____.

- My favorite part was _____.

- I was surprised when_____.

Take Off and Partner Talk Bookmark for Fiction

Before Reading

- I think this is about_____

because _____.

- This reminds me of_____ because_____.

During Reading

- So far,_____.

- Next, I think_____

will happen because_____.

- I want to know the word _____.

- I think the author chose the word _____

because _____.

?

- I am wondering_____.

After Reading

- In the beginning, _____.

- During the middle,_____.

- At the end,_____.

- My favorite part was _____.

- I was surprised when_____.

3. During reading, pause to model your thinking for each of the bookmark prompts. Say, "So far, ___ happened. Next, I think ___ will happen because ___." Then invite students to turn to a partner and use the prompts. Also pause to model the word level prompts, choosing several words: "I want to know the word _____. I think the author picked the word _____ because_____." Then invite the pairs to use the bookmark and text and try the prompts as well.

4. After reading, pause to model each of the after-reading prompts. Model using the text you've selected and show how to use each one. For example, "In the beginning,____; in the middle,____; at the end,____. I liked the part where ____. The character ___felt ____ because___. I was surprised when_____. This book was about _____. The book reminds me of_____."

5. Option: You may choose to represent each prompt with a symbol or gesture (see Figure 2.21). When modeling, write each symbol onto a sticky note and place it on the text next to the example you are about to share. Make sure students have a copy of the bookmark while you demonstrate.

For Nonfiction

1. Explain to students that when good readers talk to one another about reading, their comprehension improves. Demonstrating with a nonfiction book, display the *Take Off and Partner Talk Bookmark for Nonfiction* reproducible (see Figure 2.22) and provide a copy for each student.

2. Before reading the text, lead the class in a preview of the text by looking at the title, visuals, and text features. Make predictions using the language on the bookmark by saying, "I think I will learn ____ because_____." Add in what it may remind you of—possibly an experience or event from your life, another book, a television program, or something on the world stage. Say, "This reminds me of_____ because_____." Back your predictions with evidence from the text. Invite students to turn to a partner and repeat the prompts on the bookmark.

3. During reading, pause to model your thinking for each of the bookmark prompts. Say, "So far I have learned ____ from the text. Next, I think I will learn ____ because ___." Then invite students to turn to a partner and use the prompts. Also pause to model the word-level prompts, choosing several words: "I want to know the word _____. I think the author picked the word _____ because_____." Then invite the pairs to use the bookmark and text and try the prompts as well.

FIGURE 2.21

Fiction Partner Talk Symbols and Gestures

Before Reading—Prompts from Bookmark		Gesture
I think this is about . . . because . . . *This reminds me of . . . because . . .*	Sketch what you think.	Point to head. Look like you are thinking hard!

During Reading—Prompts from Bookmark		Gesture
So far . . .	Sketch what happened so far.	Pretend to take a picture or video.
Next, I think . . . will happen . . . because . . .	Sketch a bubble and what you think.	Point to head.
I want to know the word . . . *I think the author picked the word . . . because . . .*	Write the words.	Write a word in the air.
I am wondering . . .	? Put a question mark next to the text.	Use a first as a pretend microphone.

After Reading—Prompts from Bookmark		Gesture
In the beginning . . . *During the middle . . .* *At the end . . .*	Sketch a drawing for each beginning, middle, and end.	Pretend to take a picture or video.
My favorite part was . . . because . . .	☆ Put a star next to your favorite part.	Sketch a star in the air.
I was surprised when . . .	! Put an exclamation on a sticky note next to a part that surprised you.	Make an exclamation in the air.

Source: Literacy Strong All Year Long: Powerful Lessons for Grades 3-5 by Lori Oczkus, Valerie Ellery, and Timothy V. Rasinski. Copyright © 2018 ASCD.
Readers may duplicate this figure for noncommercial use within their school.

FIGURE 2.22

Take Off and Partner Talk Bookmark for Nonfiction

Before Reading

FINANCIAL NEWS

- I think I will learn_____

because_____.

- This reminds me of_____

because_____.

During Reading

- So far, I have learned_____.

- Next, I think I will learn _____

because_____.

- I want to know the word_____.

- I think the author chose the word_____because

_____.

?

- I am wondering_____.

After Reading

- The book or text was about

_____.

(beginning, middle, end)

☆ - My favorite part was_____.

! - I was surprised when_____.

✚ - Something new I learned was_____.

Take Off and Partner Talk Bookmark for Nonfiction

Before Reading

FINANCIAL NEWS

- I think I will learn_____

because_____.

- This reminds me of_____

because_____.

During Reading

- So far, I have learned_____.

- Next, I think I will learn _____

because_____.

- I want to know the word_____.

- I think the author chose the word_____because

_____.

?

- I am wondering_____.

After Reading

- The book or text was about

_____.

(beginning, middle, end)

☆ - My favorite part was_____.

! - I was surprised when_____.

✚ - Something new I learned was_____.

Source: Literacy Strong All Year Long: Powerful Lessons for Grades 3-5 by Lori Oczkus, Valerie Ellery, and Timothy V. Rasinski. Copyright © 2018 ASCD. Readers may duplicate this figure for noncommercial use within their school.

4. After reading, pause to model each of the after-reading prompts. Model using the text you've selected and show how to use each one: "This book (text) was about_____. I liked the part where____; I was surprised when___; Something new I learned was___."

5. Option: Represent each prompt with a symbol or gesture (see Figure 2.23). When modeling, write each symbol onto a sticky note and place it on the text next to the example you are about to share. Or you may wish to model how to make the gesture that goes with each prompt. Make sure students have a copy of the bookmark while you demonstrate.

STEP 4: Collaboration

Share the *Take Off and Partner Talk Guidelines* reproducible with students while discussing guidelines for partner talk (see Figure 2.24). Invite two students to role-play as you guide them through the demonstration using some of the talking points from the bookmarks for fiction or nonfiction. Ask the class to follow along using their bookmarks for the discussion and for the guidelines.

- Read through a text, pausing to allow the two students to model how to respond before, during, and after reading.
- Demonstrate the five guidelines one at a time with the pair.
- Look at your partner.
- Listen to your partner.
- Take turns.
- Add a comment such as: "I also think_____" or "I agree with your idea about_____."
- Ask a question such as who, what, when, where, why, or "I wonder____."

During teacher-led small group instruction, use the appropriate guidelines to help students become familiar with them as you work through a text together. Try having students first talk to partners, then the group. Also, reinforce the discussion guidelines.

STEP 5: APPLICATION

Pass out books or other texts for partners to read and discuss. Students may use sticky notes and one of the fiction or nonfiction bookmarks to read through a text silently first, marking discussion points so they will be ready to talk with their partner. Encourage students to talk before, during, and after reading, using the bookmarks to guide their discussion. Post the partner talk guidelines and circulate through the

FIGURE 2.23

Nonfiction Partner Talk Symbols and Gestures Reproducible

Before Reading		Gesture
I think I will learn_____ because_____. This reminds me of_____ because_____.	Sketch what you think.	Point to your head and look like you are thinking hard!
During Reading		
So far I have learned _____ from the text.	Sketch what happened so far.	Pretend to take a picture or video.
Next, I think I will learn _____ because _____.	Sketch a bubble and what you think.	Point to your head.
I want to know the word_____. I think the author picked the word_____ because_____.	Write the words.	Write a word in the air.
After Reading		
The book (text) was about _____.	Sketch a drawing for each beginning, middle, and end.	Pretend to take a picture or video.
My favorite part was _____ because _____.	Put a star next to your favorite part.	Sketch a star in the air.
I was surprised when _____.	Put an exclamation mark on a sticky note next to a part that surprised you.	Make an exclamation mark in the air.
Something new I learned was _____.	Write a plus sign on a sticky note next to a part where you learned something new.	Make a plus sign with your hands.

Source: Literacy Strong All Year Long: Powerful Lessons for Grades 3-5 by Lori Oczkus, Valerie Ellery, and Timothy V. Rasinski. Copyright © 2018 ASCD. Readers may duplicate this figure for noncommercial use within their school.

FIGURE 2.24

Take Off and Partner Talk Guidelines

Take Off and Partner Talk Guidelines

LOOK at your partner.

LISTEN to your partner.

TAKE TURNS

ADD

- "I also think _____."
- "I agree _____."

QUESTION

- Ask *who*, *what*, *when*, *where*, and *why* questions.
- "I wonder _____."

Take Off and Partner Talk Guidelines

LOOK at your partner.

LISTEN to your partner.

TAKE TURNS

ADD

- "I also think _____."
- "I agree _____."

QUESTION

- Ask *who*, *what*, *when*, *where*, and *why* questions.
- "I wonder _____."

classroom, pausing to coach pairs. If you see a pair doing an exemplary job, stop the class and ask the pair to model or demonstrate. Debrief with the entire class after the session to discuss what went well and what they might do to improve.

Stroll Line. Try this discussion format when all the students are reading the same text. Have students line up, bringing their text and bookmark with them, in two lines facing each other. They have already read and marked the text with sticky notes prior to the activity. Students take turns discussing one of the points on the bookmark that you've selected. When you signal, one of the lines moves one step to the right, and the student at the end moves to the front of the line. The other line of students remains stationary. Ask students to share another point from the bookmark about the reading. Continue switching partners to discuss each prompt.

STEP 6: REFLECTION

Oral or Written Response

In their literary notebooks, students record their responses to the prompts on the bookmarks, turning them into writing prompts. Students may discuss the prompts first and then write or vice versa, depending upon the difficulty of the text and the support they need. Writing responses even after discussion is a great way to process the text.

ADAPTATION AND EXTENSION

- *Buddies:* Partner with a younger class and use the bookmarks to guide discussions during read-alouds. Have the older buddy mark a text ahead of time with places to pause and use the prompts.
- *Lunch Bunch:* Invite several students at a time to join an informal lunch bunch and have lunch in the room with you. Use the bookmarks in this lesson to guide the discussions. Just have fun with this informal setting!
- *English Language Learner Suggestion*: Using either the fiction or nonfiction *Talk Symbols and Gestures* (Figure 2.20 or 2.23), choose one prompt from the suggested symbols or gestures to use before reading, during reading, and after reading. Throughout reading a text together, encourage students to discuss the text using only the selected prompts.
- *Struggling Reader Suggestion*: Provide an informational text to a small group of students who need extra support. Using the *Nonfiction Talk Symbols and Gestures* (Figure 2.23), support students as you read the text together.

EVALUATION

"I can . . ." Statements

- I can talk about fiction books before, during, and after reading with a partner or listening to the teacher read aloud.
- I can discuss nonfiction books before, during, and after reading with a partner.
- I can discuss confusing or interesting words I want to know when reading fiction and nonfiction.
- I can give reasons and evidence for my thinking and comments.
- I can follow the guidelines for partner discussions by listening actively, taking turns, asking questions, and adding to or elaborating on the comments made by others.

Behavior Indicators

- Participates in discussion about a read-aloud with a partner by following guidelines of eye contact, active listening, and adding to and elaborating on comments made by others.
- Explains comments with text evidence and examples.
- Shares thoughts related to comprehension of a fiction text by explaining predictions, summaries, words to clarify, connections, and questions.
- Shares thoughts related to comprehension of a nonfiction text by explaining predictions, summaries, words to clarify, connections, and questions.

~ 3

Ending the School Year Literacy Strong

*A great book should leave you with many experiences, and slightly
exhausted at the end. You live several lives while reading.*
—William Styron

*I do the very best I know how, the very best I can, and I mean to
keep on doing so until the end.*
—Abraham Lincoln

After months of hard work, the end of the school year is in sight. You may feel it is time to slow down, but now is the time to keep the momentum going to remain literacy strong. The end of the school year is an ideal time to maintain the great progress your students have made in their literacy development. It is also the time to set the stage for even more reading during vacation. This chapter presents lessons that your students will find enjoyable and engaging while continuing to move forward. Here's a look at a few classrooms that are ending the year literacy strong!

Literacy-Strong Classroom Scenarios

In literacy=strong classrooms, teachers and students continue to push ahead in their reading. Words such as *authentic, engaged, purposeful, creative,* and *fun-filled* should describe what you do with your students! Here are some quick classroom stories for inspiration as the end of the school year draws near.

Celebrate Earth Day in Words!

It's April and Mrs. Canfield's 5th grade students are excited about Earth Day. They have been discussing class projects for developing a greater awareness of saving Earth.

The students also have been studying Latin and Greek roots throughout the school year, and Mrs. Canfield feels she has the best roots to explore with students for Earth Day—*geo-* and *terra-*.

Several days before Earth Day, Mrs. Canfield writes the root *geo-* on a large sheet of chart paper and explains that it is a Greek root that literally means "earth". Then she asks her students to think of words that contain the *geo-* root. Douglas calls out "geothermal," and when Mrs. Canfield asks him to explain the meaning, he is quick to say that it refers to heat that comes from the earth. Melissa mentions that her family visited Yellowstone National Park last summer and saw geysers and hot springs that were formed by what the park ranger called geothermal forces in the park. Lisa adds *geography* to this list and told the class that her dad studied geography when he was in school, and he learned about the world and the people who lived in it. Mrs. Canfield adds *geology*, *geologist*, and *geometry*, providing brief definitions.

Two days later, working with the Latin root *terr-* or *terra-* for *earth*, students added *extraterrestrial*, *subterranean*, *terrarium*, *terrain*, and *territory* to the word chart. For the next week Mrs. Canfield and her students make an effort to add these words into their oral and written language. Mrs. Canfield puts a check mark on the whiteboard every time a student used one of the *earth* words. Frequently using these new words helps students keep the importance of Earth Day in mind.

Statues and Scenes from Reading

Mrs. Johnson's 3rd graders have worked hard in their written responses and discussions about what they have read. To add a new element of interest, she decides to have her students create a tableau after reading about Wilbur, Fern, and Charlotte in *Charlotte's Web*. They are delighted when Mrs. Johnson asks them to form small groups, choose a scene from the story, and create a tableau to represent a scene. They eagerly try to come to consensus on a scene and how to perform it. "What I really loved about using a tableau was the enthusiasm students had for turning themselves into statues that represented their scenes from the story," noted Mrs. Johnson later. "Besides creating and performing the tableau, I was really surprised that the other members of the class were so eager to figure out the scenes that were being performed in each tableau. Amazing!"

Break a Leg!

Mrs. Kent can tell that her 4th graders need something to energize them for the end of the school year. Throughout the year they have been rehearsing and performing poetry, songs, and speeches for audiences of classmates and parents. Their reading fluency has improved dramatically as students learn to read texts orally in ways that convey meaning and emotion. "I save the best for last," Mrs. Kent explains.

Over the years she has written and collected readers theater scripts based on books her students have read. For this last performance, she divides the class into groups of three to five students. Each group chooses a script on Monday to perform on Friday for classmates and parents. Throughout the week, Mrs. Kent gives students time to organize and rehearse their parts. "It's amazing how well students can work together when they have a real goal in mind," she notes. On Friday, the last hour of the school day is spent performing the scripts. This routine continues through the last five weeks of the school year, with groups changing each week, making Fridays a celebration of reading and literature. "What a great way to end each week," Mrs. Kent says. "Actually, what a great way to end the school year! The kids love it; parents love it; I love it!"

Addressing End-of-the-Year Challenges

As the end of the school year approaches, anticipation for the summer break from school begins to consume students' minds. Two major challenges for literacy-strong teachers are how to maintain and extend students' growth in and excitement for reading and how to set the stage for continued reading during vacation. We present here some of our best suggestions for making the most of these important challenges.

Questions Teachers Ask to Address End-of-the-Year Challenges

- How do I motivate students to continue to read when their minds are drifting off toward vacation?
- What valuable work can my community of literacy learners engage in collaboratively?
- What skills and strategies must I emphasize so that my students finish the year as literacy-strong readers?
- How do I measure students' growth in reading?
- How do I identify the literacy needs of my students so that when they return to school, their new teachers will be able to address their needs immediately?
- How do I continue to connect with parents and families?

Must-Have Finds to Finish the School Year Fabulously

1. Continue the Inspiration: Read to Your Students

Although the end of the school year is in sight, don't stop reading to your children. Research shows that children who are read to regularly have larger vocabularies and increased comprehension and are more motivated about reading (Rasinski & Padak, 2009). Many students look forward to the end of the school year, but end-of-the-year testing, leaving their friends, and moving on to the next grade level also create anxiety. Share books that can tap into these and other year-end topics, such as these books that teachers and parents read aloud.

- *The Crossover* by Kwame Alexander
- *El Deafo* by CeCe Bell
- *The War That Saved My Life* by Kimberly Brubaker Bradley
- *Frindle* by Andrew Clements
- *Feel the Wind* by Arthur Dorros
- *The Wrigley Riddle, Ballpark Mysteries #6* by David Kelly
- *Poppleton in Spring* by Cynthia Rylant
- *Global Warming* by Seymour Simon

2. Build Background Knowledge Through Read-Alouds of Picture Books

As students move into the upper elementary grades, informational texts begin to make up an increasingly larger portion of students' reading. Informational texts can be difficult to read if students do not have sufficient background knowledge about the topic. A great way to build background knowledge quickly is to read-aloud picture books on various topics, helping students lay the groundwork for their own informational reading.

3. Harvest Words from Read-Alouds

Vocabulary growth is crucial to reading success. What better place to find interesting and unusual words that will add to students' vocabularies than in the books that you read to your students? As you read aloud, ask students to listen for any interesting words that the authors may have used. At the end of the read-aloud, have students call out the words that they chose. Display the words on a chart and discuss their meaning with your students. Read the words frequently and encourage students to use the words in their oral and written language throughout the next several days. If you harvest 10 words per day over the last three months of the school year, you will have introduced your students to approximately 600 new and interesting words to add to their vocabularies.

4. Develop a Classroom Literacy Community: Students Share Favorite Books

As summer anticipation grows, allow students to share and recommend some of their favorite books with their classmates for summer reading. Provide a time each day for one or two students to do a quick talk about one of their favorite books from the previous year. Ask student presenters to bring in a copy of the book (so others can see it), give a summary of the book, and discuss what they liked about the book. Make a list of the titles recommended and send the list home with students on the last week of school.

5. Take Fluency (and Writing) to Another Level

Fluency continues to be an important reading competency even in the upper elementary grades. Students develop fluency through repeated practice of texts with a strong sense of "voice" that allow them to be read with expression. You may have promoted fluency earlier in the year by having your students practice and perform poetry and speeches. Now have your students work collaboratively in groups to rehearse and perform readers theater scripts, as mentioned earlier in this chapter.

Although you can easily find or purchase scripts, you can challenge your students to create their own scripts based on the stories they have read throughout the year. If the story is lengthy, students can take an episode or segment from the story to convert into a script. Students can add characters, dialogue, and even events to their scripts. In developing scripts from published books, students will be engaged in close reading of the original text to extract the meaning they wish to convey. The original text will act as a mentor text that will provide excellent modeling for students' own writing. What can be better—improving reading fluency, comprehension, and writing in one activity!

6. Singing Is Reading, Too!

Singing songs and reciting poetry are forms of reading—reading that is enjoyable and relatively short, and, with practice, can be mastered and done independently by most students. Find songs about spring, put the words of the song and poems on display, model reading and singing the text for students, and have students sing a new song multiple times over the course of several days. At the end of the week, have a sing-a-long in which students sing the songs they have learned, possibly recording the performance for the classroom website.

7. Involve the Community to Create Lifelong Readers

Our goal in literacy strong instruction is for our students to develop into lifelong readers who will find value in reading throughout their lives. Students can benefit from hearing the stories of others who have lived literacy strong lives, so once a week, bring in a visitor to chat with students. Invite fellow teachers and school staff members, parents and other older family members, and members of the community to share their perspectives on literacy and how reading and writing have enriched their lives from the time they left school. Perhaps these discussions will encourage students to make a greater effort to read during the summer. You might give your visitors a list of topics to discuss in a short presentation. Here are a few suggestions:

- What was your favorite book as a child?
- What is your favorite book now?
- Did you find reading difficult as a child?
- If so, how did you improve your reading?
- Describe a situation in which reading played an important role.
- Describe your personal preferences for reading.
- Describe your own personal reading habits. When and where do you read?

8. Anticipate Summer Reading

As the school year winds down, entice students to think about their summer reading plans. Invite the librarian from your local public library to visit your classroom and tell students about the library's summer reading programs and special events. The librarian can bring registration forms so students who do not have a library card can apply.

9. Continue the Parent Connection

Clearly, the need for teachers to connect with parents is as important now as it was during the earlier part of the school year. Create a Summer Reading Recommendations flyer for parents who want to help their children maintain and expand on their growth in reading. Here are a few suggestions for the flyer:

- Play family games that involve words and reading.
- Read aloud from the child's favorite book.
- Listen to the child read aloud.
- Turn on the captioning feature of the television so students can see the words as they are being performed.
- Take time for frequent trips to the local library and bookstore to borrow or purchase books and attend special events.
- If needed, search for intervention programs available for struggling readers.

10. Quick Reading Assessment: Word Recognition

Here is an easy way to check a student's progress in reading. Working individually, provide the student with a grade-level reading passage and ask him to read the passage aloud to you in his "best" (not fastest) reading voice. As he reads, mark any uncorrected word errors; also mark where he is at in the passage after one minute of reading. Toward the end of the school year, students should be reading at or above the following levels:

- 3rd Grade: 100 words read correctly in one minute
- 4th Grade: 120 words read correctly in one minute
- 5th Grade: 140 words read correctly in one minute

This assessment provides a good measure of students' growth in their foundational reading competencies. Students with scores significantly below the levels indicated may be good candidates for additional instruction or intervention in reading. Although we are essentially measuring reading speed in this assessment, we should never focus students' attention on attempting to read quickly. Speed in reading is acquired simply through authentic and engaging reading experiences.

11. Quick Reading Assessment: Fluency

Fluency is a critical competency in the primary grades, and research indicates that many young readers struggle to achieve fluency in their reading. One way to focus children's attention on fluency is to develop a rubric to display in your classroom (see the Multidimensional Fluency Chart at www.timrasinski.com/resources.html). Your rubric should focus on these aspects of oral fluency:

- Reading at an appropriate pace
- Reading with good phrasing
- Reading with good volume and confidence
- Reading with good expression

Each of these categories can be rated on a 1 to 4 scale, with 4 indicating strong performance and ratings of 1 or 2 indicating a need for improvement. When the rubric is completed, your students can rate their own fluency while reading. They could even rate your reading when you read aloud to your students. By rating and talking about fluency in your classroom, students will develop a deeper understanding of what is meant by reading fluency and how they might become more fluent readers.

12. End-of-the-School-Year Word Ladder

Finish	Take away two letters to make an animal that lives in water.
Fish	Change one letter to make another word for a dinner plate.
Dish	Change the vowel to make a short running race.
Dash	Change one letter to make another word that means to squash or smash.
Mash	Change the first letter to make a long cut on the skin.
Gash	Take away one letter to make a fuel that most cars need.
Gas	Rearrange the letters to make a word that means to droop or hang down.
Sag	Add one letter to make a hidden or unexpected difficulty or obstacle.
Snag	Rearrange the letters to make a word that means to sing in the past.
Sang	Change one letter to make to make a composition of words that are sung.
Song	Add two letters to make the opposite of weak.
Strong	

Fill in the blanks with appropriate words from the word ladder:
Now that we are close to the end of the school year, we need to keep our literacy tank filled with _____ so that we can _____ the year literacy _____!

Overview of Chapter 3 Lessons

Lesson 1. Word Study: Decoding—Stressing over Syllables: Cinquain Poetry
Lesson 2. Vocabulary: Gaming with Words—Semantic Feature Analysis
Lesson 3. Vocabulary: Analyzing Words—Land, Water, Stars Roots
Lesson 4. Vocabulary: Associating Words—Wacky Wise Words
Lesson 5. Fluency: Phrasing, Pacing, Expressing—Readers Theatre: Making Text Come Alive
Lesson 6. Comprehension: Previewing—Text Trip Maps
Lesson 7. Comprehension: Inferring and Drawing Conclusions—Tableaux: Making Texts Come to Life
Lesson 8. Comprehension: Questioning for Close Reading—ARE You Ready to Rumble? Anticipating, Reacting, and Evaluating
Lesson 9. Comprehension: Determining Importance and Summarizing—Getting the Gist: Circling Around the Main Idea
Lesson 10. Comprehension: Motivating Readers—Ready, Set Goals, Read!

LESSON 1. WORD STUDY: DECODING

Title STRESSING OVER SYLLABLES: CINQUAIN POETRY

Trailer Not all stress is bad. Stressing over syllables can be a good thing: I ob*ject*! What *object* are you ob*ject*ing? Stressing a sound gives more importance to it and allows certain words to take on a different meaning. Decoding stressed syllables can form the underlying basis of the rhythmic pattern of words. We will use poetry to grow deeper roots for understanding which syllables are accentuated by stressing it louder, longer, and even with a higher pitch. Don't stress—you will get this!

Literacy Enhancer Word Study: Decoding—Stressing Syllables, Prefix; Writing—Cinquain Poetry

Key Academic Vocabulary
(Terms spiraled from previous lessons)

Closed Syllable: A syllable that has only one vowel followed by a consonant; the vowel is usually pronounced as a short vowel sound

Decoding: Translating a printed word into its oral representation. Readers use a variety of strategies to decode words, including phonics (sound-symbol relationships), structural analysis (prefix, base word, suffix), and context.

Diphthong: A unit of sound gliding the vowel sound by the combination of a vowel digraph allowing the tongue to move and change

Haiku: A form of Japanese poetry used mainly to describe nature and the seasons in a syllabic restricted format

Multisyllabic: A word that has more than one syllable

Open Syllable: A syllable ending in only one vowel; the vowel is usually pronounced as a long vowel sound

Segmenting: Breaking a word by phoneme (sound) or syllables

Syllable: A part of a word that contains only one vowel sound; words can be made of one or more syllables

Vowel Digraph: A pair of vowel letters coming together to form a vowel team representing one sound
(New terms in this lesson)

Cinquain: A five-line poem originally based on syllabic patterns

Meter: Stressed and unstressed syllables of poetry forming a rhythmic pattern

Prefix: An affix placed in front of a root or base word to add to its meaning

Stressed Syllables: An accented syllable that is emphasized by sounding louder, with a higher pitch than the other syllables in the word; can change the meaning of the word

Learning Objectives

- Examine word analysis skills in decoding words through multisyllabic awareness.
- Explore syllable guidelines for accenting syllables.
- Investigate elements of cinquain poetry and how syllables play the key role.

Essential Questions

- How does separating words into syllables help the reader decode (read) and encode (spell)?
- How does stressing the syllable help the reader to decode, pronounce a word, and even write certain types of poetry?
- What are the necessary guidelines to write a cinquain poem?

STEP 1: PREPARATION

Organize Materials

- Wrapped present with a stone or object that will make a rattle sound
- Multimodal text sets with samples of prefixes and cinquain poetry
- Book: *Cinquain Poems (Poetry Series)* (optional)
- *Cinquain Poetry Writing* reproducible
- Word Work Journals and Writing Notebooks

STEP 2: INITIATION

Cinquain Poetry

Prior to the lesson, put a stone in a box and wrap it. Hold and shake the "present" and ask the students what they think might be inside. Tell them you are going to share what is inside the box by only giving them clues. Give them the first clue by saying how many syllables are in the name of the present. Then, give the next clue phonologically by shaking the box while orally segmenting the syllables in the name of the gift by saying each one aloud one syllable at a time (e.g., /bi/-/cy/-/cle/, /bi/-/fo/-/cals/, /bi/-/cus/-/pid/; /tri/-/pod/, /tri/-/cy/-/cle/, /tri/-/ang/-/le/, /tri/-/cepts/). Have the students combine the syllables to guess the present. Link these words back to the Latin and Greek Numerical Roots lesson in Chapter 1, Lesson 3. Ask what these words have in common (e.g., two to three syllables, numerical prefix *bi-* and *tri-*). Compare this guessing game to haiku (studied in Chapter 2, Lesson 1). Share how both games focus on syllables and also trying to guess the surprise "gift" (subject of the poem) within the "box" (the haiku). Explain that this lesson will also focus on poetry, syllables, and prefixes.

Explain to students that classic cinquain poetry, created over 100 years ago by U.S. poet Adelaide Crapsey, has a certain rhythm but does not rhyme. Display and read aloud the following cinquain poem:

Springtime

peaceful, lively

raining, planting, blooming

Earth happily reawakens

Rebirth

Reread and clap out the rhythmic syllable pattern in each line and identify the five-line unrhymed pattern (i.e., two syllables on the first line, four on the second line, six on the third line, eight on the fourth line, and two on the last line).

STEP 3: DEMONSTRATION

Stressing over Syllable Segmenting: Cinquain Style

1. Hold up the wrapped gift box again. Write the sentence, "I want to present this present." Investigate the word *present*. Ask if the word means the same thing both times in the sentence. Explain that the way you stress the sounds can change the meaning of the word. In the word *present*, it can change from a noun to a verb by changing the syllable that is stressed.

2. Discuss how most poetry has a rhythm and measured beat established by the patterns of stressed and unstressed syllables, known as the meter. Reread the cinquain poem. Have the students listen for the rhythm and pattern again and notice where the syllable sounds are the most stressed with your voice. You can also clap your hands together each time a syllable feels longer than the others.

3. Explain that a classic cinquain poem can be measured by counting the number of stressed and unstressed syllables in each line.

   Line 1 (Noun): 2 syllables, 1 stress   **Spring**/time

   Line 2 (Adjectives): 4 syllables, 2 stresses   **peace**/ful, **live**/ly

   Line 3 (Verbs): 6 syllables, 3 stresses   **rain**/ing, **plant**/ing, **bloom**/ing

   Line 4 (Expression): 8 syllables, 4 stresses   **Earth hap**/pi/ly **re**/a/**wak**/ens

   Line 5 (Synonym): 2 syllables, 1 stress   **Re**/birth

4. Highlight the words *reawakens* and *rebirth.* Isolate the *re-* prefix in both words and discuss the meaning of *re-* (i.e., *again*) and how it changes the meaning of the root word. Explain the guideline for segmenting syllables in words with prefixes (i.e., prefix will be the first syllable and also the accented syllable).

5. Continue to model dividing syllables in words that have prefixes by analyzing the letter-sound structure and vowel placements in the words. You can use a slash mark, a raised dot, or a hyphen to demonstrate the syllable segmentation.

STEP 4: COLLABORATION

Have students study words or phrases that pertain to the season and examine the syllable segmentation to begin to create their cinquain poem. Remind them to be descriptive using 32 total syllables in five lines. They can record the process on the *Cinquain Poetry Writing* reproducible in Figure 3.1. Engage in conversational coaching by asking students to discuss the following questions with diverse partners:

- How many syllables do you hear in the word ___? How do you know?
- Does our cinquain "paint a mental" image of _____? Explain it.
- How can stressed and unstressed syllables add or change the meaning of what is being read?

STEP 5: APPLICATION

Have students keep Word Work Journals in which they record and categorize the prefixes from texts they are reading or their writing pieces (e.g., interpretation or response to literature, argumentative, or persuasive). Students also can select words to analyze by syllable mapping and record their syllable and stress analysis in their journals. Have students use selected words in sentences for creating their cinquain poems.

STEP 6: REFLECTION

Oral or Written Response

Have students respond to the essential questions through oral or written response: How many syllable segments are in the word ___? Describe how the word is segmented by syllables. How do you write a cinquain poem?

ADAPTATION AND EXTENSION

- Use online tools to verify the syllable count in words and to help pronounce a word (e.g., a dictionary, a syllable dictionary, or syllable counter).
- View YouTube or other videos to guide students as they write cinquain poetry and create a class video.

FIGURE 3.1

Cinquain Poetry Writing Reproducible

Author(s):_____ Date _____

Elements of a Cinquain Poem

_____Content = nouns, adjectives, verbs, expression, synonym

_____Mechanics = spelling, grammar, punctuation

_____Syllabic format = syllables (2-4-6-8-2 within 5 lines)

Prewriting Draft: Think about words that align to each of the categories in the elements of cinquain poetry. Make a list of word choices that relate to the subject matter of your poem.

Line 1: Nouns Title, concept, theme	Line 2: Adjectives Describe	Line 3: Verbs Action	Line 4: Expressions Emotions, feelings	Line 5: Synonym Sum it up

Draft: Consider your words and begin to follow syllabic guidelines for a cinquain. Edit as needed.

1st Line (2 syllables)_____

2nd Line (4 syllables)_____

3rd Line (6 syllables)_____

4th Line (8 syllables)_____

5th Line (2 syllables)_____

Publish your cinquain poem here:

- Display a collection of books featuring cinquain poems, such as *Cinquain Poems* by Simons and Petelinsek (2015) and *Beyond the Shore: Haiku, Tanka, and Other Poems* by Kozubek and Wax (2016).
- *English Language Learner Suggestion*: Explore online game-based programs (e.g., Vocabulary Spelling City) for word analysis skills with visual, auditory, and contextual support.
- *Struggling Reader Suggestion*: Apply spelling strategies from *Words Their Way: Word Sorts for Syllables and Affixes Spellers* by Johnston, Invernizzi, Bear, and Templeton (2018).

EVALUATION

"I can . . ." Statements

- I can decode multisyllabic words.
- I can examine a syllable and determine the prefix in each syllable.
- I can write a cinquain poem.

Behavior Indicators

- Identifies the number of syllables in a word.
- Determines the prefix in a word.
- Identifies stressed and unstressed syllables in a word.

LESSON 2. VOCABULARY: GAMING WITH WORDS

Title SEMANTIC FEATURE ANALYSIS

Trailer Have you ever played the game Scattergories? Each player fills out a grid or spreadsheet with examples of items from preselected topics or categories, beginning with a chosen letter. For example, if the topic or category is "presidents" and the chosen letter is *C*, you could write "Carter," "Coolidge," or "Cleveland" in the appropriate box on the spreadsheet. The game challenges players to think in terms of items that are all within a particular category. Semantic feature analysis (SFA) is also played with a spreadsheet. However, instead of items that fit a particular category, students are challenged to think of features that would distinguish one item from others within a topic. Players must think deeply and creatively about critical features that define the meaning of particular words or concepts.

Literacy Enhancer Vocabulary: Gaming with Games—Concepts, Topics, Decoding, Spelling

Key Academic Vocabulary
(Terms spiraled from previous lessons)

Adjective: A word or phrase used to describe a noun

Anagram: A word formed from another word by using or rearranging its letters (e.g., *angel—angle*)

Consonant: Language sounds and letters that are represented by all letters of the alphabet except *a, e, i, o, u,* and sometimes *y* and *w*; letters that represent consonant sounds frequently appear at the beginning of words and syllables

Decoding: Translating a printed word into sounds by using knowledge of the conventions of letter-sound relationships and knowledge about pronunciations of words to derive written words

Noun: A word used to identify any of a class of people, places, or things

Spelling: The process of writing or naming the letters of a word

Syllables: A part of a word that contains only one vowel sound; words can be made of one or more syllables

Verb: A word used to describe an action

Vocabulary: A collection of words or phrases and the meanings they represent that make up a language or that a person has knowledge of

Vowels: Language sounds and letters represented by the letters *a, e, i, o, u,* and sometimes *y* (e.g., *cry*) and *w* (e.g., *cow*)

Word Ladder: A game-like activity where one word is transformed into another by adding, subtracting, or changing letters

Word Sort: A process used to categorize words according to features (*closed:* categories are provided and words are matched to them; *open:* categories are determined by students as they discern the common features of the words groups)
(New terms in this lesson)

Analysis: The process of studying something to identify its essential features or characteristics

Features: Characteristics that distinguish one person or item from another

Learning Objectives

- Increase students' corpus of words or concepts that they know (vocabulary).
- Explore defining and meaningful features of words or concepts.
- Improve students' abilities to identify and analyze critical semantic features in words.
- Increase students' enjoyment of exploring and learning words.

Essential Questions

- What are important topics or categories in various subject areas of study?
- What examples can students brainstorm that belong to a particular topic or category?
- How does a semantic feature analysis help you to compare and contrast?
- How are characteristics or features for the chosen exemplars selected?
- Can students engage in analyses of the exemplars using the defining characteristics or features?
- Are students able to engage in compare-and-contrast discussions about the topic and exemplars?

STEP 1: PREPARATION

Organize Materials

- Materials for creating the game chart (dry-erase board, markers, whiteboard)
- *Semantic Feature Analysis* reproducible
- *Bears Semantic Feature Analysis* reproducible

STEP 2: INITIATION

Ask students if they are familiar with the Scattergories game and describe how the game is played (see Trailer above). Create a chart with columns to represent the chosen letters for the categories (see Figure 3.2). Have students think of presidents' names that begin with the chosen letters to complete the chart. Ask students what part of the game they enjoy and why. Explain that we are going to analyze other groups of words using semantic feature analysis (SFA). Each lesson begins with the selection of a topic that falls within the classroom curriculum. For example, you may be studying individual states in the United States of America in social studies, or different types of polygons in math, or various holidays during the year.

FIGURE 3.2
Scattergories Chart

A	C	K	T	W
John Adams	Carter	Kennedy	Truman	Washington
J. Q. Adams	Clinton		Trump	
Arthur	Cleveland		Taft	

STEP 3: DEMONSTRATION

Semantic Feature Analysis

Tell your students that one of the main jobs of a scientist is to find objects that are similar (belong to the same family) and then determine characteristics or features that distinguish one from another. This is called *analysis*. As a quick example, make and display a vertical list of five or so students in your classroom (see Figure 3.3). Now ask the students, "What do these five names have in common?" The answer is that they belong to a "family" called your classroom and share the characteristic of belonging to that classroom.

FIGURE 3.3
Vertical List of Students

Ahmad				
Amanda				
Isabella				
Mitchell				
Todd				

Thinking aloud, tell your students that you want to identify features that would distinguish one or more students from the others. Brainstorming aloud, say "left-handed" and "dark hair." Adding two columns to the chart, write these features at the top of the second and third columns (see Figure 3.4). Then conduct a feature analysis by marking in the appropriate boxes: plus for *yes* and minus for *no*.

FIGURE 3.4
Feature Analysis

	Left-Handed	Dark Hair		
Ahmad	-	+		
Amanda	+	+		
Isabella	-	+		
Mitchell	+	-		
Todd	-	-		

Now, using that chart, demonstrate to your students that you have identified some features that can be used to group or identify them. Ask your students if every student has a different feature. The answer is "no" as Amanda and Mitchell are both left-handed. At this point, ask your students if they can think of a feature that would distinguish Amanda from Mitchell. Students may call out features such as "wears glasses" or "wears a shirt with a collar." Choose one of the features and write it in at the top of the fourth column, and have your students call out the analysis as you mark the chart (see Figure 3.5).

FIGURE 3.5 **Extended Feature Analysis**			
	Left-Handed	**Dark Hair**	**Wears Glasses**	
Ahmad	-	+	+	
Amanda	+	+	+	
Isabella	-	+	-	
Mitchell	+	-	-	
Todd	-	-	-	

Using the updated chart, students can now come up with descriptions of each student.

Each student now has a unique description. Tell students that this type of analysis helps us to think deeply about which features define a group of items that are related in some way. You will be asking them to use the same process with different families of related words or concepts.

STEP 4: COLLABORATION

Have your students work with a partner to do their own analysis. Distribute a copy of the *Bears Semantic Feature Analysis* reproducible to each student (see Figure 3.6). Have student teams think of features that distinguish one or more bears from the others. Ask students to identify at least three features and write them at the top of three columns. Have students then engage in the analysis by marking plus or minus for each feature. Then they should write a definition for each type of bear using the features as the essential elements of their definitions. As students work, move from one pair of students to another providing support and encouragement.

If students have identical definitions for any two or more bears, they will need to think of another feature that will distinguish them. Have students revise their definitions and share their results. Have them engage in conversational coaching:

- Were any characteristics better for helping to create their definitions than others?

- What features did they chose to highlight with their partners?
- How did students think up their characteristics?

For additional collaboration practice, prepare a *Semantic Feature Analysis* reproducible (see Figure 3.7) with a list of examples of a common category (e.g., types of snakes, types of fish, types of cars, types of toys) filled out on the left-hand column. Snakes could include garden snakes, rattlesnakes, cobras, pythons, and corn snakes. The features could be whether they are poisonous, native to North America, or constrictors.

STEP 5: APPLICATION

As students become more familiar with the analysis process, you can have them engage in an analysis any time you have a family of items. Here are some different families you might use from different content areas:

- Books we have read
- Authors we have read
- Poems we have read
- Poets we have read
- Cities in our state
- States in the United States (you don't need to use all 50)
- Countries of the world
- Types of clouds
- Types of precipitation
- Types of storms
- Types of rocks

STEP 6: REFLECTION

Oral or Written Response

Have students respond to these essential questions through oral or written response after completing an initial semantic feature analysis:

- How does a SFA help you to compare and contrast?
- How are characteristics or features for the chosen exemplars selected?
- Did you enjoy doing a SFA? Why or why not?
- Did doing a SFA make you think more deeply about the words and concepts you were analyzing? Please describe.

FIGURE 3.6

Bears Semantic Feature Analysis Reproducible

Directions: Identify a topic. Brainstorm and list examples of the topic in the first column.
In the numbered row across the top, list features that may distinguish the examples. Analyze each example and fill in the appropriate box with a plus or minus.

Topic: Bears

Features: Examples:	1 Brown fur	2 Lives in cold climates	3 Is a good swimmer	4 Favorite food includes salmon	5	6
Grizzly Bears						
Brown Bears						
Polar Bears						
Giant Pandas						

FIGURE 3.7

Semantic Feature Analysis Reproducible

Directions: Identify a topic. Brainstorm and list examples of the topic in the first column.

In the numbered row across the top, list features that may be used to distinguish the exemplars. Analyze each example and fill in the appropriate box with a plus or minus to denote the absence or presence of each feature or write a description.

Topic:_____

Features: \ Examples:	1	2	3	4	5	6

- Did you find it difficult or easy to determine good features for analyzing the words and concepts in the SFA chart? Please describe.
  - If you were asked to create your own SFA, what topic would you choose and what would be some of the exemplars you would add to the SFA chart?

ADAPTATION AND EXTENSION

- *Likert Scale.* Semantic feature analysis does not always lend itself to a "yes or no" or a "plus or minus" type of response. In many cases the features may be more nuanced, such as in describing a bear as dangerous, a president as conservative, or a state's products as agricultural. To help students respond in more nuanced ways to a SFA, you can set up a Likert scale in which students can respond to different gradations of a particular feature. Allowing for more nuanced responses will allow students to get into deeper discussions with you and classmates as they work to apply the most accurate rating to a particular word or concept. For example, here is a common scale that could be employed in a SFA:

  1. Yes, definitely
  2. Yes, somewhat
  3. Neither yes nor no
  4. No, somewhat
  5. No, definitely

- *English Language Learner Suggestion*: Use think-alouds to help students understand the process of choosing certain features to include in the analysis. For example, suggest, "Some presidents lead our country in a time of war; others do not. I think considering if they were war presidents would be a good feature on which to analyze presidents." Start with a small number of features to be analyzed, and gradually expand as students become more familiar with the analysis.
- *Struggling Reader Suggestion*: Begin with topics or categories with which students are familiar (e.g., musical instruments, school subjects, favorite foods).

EVALUATION

"I can . . ." Statements

- I can brainstorm items that belong to a particular topic for a SFA.
- I can think of features for analyzing the items belonging to a topic in a SFA.
- I can engage in a semantic feature analysis.
- I can create definitions of words from the features used in a SFA.

- I can gain a deeper understanding of the exemplars (words and concepts) in a SFA through my analysis.

Behavior Indicators

- Identifies features that can be used to analyze the words or concepts in a SFA.
- Lists exemplars (words or concepts) related to a topic used in a SFA.
- Engages in an analysis of exemplars in a SFA.
- Creates definitions of exemplars using the features from the SFA.
- Defines other features that could be used for further analysis when two or more exemplars have not been differentiated from an initial SFA.

LESSON 3. VOCABULARY: ANALYZING WORDS

Title **LAND, WATER, STARS ROOTS** *terr-/terra-; geo-; aqua-; hydra-/hydro-; astro-/aster-*

Trailer It's springtime! Farmers and gardeners are planting in their fields. Because Earth Day is celebrated in April, the end of the school year is a great time to think about word roots that deal with the essential parts of our environment—earth, land, water, and stars. When students complete these lessons, they will be more able to connect words containing these roots to their essential concept of earth, land, water or stars. Although students may be familiar with some of the roots (e.g., *aqua-*), our intent with these lessons is not simply to teach words containing specific roots, but to develop a keen eye for detecting roots within words and to independently see how the roots affect the meaning of the words. In essence, we want our students to become word detectives and connoisseurs who use their vocabulary to shoot for the stars!

Literacy Enhancer Vocabulary: Analyzing—Decoding, Spelling

Key Academic Vocabulary
(Terms spiraled from previous lessons)

Latin: An ancient language whose words and word parts have influenced words in English

Greek: An ancient language whose words and word parts have influenced words in English

Word Roots: Base words, prefixes, and suffixes in English words that are derived primarily from Latin and Greek
(New terms in this lesson)

Aqua-: A word root meaning water

Aster-: A word root meaning star

Astro-: A word root meaning star

Geo-: A word root meaning earth or land

Hydra-: A word root meaning water

Hydro-: A word root meaning water

Terr-/Terra-: A word root meaning earth or land

Learning Objectives

- Expand competency in parsing words into base and affixes.
- Learn critical English word roots and affixes derived from Latin and Greek.
- Expand vocabulary by learning English words derived from Latin and Greek.

Essential Questions

- What are the meanings of English words containing the *terr-/terra* word roots?
- What are the meanings of English words containing the *geo-/* word root?
- What are the meanings of English words containing the *aqua-/* word root?
- What are the meanings of English words containing the *hydra-/hydro-* word roots?
- What are the meanings of English words containing the *aster- /astro-* word roots?
- How does knowledge of Latin and Greek roots help students understand words in which they are located?

STEP 1: PREPARATION

Organize Materials

- List of *terr-/terra-* word roots
- Texts that correspond with root words being studied
- Word Journals

STEP 2: INITIATION

Explain to your students the concept of word roots and affixes—word patterns that have a particular meaning. Provide examples of word roots from words in Chapter 2, Lesson 3 on functional roots (e.g., *companion, collection, conspire, proclaim, exhale*). Ask students to break the words into roots and determine the meaning of the compound words by combining the meanings of the individual words. Draw the students' attention to five of the *terra-* words you put on display and have them define the words as best they can. Ask them what is common in all the words (i.e., they contain the word pattern *terr-*). Now, ask the students to determine what is common in the meaning of all the words. The answer, of course, is the concept of earth or land.

STEP 3: DEMONSTRATION

Work through each of the words on the list and define them so that the concept of *earth* or *land* is highlighted. Demonstrate to students that each word can be defined in this manner:

- Territory: A marked-off area of land under the rule of a government

- Terrain: The lay of the land
- Terrier: A breed of dog that is predisposed to dig in the earth
- *Lumbricus terrestris*: An earthworm
- Mediterranean: Sea in the middle of the known earth, surrounded by Europe and Africa
- Terre Haute: A city in Indiana located on high land above the Wabash River
- Terracotta: Baked earth or clay used for pottery
- Inter (interment): To bury in the earth

STEP 4: COLLABORATION

Have students work in pairs and small groups. Ask them to see if they can determine the meaning of the following words using a similar process of employing the concept of earth or land: *terrace, terrarium, subterranean, terrestrial,* and *extraterrestrial*. Have students think and discuss with their partner or in their groups, and then share their thinking with the class. Provide supportive and formative feedback as needed. Create a word wall that contains all the *terra-* words you have studied with your students up to this point. Read the words in unison and encourage your students to use the words in their oral and written language whenever possible.

STEP 5: APPLICATION

Create a short text like the one below or a series of sentences that contain some of the *terra* words from the word wall. Have students read these texts and do the exercises.

> My family loves to relax on the terrace in our backyard on a warm sunny day. It has several comfy chairs and terracotta pots filled with flowers to add color to our special spot. Unfortunately, we also have a terrier named Ginger. Not only is she a jumpy dog, she is also a digger. If I don't watch her closely she will dig several holes in the ground around the terrace in less than an hour. She must be looking for some subterranean critter, but she has not found any yet. We think that our terrace belongs to the whole family; Ginger, however, thinks it is her own personal territory!

> *Exercise:* Use a *terr- (terra-)* word from the word wall to make a name for this story.

> *Exercise:* Draw a sketch or diagram of what you think the writer's terrace might look like. Provide as much detail from the story as possible in your drawing.

Have students write a short text that contains at least three words from the word wall along with one question for their text. While sharing their texts in small groups, have classmates respond to the questions for each text and discuss possible answers to the essential question: "How does knowledge of Latin and Greek roots help you understand words in which they are located?"

STEP 6: REFLECTION

Oral or Written Response

Have students invent a word that contains the *terr- (terra-)* word root (e.g., *proterra; aquaterrarium*) and a definition for it (e.g., a characteristic of someone who is for or a proponent of the earth; an enclosed space that contains both earth and water). Have students reflect on why scientists may want to use word roots when inventing new ideas. For example, when Alexander Graham Bell invented an instrument for carrying sounds over long distances, he used the Greek roots for sound (*phone*) and distant or far (*tele-*) to come up with telephone. Have students write and complete the following sentence in their word journals: "I think it is important to know the *terr-(terra-)* word root because _____."

ADAPTATION AND EXTENSION

- Not all words that appear to contain a particular root have meanings related to the root. Discuss words that have the *terr- (terra-)* patterns but do not refer to earth or land (e.g., *terrible, terror, terrific*).
- Students can invent new words that contain the *terr- (terra-)* root, draw pictures of the words, and challenge one another to define them.
- Encourage students to play word games such as *Making Words* or *Making and Writing Words* (see Chapter 2, Lesson 2) using the word *territory* or *Mediterranean* as the final or target word. Other *terr- (terra-)* words can be used in making the transfer words.
- Teach word root lessons using this same format for the other word roots in this chapter—*geo-, aqua-, hydra- (hydro-), aster- (astro-)*:
  - *Geo-* (earth): geology, geode, geothermal, geometry, geodesic dome, geography, geographer, geographic, geocentric, geohydrology, geohydrologist
  - *Aqua-* (water): aquarium, aquamarine, aquanaut, aquacade, aquifer
  - *Hydra-, Hydro-* (water): hydrant, hydrophobia, hydrocephalus, hydrangea, hydrate, hydraulics, hydrogen, hydrologist, hydroelectric, hydrotherapy, dehydrate, geohydrology
  - *Astro-, Aster-* (star): astronomy, astronomer, astrology, astrologer, astronaut, astrolab, astrophysics, aster, asterisk, asteroid, disaster

- *English Language Learner Suggestion*: Put the key words on a classroom display chart. Encourage students to use the words in their oral and written language over several days. Draw attention to your students when they (or you) use the words.
- *Struggling Reader Suggestion*: Give students a set of *terr- (terra-)* words from the word wall and have them draw illustrations of the word that emphasize the concept of earth or land.

EVALUATION

"I can . . ." Statements

- I can understand what words mean that contain the word root we have studied.
- I can break longer words down into their root parts.
- I can better understand texts that contain words that have the word root we have studied.

Behavior Indicators

- Adds words and concepts that contain *terr- (terra-)* to a growing vocabulary list.
- Finds words in texts that contain the *terr- (terra-)* word root.
- Defines and understand words that contain the *terr- (terra-)* word root.
- Understands texts that contain the *terr- (terra-)* word root.

LESSON 4. VOCABULARY: ASSOCIATING WORDS

Title **WACKY WISE WORDS**

Trailer Are any of these statements familiar to you? *It's a piece of cake. Better late than never. The early bird gets the worm.* What do they have in common? They are all figures of speech that are used in everyday conversations. Authors also sprinkle them in their writing to add interest and deeper meanings to their craft. When students encounter these gems of wisdom and wit, they need to know how to deal with them. Rather than glossing over figures of speech, teach students to appreciate and savor the richness that idioms, adages, and proverbs have to offer.

Literacy Enhancer Vocabulary: Associating—Figures of Speech, Idioms, Adages, Proverbs

Key Academic Vocabulary
(Terms spiraled from previous lessons)

Adjective: A word that describes a noun (a person, place, or thing)

Metaphor: Comparison of two unlike entities; does not use the words *like* or *as*; often implies meaning and uses a form of the verb *to be*

Shades of Meaning: Words that are synonyms with varying degrees of different meanings

Simile: Comparison of two unlike entities using the words *like* or *as* to connect the ideas

Synonym: A word that has a similar meaning to another word

Verb: An action word
(New terms in this lesson)

Adages: Well-known phrases or short sayings that over time are generally accepted as universal truths

Idioms: Phrases with odd language that people don't normally put together; not taken for their literal meaning; challenging to figure out and must be learned to be able to use them correctly.

Proverbs: Popular sayings or complete sentences that pass on wisdom and are easy to understand, sometimes with a word picture.

Learning Objectives

- Identify and explain the definitions of idioms, adages, and proverbs.
- Share examples of idioms, adages, and proverbs.
- Identify the differences between idioms, adages, and proverbs.

Essential Questions

- How do idioms, adages, and proverbs make texts interesting? Why do authors use each of them?
- How can understanding these figures of speech help readers when they read and write?
- Which is your favorite type of speech: idioms, adages, or proverbs? Which do you have the most trouble understanding? Tell why.

STEP 1: PREPARATION

Organize Materials

- *Wacky Wise Words Chart* reproducible
- *Idiom Illustrator* reproducible
- *Proverb Concentration* reproducible
- Books that feature idioms, adages, and proverbs

STEP 2: INITIATION

Wise Advice

Ask students if they have an older relative or friend who often offers words of wisdom for them to follow. Model for students by providing an example from your own life such as, "My grandfather always told us that 'A penny saved is a penny earned.' I think of that saying often when I am trying to decide if I should buy something I don't really need." Invite students to talk with partners about sayings their friends or relatives have shared with them. English language learners may want to share a saying they know in their primary language. Challenge students to think of wise characters from movies and books such as Yoda from *Star Wars* and Owl from *Winnie the Pooh* as well as the sayings that they share. Tell students that they are going to learn how authors use interesting idioms, adages, and proverbs to add more power to their stories.

STEP 3: DEMONSTRATION

Read Aloud and Chart

1. Sketch a chart on the board or use the *Wacky Wise Words Chart* reproducible in Figure 3.8 to discuss figures of speech. Fill it in as you read aloud from a few different texts to demonstrate figures of speech. Ask students what they know about idioms, adages, and proverbs. Share quick definitions of each and ask how many students have heard each of the examples. Lead a discussion about each example. If you make a copy of the chart for students, conduct a close reading of the chart and have them use different colors of highlighters or pencils to mark each figure of speech. Add new ones to the chart together.

2. Discuss idioms and examples. An idiom is a saying that has funny or odd language in it. We don't really mean what we say! When we say, "You are pulling my leg," what do we mean? Tell students that the interpretation is not literal and it is often hard to figure out idioms just from the context when reading. They are unique to each language and culture so you have to learn them. Discuss each example below and add it to the chart:

   - *It was a piece of cake.* That was easy.
   - *That cost an arm and a leg.* It cost more than she thought originally.
   - *He needed to hit the books.* He had a lot of homework.

3. Discuss adages and examples. Adages are well-known phrases or short sayings that are generally accepted as universal truths. Adages have been around a long time and are not as common as proverbs and idioms. Adages are brief and to the point. Share the examples from the *Wacky Wise Words* reproducible and discuss these examples:

   - *Good things come in small packages.*
   - *Slow and steady wins the race.*

4. Discuss proverbs and examples. It is easy to mix up adages and proverbs! Actually, a proverb is an adage too! What matters most is that your students know that both proverbs and adages are pithy words of wisdom handed down through oral tradition. An adage is a believed truth that is quick and to the point. Proverbs send a message about life and often paint a word picture. Benjamin Franklin is known for his many wise proverbs, such as, "Haste makes waste." Share the examples below and from the chart:

   - *The grass is always greener on the other side of the fence.*
   - *Don't judge a book by its cover.*
   - *Strike while the iron is hot.*

FIGURE 3.8

Wacky Wise Words Chart Reproducible

Idioms	Adages	Proverbs
He is pulling my leg.	*Better late than never.*	*A penny saved is a penny earned.*
Definition: Phrases with odd language that people don't normally put together. An idiom doesn't mean what the words say. Idioms are usually phrases, not whole sentences. Every language has its own idioms to learn.	**Definition:** Well-known phrases or short sayings that are accepted as truth. Adages have been around a long time and are not as common as proverbs and idioms. Adages are brief and to the point.	**Definition:** Short statements of popular beliefs about life. You can figure these out even if they are new to you. Proverbs are complete sentences and often paint a word picture or story to visualize based on everyday life.
Examples: *I passed the test by the skin of my teeth.* (I barely finished in time.) *Sam was pulling my leg.* (Someone was not telling the truth.)	**Examples:** *Better late than never.* (Sometimes being late is better than not doing something at all.) *No risk, no gain.* (You have to gamble the possibility of loss in order to get ahead.)	**Examples:** *Don't cry over spilled milk.* (Don't worry about a problem that has already happened.) *The early bird gets the worm.* (If you do the work early, or first, you will have more opportunities.)
Our Examples: 1. 2. 3.	**Our Examples:** 1. 2. 3.	**Our Examples:** 1. 2. 3.

STEP 4: COLLABORATION

Pass out the *Idiom Illustrator* reproducible to students and work the first example together (see Figure 3.9). First discuss the idiom "when pigs fly" and sketch a pig flying in the first column of the card. Invite three students to act out the comic situation for "when pigs fly" outlined in the directions. Sketch thought and speech bubbles in the comic box. Assign idioms to each table or pair of students to complete and share with the group. Circulate and coach students on figuring out the meaning of the idioms. Explain that context clues don't always help and sometimes research may be necessary to grasp the full meaning of an idiom.

Help students with the first example on the *Proverb Concentration* reproducible and sketch a drawing together for the literal meaning of "eggs in one basket" (see Figure 3.10). Invite a few students to act out the scenario about friendship outlined on the reproducible. Students sketch on their cards. Assign cards to pairs or teams. Students report back and all students fill in their cards. Circulate and assist students as needed. When finished, students cut apart their cards and play with a partner. They turn all cards face down and take turns flipping over two cards to see if they match. If not, they put the cards back facedown. If they do match, they put them in their match pile. At the end, students see who has the most matches. As another option, one student plays alone and races the clock to match proverbs and pictures.

STEP 5: APPLICATION

At a station or their desks, students continue to use their *Idiom Illustrator* and *Proverb Concentration* reproducibles as a method for collecting more idioms and proverbs. They cut apart completed proverb cards and continue matching proverbs and their meanings. Also, students may use the *Proverb Concentration Cards* reproducible (Figure 3.11) to create their own cards and games. Provide books that feature idioms, adages, and proverbs for students to read for enjoyment. They may chart or illustrate as they take notes on the books, or they can prepare to read the book aloud to a younger buddy and explain the figurative language.

STEP 6: REFLECTION

Oral or Written Response

Lead students in a discussion about the differences between idioms, adages, and proverbs. What are some of their favorites? Why do authors use these figurative language devices in their writing? How can students use them in theirs? Students can record favorite examples of idioms, adages, and proverbs and give reasons why they enjoy them in their literacy notebooks.

FIGURE 3.9

Idiom Illustrator Reproducible

Directions: Illustrate the idioms two ways. First, sketch what the words say. For example, for the idiom "when pigs fly," sketch flying pigs. Then sketch the meaning. That sketch could be a comic, showing a child asking for a pony and the parents responding, "Sure, when pigs fly!" Use speech and thought bubbles and illustrate more examples in your literacy notebook.

Idiom: When Pigs Fly

Literal Drawing	Comic

Idiom: Piece of Cake

Literal Drawing	Comic

FIGURE 3.9 (*continued*)

Idiom: Break a Leg

Literal Drawing	Comic

Idiom: Scratch Someone's Back

Literal Drawing	Comic

Idiom: Bite Off More Than You Can Chew

Literal Drawing	Comic

FIGURE 3.10

Proverb Concentration Reproducible

Directions: Illustrate each proverb. For example, for the proverb "absence makes the heart grow fonder," you can draw a few hearts getting bigger and place them in a thinking bubble next to a stick figure. Then to show what it really means, draw a cartoon or sketch of someone calling a family member to say that he or she is missed. Cut apart the proverb cards in the first column and the illustrations in the second column. Mix up the cards and put all the cards facedown. Take turns with a partner, turning over two cards at a time. If the drawing matches the proverb, take the match and one more turn. Continue until all the cards are gone. Count your matches. Turn them over and share them.

Literal Proverb Drawing *Absence makes the heart grow fonder.*	**Drawing to Show What It Means**
Literal Proverb Drawing *The early bird gets the worm.*	**Drawing to Show What It Means**
Literal Proverb Drawing *Birds of a feather flock together.*	**Drawing to Show What It Means**
Literal Proverb Drawing *Don't count your chickens before they hatch.*	**Drawing to Show What It Means**

FIGURE 3.11

Blank Proverb Cards for Proverb Concentration

Proverb	Drawing

Proverb	Drawing

Proverb	Drawing

Proverb	Drawing

ADAPTATION AND EXTENSION

- Read aloud books that demonstrate examples of idioms and proverbs. Here are a few age-appropriate books to share with your class:
    - *Amelia Bedelia* (series) by Peggy Parish
    - *In a Pickle and Other Funny Idioms* by Marvin Terban
    - *More Parts* by Tedd Arnold
    - *The Cat's Pajamas* by Wallace Edwards
    - *Scholastic Dictionary of Idioms* by Marvin Terban
    - *My Teacher Likes to Say* by Denise Brennan Nelson
    - *There's a Frog in My Throat* by Loreen Leedy

- Ask students to interview family members for any sayings or proverbs that they remember their parents or grandparents sharing with them. Where are they from?
- Search for online resources that provide lessons on idioms and proverbs from around the world (e.g., ReadWriteThink: rwtverio.ncte.org/lessons/lesson _viewdb5d.html?id=185). Fill in the blank proverb cards in Figure 3.11.
- Make a class book or digital presentation of proverbs. Share on the class or school website or in a digital presentation. Take turns reading the proverbs to the school during announcements over the intercom. Or provide sets of proverbs for the principal to read to the school during announcements.
- *English Language Learner Suggestion:* Encourage students to share their own cultural background and learn about proverbs from around the world. Use Figure 3.11.
- *Struggling Reader Suggestion*: Play Proverb Concentration (Figure 3.10) in a small group. When students make a match, they may dramatize their proverb.

EVALUATION

"I can . . ." Statements

- I can define and identify idioms and explain their meanings.
- I can define and identify adages and explain their meanings.
- I can define and identify proverbs and explain their meanings.
- I can match idioms and proverbs and their meanings.
- I can memorize examples of common idioms, adages, and proverbs.
- I can discuss the differences between idioms, adages, and proverbs.
- I can explain why authors use idioms, adages, and proverbs in their writing.
- I can use idioms and proverbs in my writing.

Behavior Indicators

- Defines idioms and provides examples.
- Defines adages with examples.
- Defines proverbs with examples.
- Matches proverbs with their meanings.
- Matches idioms with their meanings.
- Knows and can recite some proverbs, idioms, and adages.
- Discusses the differences between proverbs, idioms, and adages.
- Explains why authors use these figurative language devices.
- Applies these devices in writing.

LESSON 5. FLUENCY: PHRASING, PACING, EXPRESSING

Title READERS THEATER: MAKE TEXTS COME ALIVE

Trailer Some stories provide such great enjoyment for readers that they frequently want to revisit and reread their favorites. Yet reading the same story from the same book may also detract from the novelty of reading a text for the first time. Have you ever read a story and later saw a movie or play that was based on the story? Did seeing a story come to life give you a fresh perspective? That experience can be recreated in classrooms through the magic of readers theater—a story presented in the form of a script. Students rehearse their assigned parts with special emphasis on reading with appropriate expression. Performing the script is easy: it involves no memorization of lines because performers are reading; there is no acting; there are no props, costumes, or scenery unless desired by the teacher or students. Student performers focus on one thing—reading—using the expression in their voices to convey meaning to the audience.

Literacy Enhancer Reading Fluency: Word Recognition Automaticity, Expressive Reading

Key Academic Vocabulary

(Terms spiraled from previous lessons)

Oratory: The art or practice of formal speaking in public

Performance: The act of presenting a play, concert, or other form of entertainment

Poetry: A genre of writing that emphasizes the expression of feelings and ideas by the use of distinctive style, rhyme, and rhythm

Rehearsal: The repeated practice reading of a text in preparation of performing the text for an audience

Rhyme: Words that have the same or similar ending sounds

Rhythm: A regular, repeated pattern of movement, sound, or language

Song: A short poem set to music

Speech: A formal address or discourse delivered to an audience

(New term in this lesson)

Script: The written text of a play, movie, or broadcast

Learning Objectives

- Increase the ability to recognize words automatically (word recognition automaticity) through repeated readings of a script.

- Improve the ability to read with appropriate expression and phrasing (prosody) while rehearsing to convey the meaning of a script through oral reading.
- Develop a greater appreciation for the role of scripts to convey meaning.

Essential Questions

- How does fluent and expressive reading add to the quality and meaning of a script?
- What do I need to do in order to make my reading of a script meaningful to an audience?
- What story, or part of a story, might I like to read as a readers theater script?

STEP 1: PREPARATION

Organize Materials

- *Readers Theater—Paul Bunyan Script*

STEP 2: INITIATION

Paul Bunyan: An American Folktale

As students near the end of the school year, they may lose interest in school and reading. One way to keep the excitement level high is to have students rehearse and perform readers theater scripts. You can find free scripts online, as well as published commercial materials. Teachers and students can also make their own scripts based on stories and other texts they may have read. To get started on readers theater, choose a story that your class knows. Using the fictional character Paul Bunyan, the giant lumberjack known for his superhuman strength, provide students with background on the folktales told about him and his loyal companion, Babe the Blue Ox. Share one of the folktales with your students, noting how his logging fame has made him the subject of many literary works, and make a list of characteristics that distinguish him from a normal person.

STEP 3: DEMONSTRATION

1. Display a copy of the *Readers Theater—Paul Bunyan Script* (p. 215) on a document camera or other display device. Model reading the script to students and ask them to follow along silently.
2. Discuss the content of the script. What did students find interesting or unusual about the story?
3. Have students look for new characteristics for Paul Bunyan that they found in the script and add them to their original list.

4. Discuss *how* you read the script. Ask students what they noticed about your reading (e.g., good volume, accurate word recognition, emphasis on words, change in tone from one narrator or character to another).

STEP 4: COLLABORATION

Divide the students into groups of three to five. Assign individual students one or more parts from the script or permit students to negotiate with one another to choose parts on their own. Provide students with 10 to 15 minutes per day for two days to rehearse the script in their group. Rehearsal should be aimed at students performing the script with accuracy, ease, and expression. Encourage students to discuss the content of the script and their individual parts with one another, and to provide positive feedback to one another. As students rehearse, circulate and provide formative feedback and modeling for them. Remind them that the purpose of their rehearsal is to perform the script for an audience in the future. As students master their assigned parts, they can alternate roles to play as many parts as possible within a script.

STEP 5: APPLICATION

Set a time and date for a performance by your students to an audience of other students, parents, and school staff. Review these successful steps of a performance from Chapter 2, Lesson 5:

1. Determine who will be invited and how invitations will be communicated.
2. Determine a location and consider the logistics including sufficient seating and size of the stage area.
3. Choreograph the performance. Will each group perform the same script?
4. Do a dress rehearsal with your students. Provide formative feedback during and after the final rehearsal.
5. On the day of the actual performance, do the following:
   a. Introduce the audience to the performance.
   b. Have one or more students provide background on Paul Bunyan as well as on any other script that may be performed. This background should also be rehearsed in advance of the performance.
   c. Remind audience members of appropriate behavior during the performance and suggest ways they can show their appreciation.
   d. Following the performance, allow audience members to share positive feedback with the performers and arrange a reception for performers and audience members.

e. Arrange for the performance area to be cleaned and returned to its original state.

STEP 6: REFLECTION

Oral or Written Response

Following the performance, ask audience members to write their own critique focusing primarily on the positive aspects. What did audience members find most notable in the readers theater performance? Share selected critiques with your students. Have students write their own responses to the readers theater experience. What did they like best? How has practicing and performing the script improved their reading? What will they do differently for future readers theater performances?

ADAPTATION AND EXTENSION

- Extend the readers theater performance by making it a regular part of your English language arts curriculum during the final months of the school year. Once a month, set the final day of the school week for a readers theater performance. Have students rehearse and perform new scripts in a manner similar to the protocol described above. You can find scripts that may be performed as readers theater (e.g., "Dr. Chase Young," "Teaching Heart," "Aaron Shepard") from many websites. After having read, rehearsed, and performed several scripts, you may challenge your students to write and perform their own scripts based on books or segments of books they have read. Stories that have plenty of dialogue easily transform into scripts.

- As students transform stories into scripts, encourage them to add new characters, new dialogue, or even new episodes. In doing so, students are actually engaging in deep comprehension by creating inferences (or educated guesses) about the content of the original text.

- *English Language Learner Suggestion*: Encourage students to write short scripts that reflect their own native culture, customs, stories, or experiences. This will allow all students to celebrate the various cultures, customs, and experiences that are present in the classroom.

- *Struggling Reader Suggestion*: Have students break a familiar poem into parts that can be performed as a script. The brevity of poetry as well as the rhythm and rhyme embedded in most poems for children make them relatively easy for students to learn to read.

EVALUATION

"I can . . ." Statements

- I can read a script with ease.
- I can read a script or a particular part within a script with expression that reflects and amplifies the meaning of the speech.
- I can read and perform my part of a script with good volume and confidence.
- I can read and perform my part of a script aloud with good posture.
- I can understand the meaning of the words in the script I read.
- I can understand the content of the script that I and my classmates read.
- I can rehearse my part of a script to the point where I can read it fluently.
- I can work cooperatively with my classmates to produce a fluent and meaning performance of a script.
- I can listen attentively to a readers theater script being performed by my classmates and offer positive feedback to the group.

Behavior Indicators

- Rehearses and performs scripts.
- Works cooperatively and positively in a readers theater group and provides good feedback to others.
- Contributes as an attentive and positive audience member.
- Finds or makes scripts to rehearse and perform for others.

Readers Theater—Paul Bunyan Script

Narrator 1:	Now I hear tell that Paul Bunyan was a mighty big lumberman.
Narrator 2:	And strong too!
Narrator 3:	He could knock down a tree with a flick of his finger.
Narrator 1:	And with his breath he could shed a tree of all its leaves.
Narrator 3:	But Paul Bunyan was lonely. He lived by himself.
Paul Bunyan:	I would like to have a partner—a friend.
Narrator 4:	One bitterly cold and snowy Minnesota morning, Paul went for his morning stroll in the woods.
Paul Bunyan:	I just love the cold weather—25 degrees below zero suits me just fine.
Narrator 3:	As he was stomping through the woods, Paul heard a soft snorting and kicking.
Paul Bunyan:	What's that?
Narrator 1:	He looked down, and what did he see?
Paul Bunyan:	Oh my, it's a tiny blue ox. He must be cold down there in the snow.
Narrator 2:	Paul picked up the tiny creature and put him in his coat pocket to keep him warm and continued on his walk. He named him Babe because he was so small.
Narrator 3:	Back at his cabin in the logging camp, Paul pulled the blue ox from his pocket and set him in front of his warm fireplace and went outside to cut down some more trees.
Narrator 1:	The baby ox fell asleep immediately.
Narrator 2:	But nothing in Paul Bunyan's camp stays small for long.
Narrator 4:	As he slept, the tiny blue ox grew,
Narrator 1:	and grew
N. 1 & 2:	and grew
N. 1, 2, & 3:	and grew
N. 1, 2, 3, & 4:	AND GREW!
Narrator 3:	By the time Paul returned to his cabin, the little blue ox had grown to ten times the normal size of an ox.
Paul Bunyan:	What in the world has happened to Babe? He's huge—as big as me!
Narrator 1:	Well Paul decided to keep Babe as a helper.
Narrator 2:	Babe helped Paul by hauling loads of logs that Paul would cut down in the forest.
Narrator 3:	Like Paul, Babe never got tired. He could work all day and all night too.
Narrator 4:	But most of all, Paul and Babe the Blue Ox became the best of friends.
Narrator 1:	And just like Paul and Babe, their friendship was bigger and taller than the biggest and tallest tree in all of Minnesota!

LESSON 6. COMPREHENSION: PREVIEWING

Title TEXT TRIP MAPS

Trailer In today's fast-paced digital society, maps to anywhere in the world are just a click away on our electronic devices. Many students are familiar with such "maps and apps." Just like the maps we use to find physical places, text maps or graphic organizers also prove useful when navigating through challenging texts. Research has long supported the use of graphic organizers to help students keep track of their reading comprehension (Blachowicz & Ogle, 2001). When we teach students to use text maps even before reading a text, they remain on the road to comprehension. Students learning to determine *which* map they need for fiction or nonfiction makes all the difference for a successful journey.

Literacy Enhancer Comprehension: Previewing—Text Structures

Key Academic Vocabulary:

(Terms spiraled from previous lessons)

Author: Person who wrote the text

Author's Point of View: In nonfiction, the opinion or feelings the author has toward the topic; in fiction, who is telling the story

Author's Purpose: The reason the author wrote the text, usually to inform, entertain, or persuade the reader

Caption: A text feature used to give a brief explanation to an article, illustration, or photo

Chart: A form of a table, graph, or diagram used to capture information

Graph: A diagram showing the relation between variable quantities

Heading: A text feature that divides the text into sections and tells the main idea of each section; helps the reader locate information in the text; highlighted in bold or larger text to stand out

Illustrator: The person who draws or paints the artwork to accompany the text

Index: An alphabetical list of content with references to the places where they occur

Map: A graphic representation of the content of the text using symbols or shapes

Photograph: A picture made in which the image is captured using a camera

Predict: To make an educated logical guess, or inference, about what will happen next in the text using clues from the text and one's own background knowledge

Prediction: An educated guess about what may happen in a story or other text about to be read

Preview: To look over the text before reading to predict what it will be about and to see what text features the author has included

Table of Contents: A listing of the topics and chapter titles for the text along with page numbers so the reader can find information and see how the text is organized

Text Features: The tools an author uses to help the reader navigate the text for locating and accessing meaning from the text; may consist of a table of contents, headings, photographs, bold words, maps, graphs, charts, index, and glossary

Text Structure: The organizational structure of the information in the text; fiction might contain a problem and solution and beginning, middle, and end; nonfiction may be organized around a main idea and details, a cause and effect, a problem and solution, a sequence of ideas, or a compare and contrast of ideas

Learning Objectives

- Recognize that fiction texts have a text structure that involves a setting, characters, a problem (but not always), events, resolution, point of view, and theme.
- Recognize that nonfiction texts have different text structures that vary from the main idea and detail, cause and effect, sequence, compare and contrast, and problem and solution.
- Identify which text map fits a particular nonfiction text.
- Identify which text map fits a particular fiction text.
- Use text maps to preview texts and predict what the text will be about.

Essential Questions

- How are fiction texts organized?
- How can specific fiction text maps, or organizers, help guide reading?
- What are the different ways nonfiction texts are organized?
- How can specific nonfiction maps, or organizers, help guide reading?

STEP 1: PREPARATION

Organize Materials

- Paper maps
- Picture books for fiction
- Picture books for nonfiction
- Content-area reading materials

- *Text Trip Maps: Fiction and Nonfiction* reproducible
- Bingo game cards

STEP 2: INITIATION

Map Metaphor

Ask students what they know about navigation systems on electronic devices. Discuss and show physical paper maps and navigation apps on your cell phone or device. Invite students to discuss the purposes and uses of different kinds of maps and to demonstrate the use of a variety of maps (e.g., topographical, weather). Discuss how maps help travelers plan even before setting out on a journey. Invite students to brainstorm how organizers or maps for texts may help readers before, during, and after reading. Why might a text map be important for comprehension?

STEP 3: DEMONSTRATION

For Fiction

1. Tell students that fiction books may be organized in different ways but often contain the same main elements. Show a fiction text (e.g., picture book, basal story, short story, novel) and conduct a think-aloud to demonstrate how you are figuring out text structure. Project the *Text Trip Map* reproducible in Figure 3.12 and explain the main parts of the map: beginning, middle, and end. Tell students that if you drove a car across the map, you would go from one end to the other, stopping along the way to add in the characters, setting, problem, events, and resolution. (Option: Bring in a toy car and drive it across the map as you talk about the academic language on the map. This will get their attention!) The theme lies in the center of the map, as a focus to add to throughout the reading. To demonstrate a fiction map for the intermediate level, try picture books by Patricia Pollaco or Eve Bunting as well as *Grandfather's Journey* by Allen Say, *The Journey* by Aaron Becker, and *Naked Mole Rat* by Mo Willems.

2. Using the book you've selected, demonstrate how to preview the text with text structure in mind. Preview the title, front cover, and back cover. Open the text and flip to the table of contents (if there is one), and quickly page through the text. If more information is needed to predict, read aloud a page or two and then pause to give your thoughts. Using the map, have students follow along as you discuss the possible setting, characters, and problem based on clues you've seen so far. Invite students to turn and talk to partners to repeat the characters, setting, and problem. Ask pairs to use the academic language found

on the map and to respond in full sentences as they discuss the fiction map elements for the book you just demonstrated.

For Nonfiction

1. Tell students that many authors organize their information in nonfiction texts in one of the five most common text maps: description (main idea and detail), sequence, cause and effect, problem and solution, or compare and contrast. Let students know that being able to recognize which of these structures fits the text will help them improve their comprehension.

2. Over the course of a few days, select one text at a time to represent each informational text map. Remind students that in a textbook or magazine they may see multiple organizers. Using the corresponding text map in the *Nonfiction Text Trip Map* reproducible in Figure 3.12 for each sample text, show students the various elements of each organizer. Remind them that informational texts usually contain similar text features such as a table of contents, headings, photos, charts, and an index or glossary. To demonstrate a nonfiction text, choose from content-area textbooks, weekly newspapers (e.g., *Time for Kids Nonfiction, Scholastic News*), basal anthologies, and mentor texts—picture books you already have that fit the nonfiction text organizers. See Figure 3.13 for suggestions on mentor texts.

STEP 4: COLLABORATION

Fiction Map Practice

Select a fiction text for all students to read and discuss the text structure map before reading. Invite students to turn to partners and discuss each of the terms on the map. Have partners or teams read the text together and discuss how to fill in the map. Circulate and coach students to use the academic language on the map to guide their discussions. Ask the class how using the fiction map throughout the reading process helps them understand the reading better.

Nonfiction Map Practice

Select an informational text for all students to read, and together determine which text structure fits the text. Preview the text together using the academic language found on the map. Invite students to turn and share with partners or teams as you work through the map together. Circulate and guide students as they discuss the terms on the map and apply them to the text. Read the text in pairs and as a class fill in the organizer. Ask the class how using the nonfiction map throughout the reading process helps them understand the reading better. How do text features also add to your comprehension?

STEP 5: APPLICATION

Fiction Map Experts

Students work in teams and each member chooses to focus on one fiction map element such as setting, characters, problem, or events. Before reading, students predict and preview the text and share their ideas. During reading, they pause and again chime in with their respective parts and ideas. After reading, the group creates a giant-sized fiction map for their text.

Nonfiction Map Experts

Students work in teams to use a nonfiction organizer to preview, work through, and discuss a nonfiction text. Teams make a giant-sized organizer to share with the class. Groups may work on texts that are organized the same way (e.g., cause and effect) or teams may report on different types of texts (i.e., one team shows compare and contrast and another chooses sequence). Invite teams to share the text features included in their chosen text. Try this activity with weekly news articles, content-area textbooks, or nonfiction picture books.

STEP 6: REFLECTION

Ask students to sketch the generic text maps for fiction and nonfiction in their literacy notebooks. Have students fill in text maps for texts the class is reading. Ask them to write paragraphs about texts they've read using the text map academic language to guide them. Incorporate the vocabulary found in the language bank in Figure 3.14 to help write the paragraphs.

ADAPTATION AND EXTENSION

- Play Info Text-O game with the nonfiction organizers.
  1. Create a card with a 3 × 3 grid (you may use the online generator at www.bookunitsteacher.com/wp/?=1650) and give to your students.
  2. Choose four text features (e.g., headings, maps, charts, and photographs) and ask students to randomly record those and an organizer name (e.g., description, sequence, compare and contrast, cause and effect, problem and solution) in each box.
  3. Next, ask students to mark the center box as FREE (voiding student's previous choice).

4. Students can use tokens or ripped up pieces of paper for markers.

5. Display a nonfiction text and read it aloud. Have students work independently or talk with partners to figure out which of the text structures fits the text and mark it on their cards.

6. Also, show text features on the document camera and ask students to identify them and mark their cards.

7. To win, markers can be across, down, diagonal, or cover the full card.

8. Clear cards of markers and play again.

- *English Language Learner* and *Struggling Reader Suggestion*: Play Info-Text O with small groups of ELLs or struggling readers to teach them the meanings of the vocabulary used in the lesson. Discuss informational text organization as well as text features. Pass out informational texts keyed to students' interests and ask them to find examples of text organization and text features. Work with a small group at a table or on the floor while guiding students through the lesson.

EVALUATION

"I can . . ." Statements

- I can identify text structure elements for a fiction text: setting, characters, problem, events, resolution, and theme.
- I can identify five text structures for nonfiction texts: description, cause and effect, problem and solution, compare and contrast, and sequence.
- I can identify which text map fits a particular nonfiction text.
- I can use text maps for fiction and nonfiction to preview texts and predict what they will be about.

Behavior Indicators

- Identifies fiction elements found on a fiction map and applies them to a fiction text: setting, characters, problem, event, resolution, and theme.
- Uses a fiction map to preview a text to make logical predictions.
- Names the five graphic organizers for nonfiction texts: description, sequence, problem and solution, compare and contrast, and cause and effect.
- Studies a text and identifies which of the nonfiction organizers fits the text.
- Uses a nonfiction map to preview a text and make logical predictions.

FIGURE 3.12

Text Trip Maps: Fiction and Nonfiction

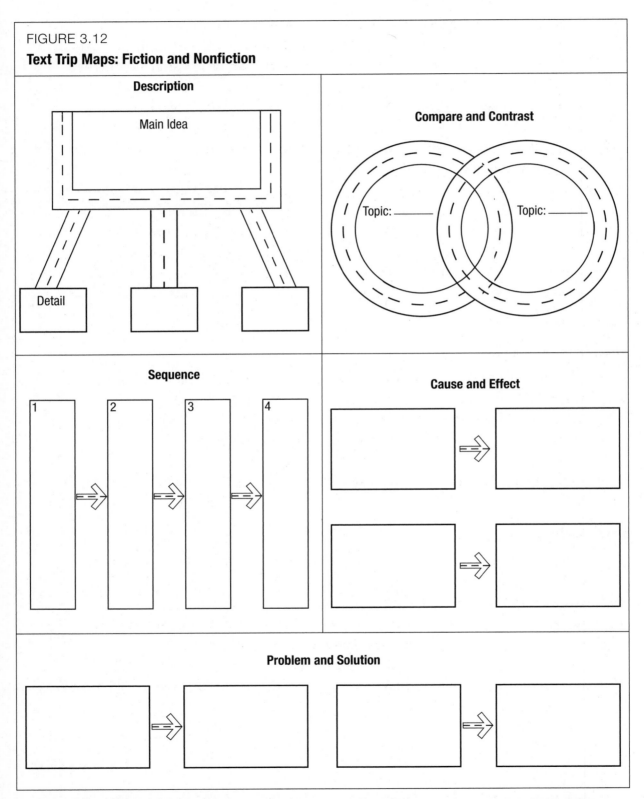

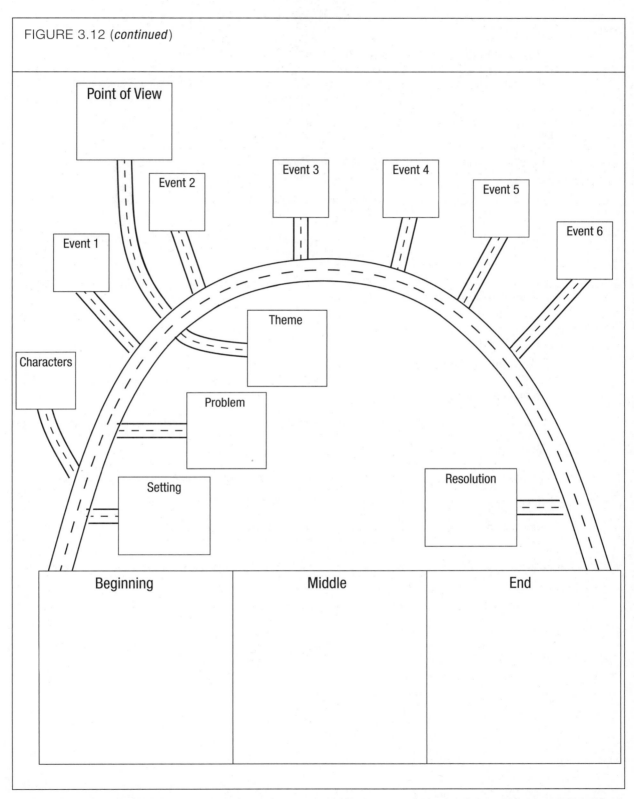

FIGURE 3.12 (*continued*)

Point of View

Event 2

Event 3

Event 4

Event 5

Event 1

Event 6

Characters

Theme

Problem

Setting

Resolution

Beginning	Middle	End

FIGURE 3.13

Mentor Texts for Modeling Nonfiction Text Structures

Main Idea and Detail	*Celebritrees: Historic and Famous Trees of the World* by Margi Preus *Feathers* by Melissa Steward
Problem and Solution	*Can We Save the Tiger?* by Martin Jenkins *Kid's Solar Energy Book* by Tilly Spetgang
Time Order Sequence	*Liberty Rising: The Story of the Statue of Liberty* by Pegi Deitz Shea *Jane Goodall* by William Rice
Compare and Contrast	*Lincoln and Douglass: An American Friendship* by Nikki Giovanni *Women's Suffrage* by Harriet Isecke
Cause and Effect	*How to Clean a Hippopotamus* by Steve Kemloms and Robin Page *Electrical Wizard* by Elizabeth Rusch

Source: Literacy Strong All Year Long: Powerful Lessons for Grades 3-5 by Lori Oczkus, Valerie Ellery, and Timothy V. Rasinski. Copyright © 2018 ASCD. Readers may duplicate this figure for noncommercial use within their school.

FIGURE 3.14

Vocabulary Language Word Bank

Fiction Vocabulary

Setting, characters, problem, event, resolution, ending, beginning, middle, end, first, next, then, finally

Nonfiction Vocabulary

Description	Main idea, detail, in addition to, most important, another, such as, in fact
Time Order Sequence	First, next, then, finally, before, after that, not long after
Compare and Contrast	Same as, alike, not only but also, similar, compared to, likewise, as well as Different from, in contrast to, instead of, however, while
Cause and Effect	Because, since, if, then, so that, for this reason, because of, consequently, in order to
Problem and Solution	The problem is, solve, a question is, one reason is, an answer is, the puzzle is, a solution is

Source: Literacy Strong All Year Long: Powerful Lessons for Grades 3-5 by Lori Oczkus, Valerie Ellery, and Timothy V. Rasinski. Copyright © 2018 ASCD. Readers may duplicate this figure for noncommercial use within their school.

LESSON 7. COMPREHENSION: INFERRING AND DRAWING CONCLUSIONS

Title TABLEAUX: MAKING TEXTS COME TO LIFE

Trailer After having read a story or chapter, we increase our understanding of the text by talking about it with others who have read the same text, or by writing about it in a response journal. But as an interesting alternative—in silence—we can use our bodies to create poses and develop gestures that reflect various episodes and meanings from a text. Those poses and gestures often help us make inferences or guesses about various parts of a text. In this lesson we explore the use of tableaux to help students deepen their understanding of texts.

Literacy Enhancer Reading Comprehension: Making Inferences Using Tableaux

Key Academic Vocabulary

(Terms spiraled from previous lessons)

Background Knowledge (Schema): The existing knowledge a person has about a particular topic

Hypothesis: A prediction usually made prior to a scientific experiment that anticipates the outcome of the experiment; the experiment is then conducted to confirm or disconfirm the hypothesis

Imagery: Internal representation of meaning based on something that is read; can include the sight, sound, smells, movements, and feelings associated with a particular scene from a text

Inference: An educated guess or prediction about some aspect of a text that is not specifically mentioned; a sophisticated form of reading comprehension

Prediction: An educated guess about what may happen in a story or other text about to be read

(New term in this lesson)

Tableau(x): A living picture; a depiction of a scene usually presented by silent and motionless participants

Learning Objectives

- Design, make, and present elaborated tableaux based on texts students read.
- Work in small groups with classmates to design, make, and present tableaux.
- Provide appropriate rationales for tableaux.
- Predict the meaning expressed in tableaux developed and presented by classmates.

Essential Questions

- What is an inference? What parts of a tableau that I create are inferences?
- What do I need to know to make a tableau about the texts I read?
- Am I able to explain the nature of the tableau I create from what I read?
- Am I able to appreciate and understand the tableaux created by my classmates?

STEP 1: PREPARATION

Organize Materials

- Several photographs of statues or sculptures of famous people or events (e.g., Lincoln Memorial, Statue of Liberty, *The Thinker* by Auguste Rodin, *Knotted Gun* at the United Nations)
- Narrative text that contains rich descriptions that lend themselves to the development of scenes that can be portrayed as tableaux

STEP 2: INITIATION

Statues and Sculptures

Show your students the photographs of statues and sculptures that you have collected and ask if they can identify them; if not, provide a brief description of the item. Then ask your students to discuss in small groups what the statue or sculpture represents (e.g., the seated Lincoln represents the president as a wise leader during the Civil War; the Statue of Liberty represents America welcoming new immigrants; the *Knotted Gun* represents a desire for peace in the world). Discuss with students how motionless statues and sculptures can represent deep meanings, ideas, and actions taken by the person represented. Tell students that they are going to have the opportunity to do the same with the texts that they read.

Describe the notion of making tableaux from words and ideas. Say the following words aloud and ask students to create a living image or statue using their own bodies to represent ideas: Play ball (baseball), Safe (baseball), Hooray!, Beware, Howdy. Have students share their tableaux with other members of the class and discuss how and why the tableaux might be different from one another. For example, the tableaux that we create are based on our own background and experience, so though we may be processing the same word, our tableaux will contain inferences that were influenced by our own background knowledge or schema related to the word.

Indicate to students that this process of making tableaux can be done when reading a text. As we read, good readers create images that we feel reflect the meaning of the passage we are reading. Those images can be developed into tableaux that can be performed, shared, and discussed with others. We may add details to our tableaux that are not even mentioned in the passage. This adding of new details is a form of inferencing.

STEP 3: DEMONSTRATION

Tableaux Performance

1. Read aloud the text you have chosen. Do not show your students any illustrations that may be part of the text. Remind them to think of images from the story that can be converted into tableaux.
2. After reading a portion of the story (or the entire story if it is short), think aloud and tell your students that as you read, you were able to come up with images in your mind and that you have thought about how those images can be turned into tableaux.
3. Perform one or more of the tableaux that you developed from your reading. Stand motionless, positioning your body to reflect the meaning you want to convey. After displaying your tableaux for several seconds, ask students if they can identify the scene from the text that you are portraying. Ask them to describe how they were able to determine the scene (e.g., the way you positioned your arms or legs).
4. If the text can be broken into several natural stopping points, create a tableau at each stopping point and ask students to identify what you are portraying.
5. When the read-aloud is complete, ask students to talk about how making tableaux while reading affected their reading and understanding of the text.

STEP 4: COLLABORATION

Have students continue the same process described above with the texts that you will have them read on their own.

1. Have students work in small groups to discuss, plan, and make tableaux at logical stopping points throughout the text.
2. Point out to students that in the process of developing a tableau, they are actually engaged in discussing the meaning of the text.
3. Have individuals or groups of students perform their tableaux for classmates.
4. Students in the audience should attempt to describe the scene being portrayed in each tableau.
5. Ask students to reflect on how actively considering and making a tableau affected how they read the text.

STEP 5: APPLICATION

Throughout the next several texts read to and with your students, have them engage in the process of planning, making, performing, and sharing tableaux in small groups. See Figure 3.15 for guidance on planning tableaux.

FIGURE 3.15

Planning Tableaux to Portray Meaning

A tableau is the representation of meaning of a text we have read, using our bodies as statues. As you read, think of scenes from the text that can be turned into a tableau. In a small group (or by yourself), plan your tableau using these questions as a guide:

- What scene or meaning will we choose to portray?
- What characters will we portray and which students will play those characters?
- All students in a group must be part of the tableau, so if there are more students than characters, brainstorm inanimate objects that students can portray (e.g., door, tree, animal).
- Decide how you will portray your individual character or thing. How will you position your body to portray the meaning you wish?
- How will members of your group position themselves with one another to convey meaning?

Perform your tableau for your classmates. Have a member of the group do a countdown: *3, 2, 1, Freeze!*

At the word *freeze*, all members of the group should become statues and make their tableau. Encourage audience members (other classmates) to guess what the group is trying to portray.

Discuss your tableau with other members of the class. Why did you choose a particular scene? How did you choose to use your body to represent meaning?

Source: Literacy Strong All Year Long: Powerful Lessons for Grades 3-5 by Lori Oczkus, Valerie Ellery, and Timothy V. Rasinski. Copyright © 2018 ASCD. Readers may duplicate this figure for noncommercial use within their school.

STEP 6: REFLECTION

Oral or Written Response

After having done several tableaux with students individually and in small groups, ask students to reflect on the process and value of doing tableaux. How did planning a tableau affect how students made meaning? Was planning and performing tableaux enjoyable? Why or why not? How might students use tableaux in other areas of their school curriculum beyond reading?

ADAPTATION AND EXTENSION

- As students become familiar with making tableaux to reflect meaning, you can make the process a bit more elaborate by making these changes:
  - As students plan their tableaux, rather than being still and silent, they can be asked to think of a physical gesture or movement that would add additional meaning to the character or item they are displaying. For

example, a performer could demonstrate throwing a ball or rock, and another performer playing the role of a door could "open" or "close" to show additional meaning. The gestures students plan should take no more than three seconds. When performing tableaux, a teacher or classmate could walk around the still life display and touch various performers on the shoulder. Upon being touched, the performer could come to life and execute the gesture. The movement students make will often reflect an inference about the original text.

○ Similarly, students performing a tableau could think of what they might say or what noise they might make if they could come alive for three seconds. A student performing the role of a character could say something in character, while the student portraying an object could make a sound associated with the object (e.g., door closing). Again, as with gestures, the words spoken or noises made during the tableau will often reflect an inference about the text.

- *English Language Learner Suggestion*: Have students create tableaux that represent customs from their native cultures. After students perform, have them provide a description of what their tableaux mean and represent in their native culture.

- *Struggling Reader Suggestion*: Tableaux do not require oral or written language to perform. Moreover, they can also be employed in nearly every area of the school curriculum. Students, especially students who struggle in reading, can be asked to create tableaux that represent scenes from history and social studies, mathematical concepts, and scientific processes. In the process of planning and performing their tableaux, students are given an avenue to think and understand the content of whatever they may be performing. Of course, as the ideas to be portrayed become more abstract, students will be challenged to think in different ways to convey meaning using their physical bodies.

EVALUATION

"I can . . ." Statements

- I can create tableaux that reflect the meaning of texts that I have read.
- I can describe why I choose a particular tableau and how I decide to perform it.
- I can work alone or with my classmates to develop and perform tableaux.
- I can engage in discussing and describing tableaux created by other students or groups in my class.

Behavior Indicators

- Plans tableaux related to the reading.
- Performs tableaux based on the reading.
- Discusses tableaux based on the reading.
- Engages in discussion about the process and value of tableaux done in conjunction with reading.

LESSON 8. COMPREHENSION: QUESTIONING FOR CLOSE READING

Title ARE YOU READY TO RUMBLE? ANTICIPATING–REACTING–EVALUATING

Trailer Are you ready to rumble? Are you ready to hear me roar? We can roar and soar by asking and answering questions as we rumble through the text! You may be thinking that we are about to enter into a "fight" with the text. For some of you, every day might feel like you are fighting the text to discover what the author is trying to tell you. Did you know that *rumble* can also mean "to discover"? So actually, we really are going to rumble through the text! We will identify question–answer relationships and how this synergy can help us resound with meaning!

Literacy Enhancer Comprehension—Questioning, Inference

Key Academic Vocabulary

(Terms spiraled from previous lessons)

Close Read: Determine purpose and notice features and language used by the author so that readers can think thoughtfully and methodically about why certain details were used in the text

Inference: A conclusion (interpretation, judgment, opinion, or prediction) based on text evidence and reasoning merged with personal background knowledge

Interpretation: An explanation of the meaning of something

Interrogate: To examine with questions; to look for answers

Judgment: The ability to make decisions or come to logical conclusions

Opinion: A view or judgment formed about something, not necessarily based on facts

Reasoning: Thinking and processing information in a logical way

Speculative Talk: Make an inference by suggesting or hinting at connections and conclusions; elements of imaginative thinking to support understanding

Text-Based Evidence: Evidence derived from key facts and details in the text

Text-Dependent Questions: Sentences in interrogative form that can only be answered by referring explicitly back to the text being read

(New terms in this lesson)

Anticipate: To expect or predict

Cite: To quote from a specified source as evidence for or justification of an argument or statement

Question–Answer Relationship (QAR): A tool to ask and answer questions considering both information in the text and reader's background knowledge

Quote: Direct words from a text; repeating what someone actually said

Learning Objectives

- Confirm or change predictions about text.
- Demonstrate the relationship between questions and answers.
- Use explicitly stated information, background knowledge, and connections to the text to ask and answer questions.
- Quote accurately from a text when explaining what the text (author) says explicitly and when drawing inferences from the text.

Essential Question

- What is the relationship between questions and answers?
- How does asking and answering different types of questions about the text help to comprehend it?
- When is it valuable to cite evidence?

STEP 1: PREPARATION

Organize Materials

- Boxing gloves (optional)
- Multimodal text
- Predetermined "proof statements" to align with text
- *Anticipation–Reaction–Evaluation (ARE) Guide* reproducible
- Supplies to create a class anchor chart (e.g., chart paper, markers)
- *Concepts for Analyzing Questioning* reproducible

STEP 2: INITIATION

Anticipation and Reaction Using Proof Statements

Proof statements about a text are true or false statements that students will need to validate during reading. Prior to meeting with students, identify the main topic or concept of a text and create four proof statements for students to validate, using these four categories:

1. Literal Statements—stated directly in the text
2. Literal Lateral Statements—stated directly in and through the text
3. Literal and Inferential Statements—stated directly in the text and can be inferred

4. Individual Experiential Statements—activating opinions based on prior knowledge and experience without the text evidence to support thinking

Put on boxing gloves and ask if the students are ready to rumble with the text. Display the cover or title of the text. Slowly take off the gloves while explaining that we won't actually have a match that requires physical fighting, but we will be demonstrating a "match" between "questions and answers" and how they correspond to each other. Explain that the word *rumble* also means "to discover." Share how we will be discovering the truth about certain statements based on the text we are reading and also exploring the question–answer relationship.

State or read one of the proof statements you created. Ask students to respond with their answer, guess, or prediction by stating if they agree or disagree with the statement. Alternative responses could be true or false, deal or no deal, thumbs up or thumbs down. After they respond, have them justify with their partners why they responded the way they did.

Begin reading aloud, having the students lean in and listen to confirm or possibly change their thinking based on what is being read. After reading a section, ask students, "Were you able to confirm your thinking? If so, what parts of the text gave you confirmation? Or did you have to change your thinking? Why?" Revisit the text and note which category of proof statement students used to confirm their thinking and where information may be found in the text to support thinking. Establish a chart for the proof statement categories using Figure 3.16 to begin creating an anchor chart for future reference.

FIGURE 3.16
Proof Statement Categories

Proof Statements	Descriptions and Accountable Talk	Example Statements
Literal	Directly in text *Locate the exact words or phrases in the text to support your thinking.*	
Literal Lateral	Directly in and through the text *Search through the text and find multiple words or phrases to support your thinking.*	
Literal and Inferential	Directly in text and can be inferred *Search through the text and also use your reasoning to support your thinking.*	
Individual Experiential	Activate background knowledge and experience without the text evidence to support thinking *Express personal opinion based on the content without support of text evidence.*	

Source: Literacy Strong All Year Long: Powerful Lessons for Grades 3-5 by Lori Oczkus, Valerie Ellery, and Timothy V. Rasinski. Copyright © 2018 ASCD.
Readers may duplicate this figure for noncommercial use within their school.

STEP 3: DEMONSTRATION

ARE = Anticipation, Reaction, Evaluation

1. Revisit one of the generated Literal and Inferential Proof Statements that you created on the chart in the Initiation phase of the lesson to highlight the AR = Anticipation–Reaction stage of ARE.

2. Compare that Literal and Inferential Proof Statement with the "I Say" section in Figure 2.16, *Inference Dance Moves.*

3. Add a fourth column to the class anchor chart called QAR to introduce the four Question–Answer Relationships (Ellery, 2014; Herber, 1984; Raphael, 1986) and show how they represent different types and levels of questions: *Right There, Think and Search, Author and Me, and On My Own.* See Figure 3.17.

4. Revisit the Literal Proof Statement (e.g., Thermal imaging lets people see the transfer of thermal energy between solids, liquids, and gases). Model turning a proof statement into a *Right There* question. For example, if you are teaching a unit on energy, your Literal Proof Statement might be "Thermal imaging lets people see the transfer of thermal energy between solids, liquids, and gases." The *right there question* might be "What can be seen by thermal imaging?"

5. Examine the correlation between the four QAR types, proof statements, and the Inference Dance Moves (from Chapter 2). Highlight how all these categories allow the reader to visualize and realize that information from texts and their own background knowledge can contribute to answering questions. These categories can help students to search for keywords or phrases as they are locating information to answer a question or prove a statement, and to determine if they need to "read between the lines" to derive meaning.

6. Combine all three concepts for analyzing questioning onto the class anchor chart.

STEP 4: COLLABORATION

Give partners or teams a predetermined Anticipation–Reaction proof statement to anticipate, react, and evaluate. Have them record their thoughts on their *Anticipation–Reaction–Evaluation ARE Guide* reproducible (see Figure 3.18) prior to reading a section of the text to confirm or change their thinking. Have students return to the statements after they have read the text and engage in a discussion on how the textual information supported, contradicted, or modified their first opinions. Have them use accountable talk to process the stages of anticipation and reaction, and move toward the evaluation stage:

FIGURE 3.17

Concepts for Analyzing Questioning Reproducible

Proof Statements and Inference Dance Steps	Descriptions and Accountable Talk	Questions–Answer Relationships (QAR)
Literal	Directly in text: *Locate the exact words or phrases in the text to support your thinking.*	**Right There** questions: Words from the question and words from the answer will usually be found stated exactly in the text very close to each other.
I Question What It Says	Key Words: *identify, list, match, name, define, quote, cite. "According to the passage . . . Who is . . . Who are . . . Who did . . . When did . . . What did. . . What is . . . Where is . . . How many . . ."*	
Literal Lateral	Directly in and through the text: *Search throughout the text and find multiple words and or phrases to support your thinking.*	**Think and Search** questions: Require readers to derive the answer from more than one sentence, paragraph, or page.
It Says	Key Words: *compare and contrast, explain, tell why, find evidence, problem and solution, cause and effect, quote, cite. "The key details of the passage are . . . What caused . . . What was the effect . . . How would you compare and contrast . . . What examples can you locate . . . Where is it located in the text?"*	
Literal and Inferential	Directly in text and can be inferred: *Search through the text and also use your reasoning to support your thinking.*	**Author and Me** questions: Words from the book are in the question, but these questions also require input from the reader's own prior knowledge to connect with the text and derive an answer.
I Say So I Infer	Key Words: *analyze, imply, infer and draw conclusion, hypothesize, explain, reason, logical argument, prove, opinion. "The author implies . . . Use part of the text to show why you agree with . . . What did the author mean by . . . Give the reasons why . . . Why do you think the author stated . . . ? Support your rationale using text evidence . . . Why do you suppose . . . ?"*	
Individual Experiential	Activate background knowledge and experience without the text evidence to support thinking: *Express personal opinion based on the content without support of text evidence.*	**On My Own** questions: Require application from reader's background knowledge and experiences.
I Say	Key Words: *personalize, opinion, emotions, connections, schema, background. "In your opinion . . . Based on your experience . . . Have you ever . . . How do you feel about. . .What is your favorite . . . why . . . What do you already know about . . . What would you do if . . . ?"*	

Source: Literacy Strong All Year Long: Powerful Lessons for Grades 3-5 by Lori Oczkus, Valerie Ellery, and Timothy V. Rasinski. Copyright © 2018 ASCD. Readers may duplicate this figure for noncommercial use within their school.

- Do you agree or disagree with the statement presented? Why or why not?
- Try to read and confirm if your answer to the statement is true or false.
- Examine the text and refer to details in the text that support your thinking.
- What can you quote directly from the text to support your thinking?
- How do you cite textual evidence to explain what the text says explicitly?
- Which of the following quotes supports the conclusion that . . .?
- What inferences can you make about . . .?
- Where in the text does the author say . . .?
- Which key words or statements in the text support your ideas?
- Justify your thinking as you confirm or reassess your original response to the statement.

STEP 5: APPLICATION

Have individuals or partners use the *Anticipation, Reaction, Evaluation (ARE) Guide* (Figure 3.18) to create questions based on the predetermined statements that align with each of the four QAR categories.

STEP 6: REFLECTION

Oral or Written Response

Ask students to practice identifying and answering the different types of questions. Have students determine the question–answer relationship of each question and record and justify their answers in their notebooks.

- How does questioning support comprehension?
- How does a reader find answers to questions presented?
- How does a reader use quotes to explain what the text says or support inferences?
- How does a reader cite textual evidence to explain what the text says explicitly?

ADAPTATION AND EXTENSION

- Read the text and write your own QAR questions. Then swap your QAR questions with another student and find and categorize the answers. Compare questions and answers when finished.
- *English Language Learner Suggestion*: Present examples of Open Questions (Ellery & Rosenboom, 2011; Small, 2011) or a broader question that encourages choice and varied levels of responses. Provide students with answers to the content question, and students will respond with questions:

FIGURE 3.18

Anticipation, Reaction, Evaluation (ARE) Guide

Directions:
1. Read the anticipation statement and decide if you agree or disagree with it.
2. In the Self-Reflection column, place a + if you agree with the statement or think the statement is true. Place an X in the Self Reflection column if you disagree with the statement or if you think the statement is false or not true.
3. Read the text to confirm or change your opinion of the statement. Place a + in the Text Reaction column if the statement in the text is true and an X if it is not true.
4. Record your analysis of the process in the Evaluation column.

Anticipation Statement	Self-Reflection	Text Reaction	Evaluation
1.			
2.			
3.			

○ *Prompt:* "The answer is _____. What might the question be?"
Example: "The answer is C-Squared. What might the question be?"

○ *Prompt:* "How are _____ and _____ alike? How are they different?"
Example: "How are immigration and relocation alike? How are they different?"

○ *Prompt:* "Initiate a one-minute conversation using the concepts of _____, _____, and _____."
Example: "Initiate a one-minute conversation with your partner, using the concepts of mean, median, and mode."

- *Struggling Reader Suggestion:* Use online games for identifying question–answer relationships and to practice rephrasing answers into questions (e.g., jeopardylabs.com/browse/).

EVALUATION

"I can . . ." Statements

- I can ask and answer questions to establish a purpose for reading.
- I can gather facts from the text; develop questions based on the facts, my background knowledge, or connections; and find the answer to my question within the text.
- I can determine the author's message by asking and answering questions about the text.

Behavior Indicators

- Answers literal and inferential questions and identifies how and where the answers were found.
- Demonstrates the relationship between questions and answers.
- Quotes accurately from a text when explaining what the text explicitly says and when drawing inferences.

LESSON 9. COMPREHENSION: DETERMINING IMPORTANCE AND SUMMARIZING

Title GETTING THE GIST: CIRCLING AROUND THE MAIN IDEA

Trailer Oh, snap! That's a wrap! How can readers identify key details within the text to begin grasping the theme? The answer is only a snap away when teachers apply this lesson in their classrooms. Readers learn how to get the "gist" of identifying details to discover the central message as they circle around the main idea (see Figure 3.19). For a circle or wheel to move smoothly, its spokes need to be strong. This lesson will prove once again how essential spokes are for forward progress toward a strong summary of what is being read!

Literacy Enhancer Comprehension: Determining Importance and Summarizing—Key Details, Main Idea, Theme, Central Message

Key Academic Vocabulary

(Terms spiraled from previous lessons)

Cause and Effect: A relationship between actions in which one event (the cause) makes another event happen (effect)

Chronological: Organized within a sequential order of time

Compare and Contrast: To analyze two or more objects on similarities and differences

Contribute: To help achieve or provide something; to bring about the sequence of events

Essential: Absolutely necessary for the meaning and purpose

Fable: A story passed down among generations to teach about morals and valuable lessons using animals that personify people, plants, or forces of nature

Information: Gathered knowledge; facts and ideas

Key Detail: An important feature, fact, or item that supports the overall meaning

Moral: A practical lesson contained in a story

Recount: To give detailed descriptions of information from a text in chronological order and past tense to convey the message of the text

Retelling: Recalling in a sequential order what is happening in a text

Sequencing: Placing information in a certain order

Sift: To filter and examine which detail is most important

Story Elements: Parts or ingredients of a story (i.e., character, setting, event, plot, problem, solution)

Text-Based: Evidence derived from key facts and details in the text
(New terms in this lesson)

Central Message: Main thought or principal theme the author is trying to tell or teach

Gist: The main topic, idea, or the overall central message of a text

Main Idea: The gist or important information or central thought that tells about the overall idea of a paragraph or section of text

Summarize: Brief statement of the main points of a text using fewer words and concise form

Learning Objectives

- Determine one or more main ideas within a text and explain how these ideas are supported by key details.
- Construct the chronological events and summarize the text.
- Identify the central message the author is trying to establish or teach from the text.

Essential Questions

- What is the main idea?
- What is the relationship between the key details and the main idea in a text?
- What is the summary of the text?
- What are the characteristics of an effective summary?
- What is the central message the author wants the reader to know from the text?

STEP 1: PREPARATION

Organize Materials

- Index cards for words or pictures from unit of study
- Multimodal text set on topic of study
- *Circling Around the Main Idea* Reproducible (Figure 3.19)
- Literacy Notebooks
- Supplies to create a class Anchor Chart (e.g., chart paper, markers)

STEP 2: INITIATION

It's a Snap!

Ask students to snap their fingers while focusing on how many fingers are active when they are snapping. Have them try to snap their thumb and index finger without moving any other fingers and share their observations with partners. Continue having them snap with the other fingers, noting how many of the fingers play some part in creating a strong snap. Ask, "How does snapping relate to reading?" Display several illustrations from the text. Examine one image at a time by thinking aloud, describing certain details that you notice from the illustration. Count out using your fingers as you describe each of the three to five details from the images. Explain how the details represent key facts and when you snap your fingers together it is like bringing all the facts together, forming the main idea, and "getting the gist"!

Share how in this lesson we are going to summarize each collection of details for the main idea, which will lead to understanding the author's purpose of the central message. Remind students that the information we are collecting is like the details on our "stones" in the Sifting What Matters lesson (see Chapter 1) and the "ingredients" found in the Recount Recipe lesson (see Chapter 2).

STEP 3: DEMONSTRATION

Circling Around the Main Idea

1. Select a text and display the *Circling Around the Main Idea* reproducible (Figure 3.19) (Ellery, 2014; Irwin & Baker, 1989). Model the concept of compiling important information to gather the main idea. Ponder these details from a passage and sift through to find the important key details to record in the first section on the wheel. Compare how these points are like each of the three to five fingers needed to create a strong snap in the concept of "getting the gist."

2. Think about the points in the section and how they all come together to share the important information that gives the "gist," highlighting what is essential, and making up the overall idea of a paragraph or section of text.

3. Record what is essential from these details on the spoke of the wheel directly relating to the section with the gathered information to capture the gist.

4. Continue to the next section of the wheel and have students sift salient information. Investigate with students how to read closely to determine what the author is trying to convey as essential. Continue the process to complete a class *Main Idea Wheel.*

FIGURE 3.19

Circling Around the Main Idea Reproducible

Directions: Around the outer ring, record the *section* of the text that you are analyzing (i.e., page number, chapter title, subheading). Inside the wheel, record the *details* from the essential idea. Inside the spokes, summarize what's *essential* from the details. Write the *main idea* in the center.

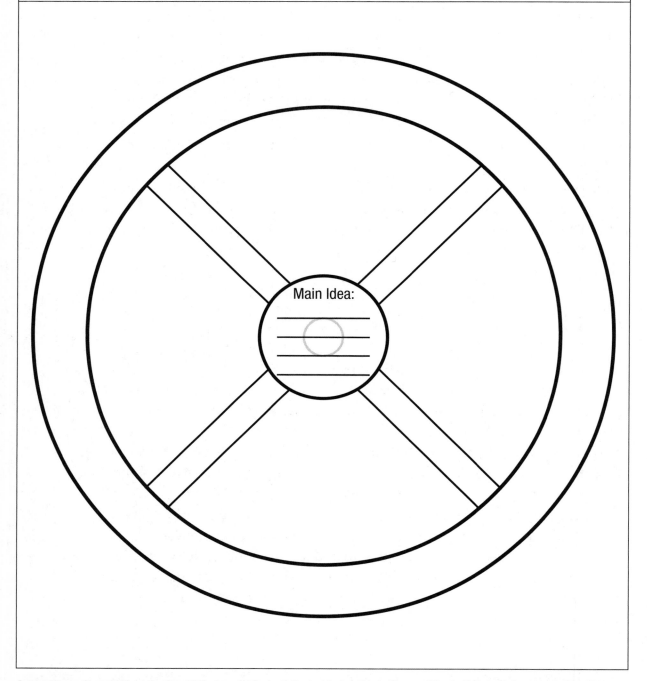

Main Idea:

5. Read each of the spokes and connect them together to create a group summary based on the essential details of the text. Generate a class anchor chart on the characteristics of an effective summary (e.g., key details, main ideas based on key details, chronological order, concise, precise story elements).

6. Examine the key details and main idea within the text as clues to support the overall big idea for the author's purpose and reason for the central message.

STEP 4: COLLABORATION

Divide students into groups. Assign each group a different section or chapter of text to determine the essential details and record on a *Main Idea Wheel*. Students justify with text evidence why they feel a part is worthy to be a detail inside the spoke on each section. Have them determine from the details what is essential to summarize on each spoke. Engage in conversational coaching by asking students to discuss the following questions with diverse partners:

- What is the relationship between the details (i.e., what's on the fingers) and the main idea (i.e., the snap)?
- How do the key details help convey the central message?

STEP 5: APPLICATION

Students create their own *Main Idea Wheels* based on a text they are independently reading. Have them reflect on the ideas and statements they wrote on their spokes and on how these ideas supported their process of making meaning from the text.

STEP 6: REFLECTION

Oral or Written Response

Have students reflect and respond in their Literacy Journals on the process to recognize how ideas are organized in an informational text. Remind them they can describe or graphically represent the relationship between the main idea and details using the *Main Idea Wheel*. Have them explain how the main idea is supported by key details, and answer the essential questions:

- What are the characteristics of an effective summary?
- What is the central message the author wants the reader to know from the text?

ADAPTATION AND EXTENSION

- *English Language Learner Suggestion*: Create an ad about the topic of study using an online resource for visual support, such as Voki. Have the students design a talking avatar to provide details that describe the main topic.

- *Struggling Reader Suggestion*: Watch a movie trailer and discuss how it gives a brief overview of the content of the movie. Use a tablet and assign a certain text. Have the students use the text and apply a movie app to create a "text" trailer with the topic and essential details to give a reader the gist of the subject matter of the text.

EVALUATION

"I can . . ." Statements

- I can find how the main idea is supported by details.
- I can explain how the main idea is supported by key details to summarize the text.
- I can use details to summarize the main idea in a text.
- I can explain the relationships between two or more individuals, events, ideas, or concepts in an informational text.
- I can use specific information from the text to support my explanation of the relationships and interactions between two or more individuals, events, ideas, or concepts in historical, scientific, or technical text.

Behavior Indicators

- Uses supporting details from the text to clearly explain main idea.
- Determines two or more main ideas of a text.
- Develops effective summaries that are supported by key details in the text.

LESSON 10. COMPREHENSION: MOTIVATING READERS

Title **READY, SET GOALS, READ!**

Trailer Our students set goals often in their everyday lives and activities. They set goals such as swimming across the pool without stopping, saving money for a special toy or outing, or reaching the next level in a video game. Goal setting requires planning small, realistic action steps to make reaching one's target possible. The same holds true for student's reading goals. Broad goals such as "I want to be a better reader" or simply "I want to read more books" tend to be too vague and not motivating for students. However, by breaking goals into smaller, measurable attainable steps, students recognize and experience success along the way. Harness the power of goal setting!

Literacy Enhancer Comprehension: Motivating Readers—Goal Setting, Text Features, Book Talks, Predicting, Summarizing

Key Academic Vocabulary

(Terms spiraled from previous lessons)

Author: The person who wrote the book

Fiction: The genre that includes stories that are make-believe, also poetry

Illustrator: The person who illustrated the book

Nonfiction: The genre that includes factual or real information that is portrayed to answer, explain, or describe

Predict: To use information from a text to infer what the text will be about or what one might learn from it

Summarize: To tell what has happened in the text by sharing important points and details

Title: The name of the text; tells what it is about or gives clues to the content
(New terms for this lesson)

Accuracy: The ability to read words correctly without making errors

Goal: An ideal or objective to achieve

Plan: A specific action that is measurable for working towards a goal

Prosody: The aspect of fluency that includes phrasing, yielding for punctuation, and placing emphasis and expression in the proper places in the reading of the text

Rate: The speed at which one reads; includes volume, expression, and natural sounding pace

Stamina: The ability to focus on reading for set amounts of time

Learning Objectives

- Identify and establish personal, measurable reading goals that center around reading more books and a variety of book genres.
- Identify and establish personal, measurable reading goals that center around reading stamina (e.g., number of minutes of uninterrupted reading).
- Identify and establish personal, measurable reading goals that center around increasing the volume of reading (e.g., books, pages) and the rigor of the material.
- Identify and establish personal, measurable reading strategy goals that center around comprehension, fluency, and decoding words.

Essential Questions

- What are some ways you can improve your reading by setting goals?
- What goals can you set for reading a variety of genres and increasingly more challenging materials, improving your stamina and fluency?
- What goals can you set to help you increase the time you spend reading?
- How can you set specific goals to improve your comprehension, fluency, and decoding?

STEP 1: PREPARATION

Organize Materials

- *Ready, Set Goals, Read!* reproducible
- *My Reading Strategy Goals Bookmark* reproducible

STEP 2: INITIATION

The Importance of Setting Goals

Bring the sports section from the newspaper to show students. Invite them to share examples of athletes they follow and to discuss why and how professional athletes set goals to improve their performance. Share an example of a hobby or activity you enjoy and specific measurable goals. For example, your goals might include increasing the number of steps you walk daily as measured by your smartphone, or knitting increasingly more difficult projects such as scarves, then graduating to sweaters.

Discuss how students set goals for their sports or activities. Include a variety of their interests such as skiing, swimming, knitting, sewing, cooking, art, and biking. Assign each team of students a sport or activity to discuss or allow students to meet with others who share the same interests. Teams discuss at least two specific goals for their sport or activity and create a chart to share. *Prompt:* "Our activity is _____. The goal is _____. The plan is to _____ (a number increase)." *Example:* "Our activity is running. The goal is to run for an hour. The plan is to increase our running time by 15 minutes every week until we are able to run for an hour." Circulate and coach groups to make their goals specific and measurable. Invite groups to share their charts with the class.

STEP 3: DEMONSTRATION

How to Set Reading Goals

1. Display and share with students *Ready, Set Goals, Read!* reproducible (Figure 3.20) and *My Reading Strategy Goals Bookmark* (Figure 3.21). Explain that you are going to use them to model how to set different kinds of goals for reading. Tell students that good readers set goals that can be measured, just like athletes.

2. Demonstrate how to set goals for comprehension, fluency, and decoding using *My Reading Strategy Goals Bookmark* (see Figure 3.21). Show how to cross-reference using a book log (see *My Reading Book Log* Figure 1.17, p. 82) to demonstrate the importance of reflecting on one's reading to set goals. As you model how to set goals, use examples from your own reading, share the goals of a hypothetical student, or invite a volunteer to set goals with you in front of the class.

3. Next, discuss each goal and the number of books, the different kinds and genres of books, time spent reading, and the level of challenge. Encourage students to consider including fiction and nonfiction as they set reading goals. Before you conduct your think-aloud, ask students to read the strategies and to discuss them with a partner. Then model and demonstrate each strategy using a text the class is familiar with or one you wish to introduce, thinking aloud as you go. Use a favorite picture book or a chapter book such as any book from the *Diary of a Wimpy Kid* series by Jeff Kinney or J. K. Rowling's *Harry Potter* series. Conduct the demonstration several times using both fiction and nonfiction.

STEP 4: COLLABORATION

Display several genres of books such as fantasy, nonfiction, historical fiction, and mysteries in different spots around the classroom. Label the displays and make sure there is one book for each student. Give a brief book talk about each genre and share a title or two from each book group. Have students rotate to each book station to briefly preview the texts on display. Designate a signal for students to rotate to the next station. When students have visited all genres, have them go back to their seats

FIGURE 3.20

Ready, Set Goals, Read! Reproducible

Obstacles to Reading Goals	Overcoming Obstacles

Obstacles to Reading Goals

Not sure of what kinds of books to read
Don't like certain genres
Only like one kind of book

Lots of after-school activities

Noisy at home

No place to read at home

No books at home

Distracted at school

Wasting time on selecting books
Don't know what books to read next

Unfamiliar with chapter books, nonfiction

Fear reading more challenging books

Need strategies
for reading
harder books

Overcoming Obstacles

Ask friends, teachers, and librarians for book reviews

Set a time to read, even for 15 minutes

Find a place at home to read or wear headphones

Check out books from the library

Read at the library and in class

Keep a list of books you want to read
Keep a list of authors to read

Try a harder book about a topic you want to read

Listen to a harder book on tape

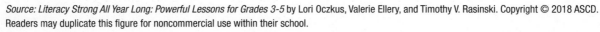

FIGURE 3.21

Ready, Set Goals, Read! Bookmark Reproducible

Name_____ Date_____

Number of Books
My Goal: I want to read more books.

My Plan
I want to read #____ books by_____ or every _____ .
List of the books I want to read:
- _____
- _____

Kinds of Books
My Goal: I want to read different kinds of books.

My Plan
I will read #____ of ____ (genre) books by_____ or every_____ .
Circle genres: adventure, autobiography, biography, fables, fairy tales, mysteries, nonfiction, poetry, realistic fiction, science fiction, graphic novels, other _____ .

List of different kinds of books I want to read.
- _____
- _____

Time Spent Reading
My Goal: I want to spend more time reading.

My Plan
- I will read for ___ minutes daily at school.
- I will read for ___ minutes daily at home.

Challenge of Books
My Goal: I want to read harder books.

My Plan
I will read # ___ books that have:
___ more pages or chapters
___ more words on the page
___ hard concepts

List of harder books I want to read.

- _____
- _____

Ready, Set Goals, Read! Bookmark Reproducible

Name_____ Date_____

Number of Books
My Goal: I want to read more books.

My Plan
I want to read #____ books by_____ or every _____ .
List of the books I want to read:
- _____
- _____

Kinds of Books
My Goal: I want to read different kinds of books.

My Plan
I will read #____ of ____ (genre) books by_____ or every_____ .
Circle genres: adventure, autobiography, biography, fables, fairy tales, mysteries, nonfiction, poetry, realistic fiction, science fiction, graphic novels, other _____ .

List of different kinds of books I want to read.
- _____
- _____

Time Spent Reading
My Goal: I want to spend more time reading.

My Plan
- I will read for ___ minutes daily at school.
- I will read for ___ minutes daily at home.

Challenge of Books
My Goal: I want to read harder books.

My Plan
I will read # ___ books that have:
___ more pages or chapters
___ more words on the page
___ hard concepts

List of harder books I want to read.

- _____
- _____

FIGURE 3.22

My Reading Strategy Goals Bookmark

My Reading Strategy Goals

Comprehension
Before Reading
____I will look at the cover, title, inside pages and text features (nonfiction) to make predictions.
During Reading
____I will pause to clarify any words or ideas I need to figure out.
____I will pause to summarize and predict.
After Reading
____I will pause to summarize, predict, and question.
____I will summarize the main ideas in order.
____I will share my opinions/ideas with text evidence.

Fluency
Rate
____I will read with expression.
____I will read with volume.
____I will read at a natural sounding speed.
Accuracy
____I will read the words as correctly as I can.
Prosody
____I will read words in phrases.
____I will follow the punctuation.
____I will read some words with more emphasis and expression.

Decoding
____I will use a variety of strategies for figuring out words including
____chopping words into familiar parts
____rereading
____reading on
____thinking of synonyms
____sounding out
____looking the word up in a dictionary

My Reading Strategy Goals Bookmark

My Reading Strategy Goals

Comprehension
Before Reading
____I will look at the cover, title, inside pages and text features (nonfiction) to make predictions.
During Reading
____I will pause to clarify any words or ideas I need to figure out.
____I will pause to summarize and predict.
After Reading
____I will pause to summarize, predict, and question.
____I will summarize the main ideas in order.
____I will share my opinions/ideas with text evidence.

Fluency
Rate
____I will read with expression.
____I will read with volume.
____I will read at a natural sounding speed.
Accuracy
____I will read the words as correctly as I can.
Prosody
____I will read words in phrases.
____I will follow the punctuation.
____I will read some words with more emphasis and expression.

Decoding
____I will use a variety of strategies for figuring out words including
____chopping words into familiar parts
____rereading
____reading on
____thinking of synonyms
____sounding out
____looking the word up in a dictionary

to fill out their bookmarks. Discuss as a class their reflections and allow students to select books to read. Try this activity throughout the year to continue to inspire your students to select different genres of books to read.

Charting Obstacles/Solutions

With students working in pairs or teams, discuss the *Ready, Set Goals, Read!* bookmark. Select one goal at a time to brainstorm obstacles and share solutions before moving on to the next. For example, list problems students may have reaching their target number of books or finding time to read. Then brainstorm ways to fix that problem such as finding more time to read and choosing books by an author whose books you devour quickly. Discuss possible obstacles and solutions to reaching goals by creating a chart like the one in Figure 3.20. Discuss ways to overcome obstacles. For example, perhaps students aren't sure where to get ideas for different genres of books to read, or they may not know about authors or books that may interest them. Some students might be busy at home with extracurricular activities and have a hard time carving out reading time, and others may have trouble settling down in school to read.

STEP 5: APPLICATION

Use the bookmarks in this lesson to conference with individual students throughout the school year. Coach students as they set goals for reading comprehension, fluency, and decoding using the *My Reading Strategies Goals* bookmark. As you confer with students, refer to your observations during class to help pinpoint goals.

STEP 6: REFLECTION

Oral or Written Response

Invite students to write reflections on their book choices in their literacy notebooks. Encourage them to rank order and compare and contrast titles from their book logs and bookmarks. Here are a few prompts for their reflections:

- I notice I enjoy reading mostly _____ [genre] at this time because _____.
- I like this type of book because _____.
- Some titles I especially enjoyed include _____ and _____.
- The best book I've read lately is _____. I like it the most because _____.
- A book I really want to read next is_____ because _____.
- I am making progress on my reading goals because now I am better at _____ _____ and also _____.

ADAPTATION AND EXTENSION

- *Lunch Bunch:* Invite students who have similar genre goals to eat lunch with you to discuss the books they are reading now and books they might enjoy. For example, students who wish to read more mysteries meet as a group with you.
- *Take a Selfie:* In this case, a selfie is a photograph taken of the reader with his or her book. (Miller, 2009). A "shelfie" may also be a photograph of the book and only the student's first name if you don't want to reveal student faces or identities. Post shelfies in the classroom, hallway, or on the school or class website.
- *Poetry Break*: Encourage students to love poetry as a genre all year long with poetry breaks. Either pass out poetry books or have students store poetry in their desks so they will be ready when you choose a random time to signal for a poetry break. Steven L. Layne shares the following idea in *Best Ever Literacy Survival Tips: 72 Lessons You Can't Teach Without* (Oczkus, 2012):

  > My elementary and middle school classes loved poetry breaks, when I would cease instruction in a manner that appeared completely impromptu and wildly yell something like "POETRY BREAK!" They were trained to know that this meant everyone was to grab any poetry book from my large collection, find a comfy spot, and read some poems—or grab a partner and read them aloud together. (p. 6)

- *Nonfiction Break*: This idea is a spin-off of the poetry break. Alert students at a random surprise moment that it is time for a nonfiction break! Students pause their work and read high-interest nonfiction texts that you pass out or that students already have at their desks. As an option, they can look up articles of interest online. Add a healthy snack to the nonfiction or poetry breaks to add more fun to the surprise reading moments in your classroom.
- *English Language Learner Suggestion*: Discuss the academic language associated with goal setting, including *goal, plan,* and *challenge*. Use the *Ready, Set Goals, Read! bookmark* to help students set reading goals.
- *Struggling Reader Suggestion*: On separate days, meet with struggling readers in a small group to model and discuss one area of goal setting in each meeting using the *Ready, Set Goals, Read! Bookmark*. Discuss in separate sessions number of books, kinds of books, time spent reading, and challenge of books. Use appropriate examples from your own reading.

EVALUATION

"I can . . ." Statements

- I can set and reach realistic goals for increasing the number of books I read.
- I can set goals for reading different types of genres.
- I can set goals for reading increasingly more challenging types of books.
- I can set goals for increasing my reading minutes at school and at home.
- I can set goals for using comprehension strategies before, during, and after reading.
- I can set goals for improving my reading fluency in rate, accuracy, and prosody.
- I can set goals for using a variety of decoding strategies to figure out words.

Behavior Indicators

- Identifies a goal for reading more books by setting a target number and a time-line for reaching the goal.
- Identifies a goal for reading different kinds of genres of books in a given time frame.
- Identifies a goal for spending more time reading by setting minute goals for reading at school and at home.
- Identifies a goal for reading more challenging books by identifying what makes them challenging, such as more words on the pages, more pages, or chapters.
- Sets a goal to read more challenging books in a given time frame.

~ 4

Stopping the Summer Slide

"A reader lives a thousand lives before he dies," said Jojen. "The man who never reads lives only one."
—George R. R. Martin, *A Dance with Dragons*

Until I feared I would lose it, I never loved to read. One does not love breathing.
—Harper Lee, *To Kill a Mockingbird*

Summer is a great time for playing, swimming, bike riding, picnicking, and many other fun activities. For many students, though, summer is not a time for reading. This is indeed unfortunate, for research has shown that if children do not continue reading during the summer months, they are likely to regress in their reading achievement—ending the summer reading with less proficiency than at the beginning (Allington & McGill-Franzen, 2013; Kim & White, 2011). According to some studies, students can lose upward of three months of reading achievement over a summer by not engaging in reading; between grades 1 and 6, the cumulative regression in reading achievement can be well over a year (Mraz & Rasinski, 2007). Of course, there is a flip side to summer reading, too. The students who do engage in reading and reading-related activities maintain and increase their reading achievement over the summer.

Knowing the results of those studies, we believe the part of our students' lives we call "summer" should be a time to continue students' growth as readers. Through the previous chapters, we have provided you with lessons on various key competencies for reading success. These lessons have spiraled through the school year so that the individual competencies continue to be the focus of instruction throughout the year. In

Chapter 4, you will find that we have continued our focus on the same essential reading competencies but with an emphasis on how parents (and teachers) can continue their students' reading development through the summer. Here you will find instructional tools and approaches that you can share with the parents of your students to make reading fun and educational, and to keep your students literacy strong!

Literacy-Strong Summer Scenarios
Family Games

In Mrs. Close's flyer for parents about summer reading, she included a list of family games that would encourage her 4th grade students to play with words. The games included Boggle, Balderdash, Wheel of Fortune, Scrabble, and online games such as Text Twist, Words with Friends, and Wordo (see Lesson 2). She recommended that families choose one evening a week as Family Game Night and spend an hour or so playing various word games that are at a suitable developmental level for the children.

"Of all the recommendations I made for parents, this one really surprised me," Mrs. Close mentioned in an interview. "When I sent home a survey at the end of the summer, about half the parents indicated that they actually did Family Game Night with their children. Many had not thought that playing board games such as Scrabble could help their child's reading." Interestingly, when the next school year began, many of the 5th grade teachers reported to Mrs. Close that the students had lobbied for the opportunity to continue playing word games in school. "When students begin begging to engage in word learning, even if it's a game, you know you are on to something!"

Parent and Partner Reading

Joan Siefert knows that reading development is a cumulative thing. The more reading her 3rd grade students do, the more they grow. It doesn't matter what you read, as long as you read something. She also knows that reading with someone else can be a big motivator. As a result, she searched for texts that students could read with a partner over the summer. Some of her favorites include the following titles.

- *I Am the Dog, I Am the Cat* by Donald Hall
- *You Read to Me and I'll Read to You: Very Short Stories to Be Read Together* by Mary Ann Hoberman
- *You Read to Me and I'll Read to You: Very Short Fables to Be Read Together* by Mary Ann Hoberman
- *Joyful Noise* by Paul Fleischman

- *I Am Phoenix* by Paul Fleischman
- *Pain and the Great One* by Judy Blume
- *Once Upon a Cool Motorcycle Dude* by Kevin O'Malley
- *Partner Poems for Building Fluency* by Timothy Rasinski, David Harrison, and Gay Fawcett

Ms. Siefert sent these titles to parents near the end of the school year, described the nature of the books, and invited parents to read them with their children. Over half of the parents took the bait and had a ball reading with their children. "We had moms reading with sons, dads with daughters, and just about all different combinations you can think of. I even had a couple parents contact me for other books that could be read as partners."

Anticipating the Coming Year

Fourth grade teacher Calvin Stark is not one to put things off. As soon as the second-year teacher was informed of the members of his class for the coming year, he immediately went to work to connect with parents. He created an introductory letter to parents in which he identified topics he intended to cover with students over the coming year—the Great Depression, the Vietnam War, weather and climate change, and the federal government, among others. In his letter, he asked parents if they had experience in these areas and would be willing to share their expertise with his class, and if they had any items or artifacts related to the topic that they could share.

Mr. Stark was overwhelmed with the response he received—not just parents' willingness to talk with students, but also to bring in items that helped to add depth and context to what students were reading. "Several students had grandparents who were Vietnam veterans. They were more than happy to come to the class to talk about their experience in the war. When we studied the Great Depression and read books such as *Out of the Dust* (by Karen Hesse) and *Children of the Great Depression* (by Russel Freedman), parents brought in artifacts that had belonged to their own parents and grandparents who had lived through the Depression. Imagine the conversation we had in class when I held up a hair curling iron that did not have an electric cord attached to it and a doily from a flour sack made by a student's great-grandmother!

"What parents contributed really added to students' understanding of these events and how the texts that we read related to them. But more important I discovered that parents and family members want to be involved in their children's school lives. They just need an open invitation." As a result, Mr. Stark plans to make his introduction and summer invitation to parents a regular part of his teaching.

Addressing Summer Reading Challenges

Summer can be "make or break," especially for students who struggle with reading. If 3rd, 4th, and 5th graders choose not to read during the summer, they are likely to fall further behind in their reading development. If, on the other hand, struggling readers can be motivated to read as little as 20 to 30 minutes per day throughout the summer, it is likely that they will make progress in their reading and set the stage for growth when the next school year begins. The essential challenge, then, is how to keep students reading when they have so many other activities to distract them.

Questions Teachers Ask to Address Summer Reading Challenges

- How can I, as the child's teacher, communicate with families and affect reading at home during the summer months?
- How can families find time for reading and reading-related activities?
- In what ways can families integrate literacy into typical summer activities?
- What resources are available in my community to promote literacy during the summer months?
- How can I track students' reading during the summer months?

Essentials for Sustaining Strength Through the Summer

1. You've Got Mail!

Children love receiving mail—snail mail or electronic mail. Before the end of the school year, collect students' (or families') email addresses or have parents write their child's name and mailing address on two or three postcards. Then, over the course of the summer, drop notes to your students reminding them to read, perhaps even suggesting a couple titles that your students would enjoy. Check with your community library to be sure the titles are available.

2. Family Read-Alouds

The power of reading to children of all ages, whether in school or at home, cannot be overstated. Children love to be read to by parents as well as teachers, and they benefit by having larger vocabularies, improved comprehension, and more enthusiasm about reading. Encourage parents to read to their children nightly. They can take turns reading or both can read to their children every evening. Not only are the children strengthening their literacy, but the parents are creating wonderful memories that will last a lifetime. Provide parents with the titles and authors of books you know children would love to hear.

3. Family Reads: Make It Interactive

Some books and poems are meant to be read by more than one reader. Like Joan Siefert, you can encourage parents to find such books, divide up the reading parts, and read with their children. It is great fun to share a poem or story with family members in this way. Having read a book or poem once, family members can switch parts and read it again and again.

4. Family Reads: Parents as Listeners

Research has shown that children can improve their reading by reading to their parents (Rasinski & Padak, 2009). Parents who listen to their children read in a positive and supportive manner allow children to demonstrate their growing competence in reading. Encourage parents to take a few minutes to listen to their children read and to follow the reading with positive, enthusiastic, and encouraging comments. When children feel safe and successful in their reading, they are more likely to read more. Brainstorm with parents to create a list of thoughtful comments they could make in response to their children's reading (e.g., "I love how you read that story with expression"; "Wow, you impressed me with your word decoding. There were some difficult words in that passage"; "It is fun to listen to you read. I hope we can do this every evening").

5. Summer Songs and Rhythmical Words

Just as the summer air is filled with the rhythmical sounds of birds, crickets, and other insects, it can be filled with the sounds of song and poetry. There are so many poems available for children and families to read, rehearse, recite, and celebrate. Simply do an online search for "summer songs for children," "patriotic songs," and "summer poetry for children," and you and parents will discover more than enough rhythmical words to challenge even the most enthusiastic crickets! The rhythm, rhyme, and brevity of poems and songs make them easy for all children to learn to read.

6. Summer Is the Right Time for Writing

Writing and reading are reciprocal processes. To write, we need to read. Think of all the things that children can write over the summer months with their parents and other family members. Here's a list of writing activities that your students might find enjoyable:

- Write a daily journal, recording personal thoughts and observations during nature walks or at family gatherings.
- Write a daily journal describing all the activities during a summer trip.

- Keep a dialogue journal, alternating days on which the parent and student make their entries.
- Write letters (snail mail or electronic) to family members across the country. Students may receive replies from their family members as well—what a treat!
- Write and perform poetry. Learn how to write parodies of popular poems at www.gigglepoetry.com.

7. It May Be Television, but It's Still Reading

What happens when you turn on the captioning feature on your home television? Instant reading material! When watching captioned television, children will hear the words being uttered by the speaker while seeing the same words appear on the screen. It is natural for our eyes to be drawn to the words on the screen. It may not be the most effective way for children to read, but it is reading. Parents can easily ensure that when the television is on in the summer, the captioning feature is also on to give their children an extra dose of reading.

8. Check Out Your Community

Parents need to be aware of the community resources they can turn to in helping their children remain literacy strong. Community libraries offer a wide range of engaging programs to keep children reading over the summer months. Other organizations and programs also may support summer literacy. Check out the local bookstores, the local newspaper, the city government, the parks and recreation department, places of worship, and the local university. Teachers and principals may wish to contact some local organizations in advance to determine if they would be willing to support literacy learning in some way. In many instances, these organizations only need to be asked.

9. Monitor Summer Reading

It is a good idea to attempt to track the reading that students do over the summer. Perhaps provide parents with a monthly calendar filled with literacy ideas. You can ask parents to estimate and report the number of minutes their children read each day of the summer. The calendar itself can act as a reminder for parents to keep literacy in mind. At the end of the summer, teachers can use the calendars to determine just how successful they were at encouraging children and families to engage in summer reading and writing.

10. Build That Reading Foundation: The Fluency Development Lesson

Research has shown that many, if not most, 3rd through 5th grade students who struggle in reading exhibit difficulties in foundational reading competencies (e.g., word knowledge and recognition, reading fluency). The Fluency Development Lesson (FDL) accelerates students' growth in these areas, employing short reading passages (poems, story segments, other texts) that students read and reread over a short period of time. Here is the format for the lesson in a school setting:

1. The teacher introduces a new short authentic text *with voice* (meant for rehearsal and performance) and reads it to the students two or three times while the students follow along. Text may be a poem or a segment from a basal passage or literature book.

2. The teacher and students discuss the nature and content of the passage.

3. Teacher and students read the passage chorally several times. Antiphonal reading and other variations are used to create variety and maintain engagement.

4. The teacher organizes student pairs. Each student practices the passage three times while his or her partner listens and provides support and encouragement.

5. Individuals and groups of students perform their reading for the class or other audience.

6. The students and their teacher choose three or six words from the text to add to the word bank or word wall.

7. Students engage in word study activities (e.g., word sorts with word bank words, word walls, flash card practice, defining words, and word games).

8. The students take a copy of the passage home to practice with parents and other family members.

9. Students return to school the next day and read the passage to the teacher or a partner who checks for fluency and accuracy.

10. The next day, students are led by the teacher in reading the previous day's text a few more times. Then the teacher introduces a new poem and the lesson begins anew (Rasinski, 2010).

The FDL can be adapted for home use, and parents can be trained to use it with their children. Since children would be doing the lesson at home, a parent would be taking on the role of the teacher, working through step 7, and there would be no student pairing. Alternatively, parents could hire tutors to work with their children in reading using the structure of the FDL.

11. Books for Summer Reading

Here is a list of books that parents can use for reading aloud to students during the summer break:

- *The Truth About My Unbelievable Summer* by David Cali
- *One Good Thing About America* by Ruth Freeman
- *Now You See Them, Now You Don't: Poems About Creatures That Hide* by David Harrison
- *Echo* by Pam Munoz Ryan
- *Tornadoes* by Seymour Simon
- *One Crazy Summer* by Rita William-Garcia

12. Summer Word Ladder

Number a blank sheet of paper, from 1 to 12 vertically. Write the word *summer* next to number 1. Then make 11 more words by adding, subtracting, and changing letters from the previous word. Listen closely for the clues given by the teacher. Then sort the words you made into categories—words that have something to do with summer and those that don't. Be prepared to explain your choices.

1. Summer — Add an *L* and change the second *M* to a *B* to make another word for sleeping.
2. Slumber — Take away one letter to make wood that is used for building.
3. Lumber — Add one letter to make a person who works with pipes involved in the distribution of water in a building.
4. Plumber — Take away three letters to make a kind of fruit.
5. Plum — Rearrange the letters to make another word for a mass or blob.
6. Lump — Change one letter to make a word that describes how a person with an injured leg might walk.
7. Limp — Take away one letter to make a body part used for kissing.
8. Lip — Change one letter to make another word that means to tear or pull apart.
9. Rip — Change one letter to make a word that means to free yourself from something.
10. Rid — Change one letter to make a color.
11. Red — Add one letter to make a great activity to do during the summer.
12. Read

Overview of Chapter 4 Lessons

Lesson 1.   Word Study: Decoding—Syllable Scoop Search

Lesson 2.   Vocabulary: Gaming with Words—Family Wordo

Lesson 3.   Vocabulary: Analyzing Words—Finding Word Roots Throughout the Summer

Lesson 4.   Vocabulary: Associating Words—Words and Their Crazy Relatives

Lesson 5.   Fluency: Phrasing, Pacing, Expressing—Celebrating USA on Independence Day

Lesson 6.   Comprehension: Previewing—Preview Power

Lesson 7.   Comprehension: Inferring and Drawing Conclusions—Summer Book Buddies

Lesson 8.   Comprehension: Questioning for Close Reading—Question Generator

Lesson 9.   Comprehension: Determining Importance and Summarizing—Movie Message Madness

Lesson 10.   Comprehension: Motivating Readers—Splash into Summer Reading!

LESSON 1. WORD STUDY: DECODING

Title SYLLABLE SCOOP SEARCH

Trailer I scream. You scream. We all scream for ice cream! The cool sensation of ice cream helps to beat the summer heat. One scoop, two scoops—the higher the better. In this lesson we will keep this summer treat a part of the learning experience by searching for words with certain "ingredients" to make up just the right scoop to place on our cones. Each scoop will contain a delicious sprinkle of syllables to satisfy our sweet tooth for decoding and spelling accuracy.

Literacy Enhancer Word Study: Decoding—Syllables

Key Academic Vocabulary
(Terms spiraled from previous lessons)

Cinquain: A five-line poem originally based on syllabic patterns

Closed Syllable: A syllable that has only one vowel followed by a consonant; the vowel is usually pronounced as a short vowel sound

Decoding: Translating a printed word into its oral representation. In word decoding, readers use a variety of strategies including phonics (sound symbol relationships), structural analysis (prefix, base word, suffix), and context

Diphthong: A unit of sound gliding the vowel sound by the combination of a vowel digraph, allowing the tongue to move and change

Haiku: A form of Japanese poetry used mainly to describe nature and the seasons in a syllabic restricted format

Meter: Stressed and unstressed syllables of poetry forming a rhythmic pattern

Multisyllabic: Having more than one syllable

Open Syllable: A syllable ending in only one vowel; the vowel is usually pronounced as a long vowel sound

Prefix: An affix placed in front of a root or base word to add to the meaning of it

Segmenting: Breaking a word by phoneme (sound) or syllables

Stressed Syllable: Accented syllable that is emphasized by sounding louder, with a higher pitch than the other syllables in the word; can change the meaning of the word

Syllable: A part of a word that contains only one vowel sound; words can be made of one or more syllables

Vowel Digraph: A pair of vowel letters coming together to form a vowel team representing one sound

Learning Objectives

- Examine word analysis skills in decoding words through multisyllabic awareness.
- Explore syllable guidelines for accenting syllables.
- Investigate elements of haiku and cinquain poetry and how syllables play the key role.

Essential Questions

- How does separating words into syllables help the reader decode (read) and encode (spell)?
- How does stressing the syllable help the reader to decode, pronounce a word, and even write certain types of poetry?

STEP 1: PREPARATION

Organize Materials

- *Syllable Scoop Search* reproducible
- *Parent Letter for Decoding* reproducible
- Selected text aligned to topic of study
- Word Work Journals or Writing Notebooks

STEP 2: INITIATION

Summer Seasonal Cinquain Poetry

Review how a classic cinquain poem can be measured by counting the number of stressed and unstressed syllables in each line.

Line 1 (Noun): 2 syllables, 1 stress	**Sum**/mer
Line 2 (Adjectives): 4 syllables, 2 stresses	**Laz**/y, **live**/ly
Line 3 (Verbs): 6 syllables, 3 stresses	**swim**/ming, **read**/ing, **play**/ing
Line 4 (Expression): 8 syllables, 4 stresses	/**on**/ /**fam**/i/ly /**fun**/ /va/**ca**/tion
Line 5 (Synonym): 2 syllables, 1 stress	**Re**/freshed

Highlight the word *refresh* from the cinquain poem. Isolate the *re-* prefix and review the meaning of *re-* ("again") and how it changes the meaning of the root word. Ask students to think of ways they can get refreshed in the summer (e.g., going to an ice cream parlor, swimming in a pool, drinking lemonade). Share how this lesson will focus on ice cream and scooping up syllables for our flavorful cones.

STEP 3: DEMONSTRATION

Refreshing Summer Syllable Scoops

1. Model dividing syllables in words using the *Syllable Segmentation* reproducible found in Chapter 2, Lesson 1. You can use a slash mark, a raised dot, or a hyphen to demonstrate the syllable segmentation.
2. Review the ice cream cone choices from the refreshing summer *Syllable Scoop Search* reproducible (see Figure 4.1). Explain how the cone choices provided add the foundational flavor for the types of syllable scoops we will search for as we top off our refreshing ice cream cones.

STEP 4: COLLABORATION

Have students study words or phrases that pertain to the season and examine the syllable segmentation to create their own haiku or cinquain poem. They can record the process on the *Haiku Writing* reproducible from Chapter 2 or the *Cinquain Poem* reproducible from Chapter 3. Engage in conversational coaching by asking students to discuss the following questions with diverse partners:

- How does separating words into syllables help the reader decode (read) and encode (spell)?
- What strategies can I use to help me decode unknown words in my reading?

STEP 5: APPLICATION

Students can select words to analyze from their haiku or cinquain poem by syllable mapping and record their syllable and stress analysis in their Word Work Journals. Have students create a *Syllable Scoop Search*, writing their own description for a "flavorful cone" and then searching for words to make up each ice cream scoop.

STEP 6: REFLECTION

Oral or Written Response

Have students respond to the essential questions through oral or written response in their Word Work Journals:

- How many syllable segments are in the word ___? How are the words segmented?
- How does stressing the syllable help the reader to decode, pronounce a word, and even write certain types of poetry?

ADAPTATION AND EXTENSION

Revisit the Decoding lessons and the Adaptation and Extension sections in earlier lessons for a variety of examples of how to strengthen students' abilities for this strategy of decoding: Vowel Teams in Chapter 1, Syllable Structure in Chapter 2, and Stressing Over Syllables in Chapter 3.

- *Parents and Tutors:* Send the *Parent Letter for Decoding* (Figure 4.2) to solicit additional support for these skills at home.
- *Parents and Tutors*: Send a letter to parents and offer a weekly plan of activities that can be used to improve students' decoding strategies and to help bring meaning to a text.
- *Small-Group Instruction:* Provide examples of how to segment syllables. Search through texts and find words to match the characteristics on the syllable segmentation.
- *Independent Work*: Have students do a *syllable scoop search*, writing their own description for a "flavorful cone" and then searching for words to make up each ice cream scoop.
- *English Language Learner Suggestion*: Have students practice Sound Segmenting (Ellery, 2014). Show a picture card that represents a word. Have the student say what the object is in the picture. Roll a ball of clay into a long horizontal log to represent the word. Have the student break off a piece of the clay as he or she says each syllable segment in the word. Next, have the student pick up the first syllable part of the clay and share the syllable it represents. Then, have them pick up the second syllable representation and orally pronounce that syllable, continuing until all syllables have been expressed. Once all the syllables have been segmented, have them begin to blend each syllable together by pinching the clay to connect all syllables to its original form. Finally, have them orally pronounce the word again and locate it in the text and read it in the sentence contextually.
- *Struggling Reader Suggestion*: Select words from a text and break each word into syllables. Write each syllable on an index card or sticky note, mix them up, and place in stacks. Have the students pick cards from the pile and begin to sort and rearrange them to create a word. They can record the blended word in their Word Work Journals, placing a slash mark between each syllable to demonstrate the syllable break.

EVALUATION

"I can . . ." Statements

- I can decode multisyllabic words.
- I can identify the vowel digraph in a word.
- I can examine a syllable and determine the affix in each syllable.

Behavior Indicators

- Identifies the number of syllables in a word.
- Determines the affix in a word.
- Identifies stress and unstressed syllables in a word.

FIGURE 4.1

Syllable Scoop Search Reproducible

Name: _____ Text: _____

Directions: Search through the text and find words to match the characteristics on the cone. Draw a scoop of ice cream with a word to match each of the cones. Have each scoop represent only one word, and each cone can have one or more scoops—the higher the yummier! Enjoy!

Has 2 syllables, both are closed	Has 2 syllables, both are open	Has 1 syllable with a vowel digraph
Has 2 syllables with a double consonant	Has 2 syllables and is a compound word	Has 3 syllables with a prefix or suffix

---

FIGURE 4.2

Parent Letter for Decoding Reproducible

Dear Parents,

You may find this weekly plan of activities useful during the summer to enhance your child's ability to decode words and bring meaning to a text. This lesson arrangement will encourage your child to apply the writing, spelling, and decoding skills learned this year in class. Each week, add a different list of words, poems, or books for your child to use while practicing the skills.

Monday: Using selected text, search for words with vowel digraphs and list them in a Word Journal (e.g., spiral notebook). Select a word from the list and ask the following questions: What is the vowel digraph in the word_____? What other words have the same vowel digraph as the word _____? How do you position your mouth for the vowel digraph in the word _____? Is it a diphthong? Repeat with other words in the list.

Tuesday: Using words from the vowel digraph word list in their Word Journals, have students select three words with the same vowel digraph and use them in sentences, poetry writing, or creating their own riddles.

Wednesday: Go on a nature walk with your child or display nature photographs of a season of the year. Have your child record the observations of nature in their Word Journal. Have your child write a haiku using the words recorded. Ask your child: How many syllables are in _____? Does the haiku paint a mental image of _____? Explain it.

Thursday: Using the words collected during the nature walk, sort them using syllable patterns, number of syllables, stressed or unstressed syllable patterns, or by affixes.

Friday: Have your child write a cinquain. Ask: How many syllables do you hear in the word_____? How do you know? Does your cinquain paint a mental image of _____? Explain it. How can stressed and unstressed syllables add or change the meaning of what is being read?

Sincerely,

Your Child's Teacher

LESSON 2. VOCABULARY: GAMING WITH WORDS

Title FAMILY WORDO

Trailer Nearly everyone has played Bingo—a simple game in which letters and numbers are randomly called out and players cover those spots on their cards with chips or markers. When a row, column, or diagonal of the Bingo card is covered with markers, the player calls out "Bingo" and (after markers are verified) is declared a winner. Often a prize is given to the winner. The concept of Bingo can be applied to a vocabulary learning and reinforcement game called Wordo. The simplicity and ease of learning Wordo makes it particularly suited for play at home with family members of all ages.

Literacy Enhancer Vocabulary: Gaming with Words—Decoding, Spelling

Key Academic Vocabulary
(Terms spiraled from previous lessons)

Adjective: A word or phrase used to describe a noun

Anagram: A word formed from another word by using or rearranging its letters (e.g., *angel* turns into *angle*)

Analysis: The process of studying something for the purpose of identifying its essential features or characteristics

Consonants: Language sounds and letters that are represented by all letters of the alphabet except *a, e, i, o, u,* and sometimes *y* and *w*

Decoding: The process of translating a printed word into sounds by using knowledge of the conventions of letter sound relationships and knowledge about pronunciations of words to derive written words

Definition: A statement that explains the meaning of a word

Features: Characteristics that distinguish one person or item from another

Noun: A word used to identify any of a class of people, places, or things

Spelling: The process of writing or naming the letters of a word

Syllable: A part of a word that contains only one vowel sound; words can be made of one or more syllables

Verb: A word used to describe an action

Vocabulary: A collection of words or phrases and the meanings they represent that make up a language or that a person has knowledge of

Vowel: Language sounds and letters represented by the letters *a, e, i, o, u,* and sometimes *y* (e.g., *cry*) and *w* (e.g., cow)

Word Ladder: A game-like activity where one word is transformed into another by adding, subtracting, or changing letters.

Word Sort: A process used to categorize words according to features (*closed* means that categories are provided and words are matched to them; *open* means that categories are determined by students as they discern the common features of the words groups)

Wordo: A Bingo-like game in which players attempt to develop a row or line of words on a playing grid

Learning Objectives

- Reinforce students' corpus of words or concepts (vocabulary).
- Devise semantic and structural clues for words under study.
- Increase students' enjoyment in exploring and learning words with friends and family members.

Essential Questions

- What are the meanings of sets of words under study?
- What are the structural elements of words under study?

STEP 1: PREPARATION

Organize Materials

- *Wordo Cards (4 x 4)* reproducible
- *Wordo Cards (5 x 5)* reproducible
- Five sets of words from different academic categories
- *Wordo Directions and Family Letter* reproducible
- Word Journals

STEP 2: INITIATION

Wordo

Get students thinking about the game by teaching them to sing the song, Wordo to the tune of "Bingo." Students should clap for the letters that are deleted from each succeeding verse.

> There was a teacher had a game
> And Wordo was its name-O

W-O-R-D-O, W-O-R-D-O, W-O-R-D-O
And Wordo was its name-O

Wordo is a lot of fun
And Wordo is our game-O
W-O-R-D-_, W-O-R-D-_, W-O-R-D-_
And Wordo is our game-O

Wordo helps you learn hard words
And Wordo is our game-O
W-O-R-_-_, W-O-R-_-_, W-O-R-_-_
And Wordo is our game-O

We play Wordo in our school
And Wordo is our game-O
W-O-_-_-_, W-O-_-_-_, W-O-_-_-_
And Wordo is our game-O

We'll play Wordo in our homes
And Wordo is our game-O
W-_-_-_-_, W-_-_-_-_, W-_-_-_-_
And Wordo is our game-O

We'll play Wordo every day
And Wordo is our game-O
_-_-_-_-_, _-_-_-_-_, _-_-_-_-_
And Wordo is our game-O

STEP 3: DEMONSTRATION

1. Several weeks before the end of the school year, begin playing Wordo on a regular basis with your students using the materials described above. Choose words that the class has already studied and explored for each Wordo game. Figure 4.3 displays Wordo (4 × 4) cards and Figure 4.4 displays the Wordo (5 × 5) cards for more advanced students. Choose the card most appropriate for your students and make copies for them to take home to play with family members (we recommend a minimum of 25 copies per student family). If

using the (5 × 5) card, you will need at least 24 or more words per game set; 15 or more words if using the (4 × 4) card. As you will be asking your students to play Wordo for five weeks, develop five sets of words, one for each week. You may wish to divide your word sets into academic areas or categories (e.g., math, science, social studies, language arts). Make a copy of the word sets for each student in your class. After playing several rounds of Wordo, ask your students to share what they think of the game and how they think they might play it at home during the summer with their family.

2. When you have led students in playing Wordo for several days, invite volunteers to take on the role of master of ceremony (MC) or moderator. The MC will need to preview the words to create clues to present to classmates.

STEP 4: COLLABORATION

Divide your class into groups of four or five students. Have each group play several rounds of Wordo using a list of words that you provide. Every student should have a chance to be MC. Have students engage in conversational coaching using the essential questions:

- What are the meanings of sets of words under study?
- What are the structural elements of words under study?

STEP 5: APPLICATION

Near the end of the school year, provide students and their families with a packet that includes *Wordo Directions and Family Letter* reproducible (Figure 4.5), multiple copies of Wordo card reproducibles, and most important, the five sets of words that students and their families will use while playing the games.

STEP 6: REFLECTION

Oral or Written Response

At the beginning of the next school year, ask students to respond in writing to their Wordo game experience at home. The responses could include answers to the following questions:

- Did you enjoy playing Wordo games with your family over the summer? Why or why not?
- How often did you play with your family?
- How many people in your family played the game? Who were they?
- Did the other members of your family enjoy playing the game?

- What suggestions do you have for making this and any word games better for next summer?

ADAPTATION AND EXTENSION

- Encourage students who have younger siblings to make a Wordo game appropriate to share, using easier words and a 4 × 4 card structure.
- Invite other community members and agencies to play Wordo games during the summer months. The local community library could hold a tournament once a week for students. Other word and reading games could be included in the weekly game event.
- *Small-Group Instruction:* Take turns being the moderator and coming up with clues for the words.
- *Parents and Tutors:* Expand to a 6 × 6 matrix card and use 35–36 words. Or, play other word games like Scrabble, Boggle, and Balderdash.
- *Independent Work:* Have students find words in their current reading or current events to use in new games.
- *English Language Learner Suggestion*: Send home suggestions for words to be used in the home Wordo game. The list of words should include words you think are critical for ELLs to continue their progress in mastering English.
- *Struggling Reader Suggestion*: Send suggestions of words for the home games. The list of words should include those you think are essential for struggling readers to master. To progress in reading, high-frequency words should be mastered as soon as possible. You may wish to select words from the Fry Instant Word List (available online) to send as suggestions for the home games.

EVALUATION

"I can . . ." Statements

- I can read and understand the words we use in our games.
- I can brainstorm clues and come up with definitions for the words used in word games when I am the MC.
- I can teach other members of my family and my friends to play Wordo games.
- I can create my own game to play with others.

Behavior Indicators

- Plays Wordo games on a regular basis with family members over the summer.
- Develops mastery of the words used in Wordo games over the summer.
- Leads Wordo games as the master of ceremony.
- Creates Wordo games to play with others.
- Finds enjoyment in playing Wordo games with others.

FIGURE 4.3

Wordo Game Card Reproducible

W	O	R	D	O

Source: Literacy Strong All Year Long: Powerful Lessons for Grades 3-5 by Lori Oczkus, Valerie Ellery, and Timothy V. Rasinski. Copyright © 2018 ASCD. Readers may duplicate this figure for noncommercial use within their school.

FIGURE 4.4

Wordo Game Card (5 × 5) Reproducible

W	O	R	D	O

Source: Literacy Strong All Year Long: Powerful Lessons for Grades 3-5 by Lori Oczkus, Valerie Ellery, and Timothy V. Rasinski. Copyright © 2018 ASCD. Readers may duplicate this figure for noncommercial use within their school.

FIGURE 4.5

Wordo Directions and Family Letter Reproducible

Dear Students and Family Members,

Wordo is a word game that will help students maintain their vocabulary over the summer. Thank you for playing Wordo regularly as a family.

Materials

- Wordo game cards (enclosed)
- Five word sets (enclosed, use one set per week)
- A set of index cards or paper cut into card size
- Markers for covering words (e.g., bingo markers, poker chips, buttons, dried beans)

How to Play

For each game you will need a leader—the master of ceremonies (MC)—and at least two players. Participants should rotate into the MC role. If possible, plan to play the games several times a week, using a different set of words each week. Play time for each game is about 30 minutes.

The MC writes the words for the week on index cards (one word per card) and thinks of clues for each word. The clues can be the meaning of the word, other words that mean the same, rhyming words, and sentences that include the target word (without using the target word in the clue). Other options might be structural clues such as number of syllables, grammatical category, or presence of a prefix or suffix.

Each player gets one card and randomly records the words for the week on the game card (one per box). Players may choose to mark one box as the "free" spot (and not use one word on the list). When the cards are filled, the players are ready for the game.

The MC randomly selects one word at a time from the word deck and calls out the word or one of the clues. Players hear the word or clue, find it on their cards, and cover the box with a marker. The MC continues calling out randomly selected words from the word card deck and players cover the corresponding words on their cards.

The game continues until one player has a full column, row, or diagonal set of boxes covered and calls out "Wordo!" The player's card is checked for accuracy and declared the winner. A small prize may be given, cards are cleared, and a new game proceeds.

LESSON 3. VOCABULARY: ANALYZING WORDS

Title FINDING WORD ROOTS THROUGHOUT THE SUMMER

Trailer Summer—when students may have some free time—is a great opportunity to engage in pleasure reading. We want to stop the summer reading decline that many students experience, so consider incorporating a "treasure hunt" for students to search for the word roots they have studied throughout the year, along with a few additional roots they haven't met yet. The entire family can join in on this scavenger hunt, searching for word roots together. Students can share their findings at the beginning of the following school year and those who have found a requisite number can be awarded a prize and perhaps earn the title of "Astervocabophiles"—Star Word Lovers!

Literacy Enhancer Vocabulary: Analyzing Words, Decoding, Spelling

Key Academic Vocabulary

(Terms spiraled from previous lessons)

Greek: An ancient language whose words and word parts have influenced words in English

Latin: An ancient language whose words and word parts have influenced words in English

Word Roots: Base words, prefixes, and suffixes in English words that are derived primarily from Latin and Greek
(Word roots introduced during the school year)

Aqua-: A word root meaning water

Aster-: A word root meaning star

Astro-: A word root meaning star

Geo-: A word root meaning earth or land

Hydra-: A word root meaning water

Hydro-: A word root meaning water

Port-: A word root meaning carry

Terr- / Terra-: A word root meaning earth or land
(Prefixes introduced during the school year)

Bi-: A prefix meaning two

Co-: A prefix meaning with or together

Col-: A prefix meaning with or together

Com-: A prefix meaning with or together

Con-: A prefix meaning with or together

Ex-: A prefix meaning out of

Pro-: A prefix meaning forward or outward

Quad-: A prefix meaning four

Quar-: A prefix meaning four

Tri-: A prefix meaning three

Uni-: A prefix meaning one
(New prefixes in this lesson)

Port-: A prefix meaning carry

Pre-: A prefix meaning before

Re-: A prefix meaning again

Sub-: A prefix meaning below or under

Learning Objectives

- Expand competency in parsing words into meaningful base and affixes.
- Learn critical English word roots and affixes derived from Latin and Greek.
- Expand vocabulary by learning English words derived from Latin and Greek words.

Essential Questions

- How does knowledge of Latin and Greek roots help students understand words in which they are located?
- To what extent are words derived from Latin and Greek present in English words?

STEP 1: PREPARATION

Organize Materials

- *Word Root Scavenger Hunt Challenge* reproducible
- Texts that contain examples of word roots
- Word Journals

STEP 2: INITIATION

Digging for Word Roots

During the summer months, we want to encourage students to use their newfound knowledge of word roots in their own reading. Re-explain the concept of word roots and affixes—word patterns that have a particular meaning—and provide examples from previous lessons (e.g., *uniform, bicycle, companion, collection, conspire, proclaim, exhale, Mediterranean, geography, hydrant, aquarium*). Ask students to break the words down into roots and determine the meaning of the compound words by combining the meanings of the individual words.

Draw attention to the new roots being added for this lesson: *sub-, port-, re-,* and *pre-*. Define these roots and brainstorm with students about English words that contain these roots. Display the brainstormed words on a classroom word wall and have students copy these new roots and words in their Word Journals.

STEP 3: DEMONSTRATION

Word Root Scavenger Hunt Challenge

1. The Word Root Scavenger Hunt Challenge is a method for encouraging students to look for word roots in their own reading. Find examples of texts that contain examples of the word roots you want students to find.

2. Demonstrate the process for the scavenger hunt. Tell students that during the summer you will be challenging them to look for the roots they have studied through the school year, as well as some common roots they should already know. Make two copies of the *Word Root Scavenger Hunt Challenge* reproducible (see Figure 4.6) for each student. (Students will be using one copy of this form to record their word root hunt during the summer months, and one to use in class with partners.)

3. The *Word Root Scavenger Hunt Challenge* reproducible has spaces for you to add more word roots of your choosing. You may want to expand your students' word root knowledge and disposition by including these common word roots: *graph-* and *gram-* (write), *tele-* (distant), and *photo-* (light).

4. Display several examples of texts that contain the target word roots.

5. Identify the words containing the word roots and explain how the root affects the meaning of the words. Then demonstrate how the word, the sentence in which it appears, and the source of the sentence are marked on the *Word Root Scavenger Hunt Challenge* reproducible. Go through several examples so students can do it on their own during the summer.

STEP 4: COLLABORATION

Before the school year ends, provide students with a copy of a text that contains several of the targeted word roots. Have them work with a partner to find the target roots, fill in the appropriate spaces on one of the copies of the *Word Root Scavenger Hunt Challenge* reproducible, and share their experiences. Provide supportive and formative assistance as needed. Engage in conversational coaching discussing the essential question: "How does knowledge of Latin and Greek roots help you understand words in which they are located?"

STEP 5: APPLICATION

During the remaining days of the school year, have students continue working with their partners to complete the reproducible that they began in the section above, looking for targeted word roots. At the end of the school year, determine which pairs of students found the most words and provide them with some form of recognition.

Explain to your students that you will be asking them to do a similar task at home during the summer. When they come across word roots in their own reading, they should mark the appropriate part of the second copy of the reproducible. Tell students that family members are permitted to help them. Create a letter for parents so that they are aware of the *Word Root Scavenger Hunt Challenge* and how they and other family members might participate in the activity. When summer begins, the challenge is on.

STEP 6: REFLECTION

Oral or Written Response

When school begins the following year, have your students return their completed *Word Root Scavenger Hunt Challenge* reproducible to you. If you are not the students' teacher for the new school year, you can coordinate with the next teacher to collect the sheets. Determine which students had the most complete sheets and provide them with some form of recognition.

Have students reflect and think about their experience of studying word roots during the previous school year and the summer, and then record their thoughts in their Word Journals. Ask them to think about the extent that their study of word roots has affected their ability to understand words and texts in which the words are located. Ask, "To what extent are words derived from Latin and Greek present in English words?"

ADAPTATION AND EXTENSION

- Encourage students to play word games at home (e.g., Wordo, Chapter 4, Lesson 2) using words that contain word roots, or they can make their own word ladders (Chapter 1, Lesson 2) in which a word with a word root connects to its meaning. Below is an example:

Terrace	Take away three letters to make a running competition.
Race	Change one letter to make what is at the front of your head.
Face	Change one letter to make a kind of fabric.
Lace	Change one letter to make another name for a street.
Lane	Change the last letter to make what a terrace is made of.
Land	A terrace is a flat piece of land often used as a patio or a garden.

- *Small-Group Instruction:* Have students work in teams of two or three to complete the scavenger hunt. Or, play Wordo games with the words found in the scavenger hunt.
- *Parents and Tutors:* Create sentences using key roots and discuss with students. For example, "In yesterday's baseball game, Joe Hunter hit three triples." What does a triple have to do with threes? What is meant by a "triple triple"?
- *Independent Work:* Once students have found words in their scavenger hunt, challenge them to invent new words and concepts using the roots they have hunted for and found.
- *English Language Learner Suggestion:* During the summer, you can send e-mail messages to parents with updates on the scavenger hunt. You may create or find texts that contain the targeted roots and share these with students and parents.
- *Struggling Reader Suggestion:* You can adjust the level of the challenge by adding or subtracting word roots.

EVALUATION

"I can . . ." Statements

- I can understand what words mean that contain the word roots we have studied.
- I can break longer words down into their root parts.
- I can identify words containing word roots in the texts I read.
- I can better understand texts that contain words that have the word roots we have studied.

Behavior Indicators

- Finds words in texts that contain word roots.
- Defines and understands words that contain word roots.
- Understands texts that contain word roots.
- Adds words to a growing vocabulary list using knowledge of word roots.

FIGURE 4.6

Word Root Scavenger Hunt Challenge Reproducible

Directions: Find the *word roots* that reflect the meanings indicated in your own reading. Record the word and its meaning, along with the sentence that contains it. Family members may help you with this challenge. Students who have found sentences with the most root words will be given special recognition.

Word Root	Found word and its meaning	Sentence in which the word is found
Uni – one		
Bi – two		
Tri – three		
Quad, Quar – four		
Com – with		
Col – with		
Co – with		
Con – with		
Pro – for, forward		
Ex – out of		
Terr(a) – earth, land		
Geo – earth, land		
Aqua – water		
Hydr(a,o) – water		
Aster – star		
Astro – star		
Sub – below		
Port – carry		
Re – again		
Pre – before		

LESSON 4. VOCABULARY: ASSOCIATING WORDS

Title: **WORDS AND THEIR CRAZY RELATIVES**

Trailer: Just like families, words have some colorful relatives, too! Aunts, uncles, grandparents, and cousins are connected through the family tree, and words connect to their own relatives—synonyms, antonyms, and homographs. Recognizing the relationships between words and their kin helps students to grow in their comprehension and writing. Providing students with rich vocabulary experiences involves lots of wide reading, word learning strategies, and opportunities for developing "word consciousness." When we make word study enjoyable with silly parody verses, fun read-aloud books, and wordplay, students willingly jump in and join in the fun.

Literacy Enhancer Vocabulary: Associating—Synonyms, Antonyms, and Homographs

Key Academic Vocabulary

(Terms spiraled from previous lessons)

Synonyms: Different words that have the same or similar meanings
(New terms in this lesson)

Antonyms: Different words that are opposites

Homographs: Words that are spelled the same but have different meanings; sometimes pronounced differently

Learning Objectives

- Define and identify examples of synonyms, antonyms, and homographs.
- Sort and match synonyms, antonyms, and homographs.

Essential Questions

- What are synonyms, antonyms, and homographs?
- What are examples of synonyms, antonyms, and homographs?
- How does knowing the synonyms, antonyms, and homographs for words help to better understand words?
- How can knowing about synonyms, antonyms, and homographs help when choosing words to use during speaking or writing?

STEP 1: PREPARATION

Organize Materials

- *Words and Their Crazy Relatives Parent Letter* reproducible
- *Synonym Cards* reproducible

- *Antonym Cards* reproducible
- *Homograph Cards* reproducible
- *Homograph Sketch Maker* reproducible
- Books featuring synonyms, antonyms, and homographs
- Colorful plastic eggs
- Literacy Notebooks

STEP 2: INITIATION

We Are Family

Discuss with the class the various generic names for family members. Share and list on the board titles such as *grandpa, grandma, uncle, aunt, mom, dad, cousin, brother,* and *sister*. Ask students to share the ways family members may be alike or different (e.g., look alike, sound alike, or think alike). Tell students that they will study ways that words are related to each other like family. Knowing how words relate to other words is helpful during reading.

STEP 3: DEMONSTRATION

Word Card Parade and Song

1. Using the sets of letters in the following list, write each word in big letters on a piece of paper. Invite a few students to come to the front of the room and have each student hold one word. The class may act out the word or turn to a partner to discuss meanings. Ask students what each set of words has in common and how the words are related.
   - **Set #1: Neat, Tidy, Clean**
   What do you notice about these words? How are they related?
   Students pair-share to discuss. The whole class discusses the set of words. Ask students if they know what this group of words is called. Share that they are called synonyms—words that are different but that mean the same thing. Write the word *synonym* on the board and ask partners to share a synonym pair. Ask students to turn to partners and come up with more synonyms for the word *neat* or other examples of synonyms.
   - **Set #2: Huge, Small; Push, Pull; Hot, Cold**
   What do you notice about these words? How are they related?
   Students pair-share to discuss. The whole class discusses the set of words. Ask students if they know what this group of words is called. Explain that these words are pairs of antonyms, or opposites. Write the word *antonym*

on the board. Ask students to turn to partners and to come up with more opposite pairs.

○ **Set #3: Nail, Watch, Bass**

Provide sentences for each of these words to show the different meanings and pronunciations or show sketches of a pair—for example, a nail and a hammer and a fingernail on a hand. Or write the homographs on the board and invite students to act the pairs of sentences out to demonstrate the meaning of the words.

– He pounded the nail into the board. I painted my nails.
– He watched the game on TV. Did you lose your watch?
– She plays the bass guitar. He caught a bass.

What do you notice about these words? How are they related? Students pair-share to discuss. The whole class discusses the set of words. Ask students if they know what this group of words is called. Explain that these words are homographs. Write the word *homograph* on the board. Underline the separate parts: *homo*, which means "same," and *graph* which means "spelling." Then they can remember that the word *homograph* means "same spelling." Ask students to turn to partners and come up with more pairs.

2. Sing the song "The Words Go Matching" to the tune of "The Ants Go Marching" to help students remember the three kinds of words in this lesson: synonyms, antonyms, and homographs. Hum the song together first to remember the tune, then try the verses below:

"The Words Go Matching"
The synonyms go matching meaning by meaning, hurrah hurrah
The synonyms go matching meaning by meaning, hurrah hurrah
The synonyms go matching meaning by meaning
Like *neat* and *tidy, dusting* and *cleaning*
And they all go marching down to the book on the page, boom boom boom

The antonyms are opposites like *hot* and *cold*, hurrah, hurrah
The antonyms are opposites like *hot* and *cold* hurrah, hurrah
The antonyms are opposites
Like *push* and *pull, stands* and *sits,*
And they all mean the opposite down to the book on the page, boom boom boom

Homographs are spelled the same like twins, like twins
Homographs are spelled the same like twins, like twins
But they don't mean the same we fear
Like *bow* and *bow* and *tear* and *tear*
And they may not sound the same down to the book on the page,
boom, boom, boom

STEP 4: COLLABORATION

Students can play several easy games with classmates to become more familiar with synonyms, antonyms, and homographs. The same games can be played at home with family members. You can provide a brief letter to parents explaining the process along with a chart of definitions and examples of word relationships. For an example, see *Words and Their Crazy Relatives Parent Letter* reproducible, Figure 4.7.

Synonyms: Beat the Clock Dump and Sort

Students cut out the synonym game cards (see Figure 4.8) and put them into a small paper bag. They shake the bag, dump the words on a desk or the floor, and sort them into groups of synonyms as quickly as possible. Students try to beat and improve their own times, not the times of others. Students should read aloud their categories and defend their synonym choices. Play with 1–4 players.

Antonyms: Concentration

Students cut apart their antonym game cards (see Figure 4.9) and play concentration with a partner. They turn all cut-out cards facedown and take turns flipping over two cards to see if they are an antonym pair or match. If they do not match, they turn the cards face down again. If the cards do match, students put them in their match pile. At the end, see which student has the most matches. As an option, students can play alone to match up the antonyms, racing the clock to beat their own time. Circulate and discuss the words with students. Play with 1–4 players.

Homographs: Card Head

Students cut the homograph game cards, mix them, and put them into a pile (see Figure 4.10). Turn the pile facedown. Students take turns drawing a card and without looking at it, hold it on their forehead facing out for the other students in the group to see. The "card head" tries guessing the word by asking up to 10 yes–no questions about the homograph. Play with 1–4 players.

FIGURE 4.7

Words and Their Crazy Relatives Parent Letter Reproducible

Dear Parents and Family,

As students increase their vocabulary, they become better readers and writers! Besides reading every day, which is the best way to increase vocabulary, your child can also play word games with physical cards or on electronic devices. Your child is learning about the different ways words can be related. Just like families that are filled with interesting characters, words have some colorful relatives, too! We've been learning about relationships between words—namely, synonyms, antonyms, and homographs. This chart on word relationships provides definitions and examples of these terms.

Synonyms Different words that have the same or similar meanings	**Antonyms** Words that mean the opposite of each other	**Homographs** Words that are spelled the same but have different meanings and are sometimes pronounced differently
Examples: neat, tidy hide/cover idea/thought	Examples: hot/cold unique/ordinary deep/shallow	Examples: **address** ___to speak to a group ___where you live **duck** ___to bend, perhaps to go under something ___a bird

Here are a few easy games to play at home that will help students learn words by relating them to one another. Use the cards of synonyms, antonyms, and homographs that your child brings home or go online for lists of these types of words, and use sticky notes or index cards to have the child help make word cards. Invite your child to illustrate the word cards and store them in plastic bags or envelopes.

Concentration: Turn all cut-out cards facedown and take turns flipping over two cards to see if they are an antonym pair or synonym match. If they do not match, players put the cards face down again. If the cards do match, put them in the winner's match pile. At the end, see who has the most matches.

Card Head: Mix the cards up and put into a pile. Turn the pile facedown. Players take turns drawing a card, and without looking at it, hold it on their forehead facing out for other players to see. The "card head" tries guessing the word by asking up to 10 yes or no questions about the word on the card. As an option, set a time limit of two minutes to guess the word. Players get one point for each word guessed correctly. Keep track of points.

Beat the Clock Dump and Sort: Put word cards into a small paper bag. Shake the bag, dump the words on a table or the floor, and sort them into groups or pairs as quickly as possible. Everyone tries to beat and improve their own times, not the times of others. Practice reading the words aloud.

Have fun with words and their crazy relatives!

Sincerely,

Your Child's Teacher

FIGURE 4.8
Synonym Cards Reproducible

Directions: Use these cards to play games like Concentration, Dump and Sort, Speed Sort, Go Fish, and Charades. Illustrate the words. Make pairs with the cards. Add your own words that mean the same to expand the pairs to groups of four words.

big	large	hollow	empty	
evil	wicked	funny	silly	
hide	cover	ill	sick	
idea	thought	jog	run	
rest	relax	rug	carpet	
yell	shout	weird	odd	
sniff	smell	correct	right	
present	gift	quick	swift	
quiet	calm	rock	stone	
hear	listen	under	beneath	

Source: Literacy Strong All Year Long: Powerful Lessons for Grades 3-5 by Lori Oczkus, Valerie Ellery, and Timothy V. Rasinski. Copyright © 2018 ASCD. Readers may duplicate this figure for noncommercial use within their school.

FIGURE 4.9

Antonym Cards Reproducible

Directions: Use these cards to play games like Concentration, Dump and Sort, Speed Sort, Go Fish, and Charades. Illustrate the words. Make pairs with the cards. Create your own cards with other words that mean the same to expand the pairs to groups of four words.

fail	succeed	closer	farther	
ordinary	unique	assist	avoid	
expensive	cheap	difficult	easy	
deep	shallow	interesting	boring	
inside	outside	safe	dangerous	
smooth	rough	brave	cowardly	
give	take	positive	negative	
first	last	acceptable	unsatisfactory	
tough	delicate	shrink	swell	

Source: Literacy Strong All Year Long: Powerful Lessons for Grades 3–5 by Lori Oczkus, Valerie Ellery, and Timothy V. Rasinski. Copyright © 2018 ASCD. Readers may duplicate this figure for noncommercial use within their school.

FIGURE 4.10

Homograph Cards Reproducible

Directions: Cut out and illustrate each card. Use these cards to play games like Concentration, Dump and Sort, Speed Sort, Go Fish, and Charades. Illustrate the words. Make pairs with the cards. Sketch pictures to go with each word. Add more!

address (speak to someone)	address (street and number)	book (reserve a table or room in advance)	book (pages held together)
cave (a place in a mountain made of rock or earth)	cave (to give in)	bear (animal)	bear (to cope or endure something)
chair (furniture to sit on)	chair (to head a committee)	duck (to bend down to go under some- thing or to crouch down)	duck (a bird)
jam (stuck somewhere or in a situation)	jam (spread made with fruit)	key (unlocks doors)	key (the important part)
match (sports event)	match (starts a fire)	nail (use with hammer)	nail (on fingers and toes)
seal (sea animal)	seal (closure on something)	tire (become bored)	tire (wheel)
show (performance or broadcast)	show (to display something)	pen (write with it)	pen (fenced area for animals)

STEP 5: APPLICATION

Station Work

At a station or their desks, students continue to use their cards for each of the games. Charades also works with any of the categories of words.

Books About Synonyms, Antonyms, and Homographs

Provide books that feature synonyms, antonyms, and homographs for enjoyment. Students may chart or illustrate and take notes on the words in their literacy notebooks, or they can prepare to read the book aloud to a little buddy and explain the words. See books listed under Adaptations and Extension.

Egg-cellent Match-Ups: Synonyms and Antonyms

Use colorful plastic eggs that can be taken apart and put back together for this activity. Write one word on each half of the egg. Make sure the corresponding egg halves don't match in *color*, so that students are reading the words and matching synonyms and antonyms rather than just matching egg colors. See Figure 4.11, Colorful Eggs.

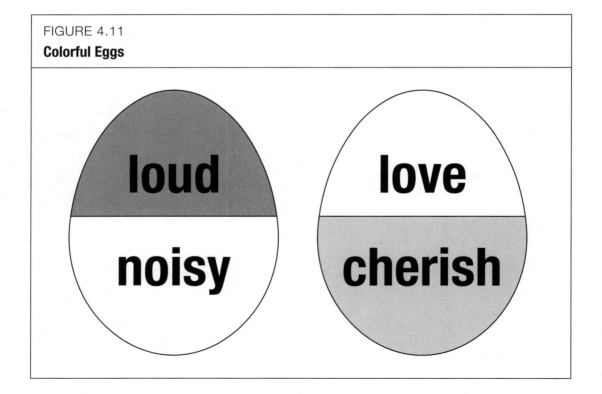

FIGURE 4.11
Colorful Eggs

STEP 6: REFLECTION

Oral or Written Response

Lead students in a discussion about the differences between synonyms, antonyms, and homographs. What are some of their favorites? Why? Why do authors use these words in their writing? How can students use them in theirs? Have students write in their literacy notebooks to record favorite examples and make sketches of synonyms, antonyms, and homographs, giving reasons why they enjoy them. See Figure 4.12 for a *Homograph Sketch Maker* reproducible.

ADAPTATION AND EXTENSION

- Use these read-aloud books to demonstrate examples of synonyms, antonyms, and homographs:
    - *Amelia Bedelia* book series by Peggy Parish
    - *Pitch and Throw, Grasp and Know: What Is a Synonym?* by Brian Cleary
    - *Stroll and Walk, Babble and Talk: More About Synonyms* by Brian Cleary
    - *If You Were a Synonym* by Michael Dahl
    - *Stop and Go, Yes and No: What Is an Antonym?* by Brian Cleary
    - *The Dove Dove: Funny Homograph Riddles* by Marvin Terban
    - *Zoola Palooza: A Book of Homographs* by Gene Baretta
- Guide students and create some shared examples for them to record in their literacy notebooks. Ask them to share favorite examples and sketches of synonyms, antonyms, and homographs.
- *Small Group Instruction:* Use the Word Card Parade and sing "The Words Go Matching" song (see pap. 287–288). Also, play games related to synonyms (Beat the Clock or Dump and Sort), antonyms (Concentration), or homographs (Card Head). Figure 4.7 has details on the games.
- *Parents and Tutors:* Share the *Words and Their Crazy Relatives Parent Letter* and Reproducible (Figure 4.7)
- *Independent Work:* Use reproducibles for games in stations, including Figure 4.8, *Synonym Cards;* Figure 4.9, *Antonym Cards;* Figure 4.10, *Homograph Cards;* and Figure 4.12, *Homograph Sketch Maker.* Students can also read and review books featuring synonyms, antonyms, and homographs.

- *English Language Learner Suggestion:* Work with students in a small group to study synonyms, antonyms, and homographs using the various reproducibles and game-like activities in this lesson. Choose just one of the types of words to study each day.
- *Struggling Reader Suggestion:* Try lessons from ReadWriteThink such as "Using Word Webs to Teach Synonyms for Commonly Used Words" (see www.readwritethink.org/classroom-resources/lesson-plans/using-word -webs-teach-282.html), and "Delicious, Tasty, Yummy, Enriching Writing with Adjectives and Synonyms" (see www.readwritethink.org/resources /resource-print.html?id=868).

EVALUATION

"I can . . ." Statements

- I can define and identify synonyms and explain their meanings.
- I can define and identify antonyms and explain their meanings.
- I can define and identify homographs and explain their meanings.
- I can sort synonyms and share their relationships and their meanings.
- I can match antonyms with their opposites.
- I can discuss the difference between meanings of homographs.
- I can explain why authors use synonyms, antonyms, and homographs in their writing.
- I can use synonyms, antonyms, and homographs in my writing.

Behavior Indicators

- Defines synonyms, provides examples, and sorts synonyms that are provided.
- Defines antonyms, provides examples, and sorts antonyms that are provided.
- Defines homographs, provides examples, and sorts homographs that are provided.
- Discusses the differences between synonyms, antonyms, and homographs.
- Explains why authors use these words.
- Tries writing using these devices.

FIGURE 4.12

Homograph Sketch Maker Reproducible

Directions: For each homograph, sketch a drawing to show what each word means. Try the first one with the word *lead*. Choose homographs from the homograph game cards to illustrate.

Homograph: lead	
Lead = be the one in charge Sketch It!	Lead = pencil lead Sketch It!

Homograph: ______	
______ = ______ Sketch It!	______ = ______ Sketch It!

Homograph: ______	
______ = ______ Sketch It!	______ = ______ Sketch It!

Source: Literacy Strong All Year Long: Powerful Lessons for Grades 3-5 by Lori Oczkus, Valerie Ellery, and Timothy V. Rasinski.

LESSON 5. FLUENCY: PHRASING, PACING, EXPRESSING—PERFORMING WITH A PURPOSE

Title CELEBRATING USA ON INDEPENDENCE DAY

Trailer One of the most important holidays in the United States is Independence Day. The country celebrates independence from England with parades, family picnics, and fireworks. In many towns, people celebrate by performing patriotic songs, poems, scripts, and speeches. You can encourage your students to add to their family and community Independence Day festivities by adding patriotic performances to their celebrations. Family members can read patriotic passages of speeches and the entire family can sing patriotic songs. This experience provides students with an authentic opportunity to use their literacy skills over the summer and maintain high levels of reading fluency. In this chapter, you will find ideas of songs, poems, and other texts that you can share with your students to make the celebration of Independence Day literacy strong.

Many holidays and celebrations have poems, songs, and other texts associated with them. Be sure to consider adding poetry, song, and other texts to your celebrations and commemorations. Many ELLs (and parents) may wish to bring in or suggest poetry and songs from their native countries so that they may share a bit of their own customs and cultures with other students.

Literacy Enhancer Reading Fluency: Word Recognition Automaticity, Expressive Reading

Key Academic Vocabulary
(Terms spiraled from previous lessons)

Choral Reading: Reading aloud in unison with others

Expression: To read orally with appropriate intonation, volume, phrasing, emphasis, and pace that reflect and amplify the meaning of the text

Inauguration: A ceremony to mark a formal induction into office

Oratory: The art or practice of formal speaking in public

Performance: The act of presenting a play, concert, or other form of entertainment

Poetry: A genre of writing that emphasizes the expression of feelings and ideas using distinctive style, rhyme, or rhythm

Rehearsal: The repeated practice reading of a text done in preparation of performing the text for an audience

Rhyme: Words that have the same or similar ending sounds

Rhythm: A regular, repeated pattern of movement, sound, or language

Script: The written text of a play, movie, or broadcast

Song: A short poem set to music

Speech: A formal address or discourse delivered to an audience

Learning Objectives

- Increase their ability to recognize words automatically (word recognition automaticity) through repeated reading of various performance texts.
- Improve their ability to read with appropriate expression and phrasing (prosody) as they rehearse to convey the meaning of texts through oral reading.
- Develop a greater appreciation for the role of songs, poetry, speeches, and scripts to convey meaning.
- Develop greater appreciation for the significance of Independence Day in U.S. culture.
- Create a better understanding of how to add to a celebratory event through performance texts.

Essential Questions

- How does fluent and expressive reading add to the quality and meaning of a text meant to be performed?
- What do I need to do to make my reading of a performance text meaningful to an audience?
- What types of performance texts do I think best add to the celebration or commemoration of a holiday?

STEP 1: PREPARATION

Organize Materials

- Computer or phone that is able to record and turn your reading and singing of songs and poems into podcasts that can be sent electronically to students and families (e.g., using audacityteam.org)
- Performance passages for Independence Day (songs, poems, speeches, readers theater scripts)
- *Readers Theater Script* reproducible (Figure 4.13) for classroom use
- Word Journal

STEP 2: INITIATION

Prior to the end of the school year, remind students that they will be celebrating an important holiday on July 4th, and provide them with background information. Invite students to brainstorm with you about activities that they and their families normally do on Independence Day. Introduce the idea of performing patriotic songs, poems, speeches, and other important texts.

STEP 3: DEMONSTRATION

1. Pass out a packet of performance texts to students and do a rehearsal of each text, modeling the reading or singing of each text over the course of several days. Discuss with students the content of each text.
2. Invite students to join you in chorally reading or singing the various texts in the packet. Use Figure 4.13, *Readers Theater Script*, to make this idea come to life.
3. Tell students that you will be meeting with their parents and will ask them to use the texts in the packet to add to each family's Independence Day celebration. Encourage students to help their parents plan for the Independence Day performance.
4. Direct students (and family members) to assign texts to individuals and small groups of family members and then continue to practice reading those texts on their own in the days prior to the Fourth of July. Students and family members may use the podcasts you have created to assist their rehearsal of the texts.

STEP 4: COLLABORATION

In your meetings and discussions with students and parents, remind them that their Independence Day performance of texts should be a collaborative effort. Parents and children should work together to make these plans:

- Assign texts to family members.
- Find time each day the week before Independence Day for family members to rehearse their texts alone and as a group.
- Listen to the online podcasts that you have created to support their practice.
- Plan the logistics of the Independence Day performance:
  - When will it happen?
  - Where will it happen (e.g., backyard, picnic ground, inside home)?
  - How will the performances be choreographed (e.g., around a campfire, from the family porch, at the dinner or picnic table)?
  - Who will be the audience (family members, others)?

STEP 5: APPLICATION

For Families

An essential purpose of this lesson is to have your students continue to engage in repeated readings through rehearsal during summer vacation. One way to support and promote summer reading rehearsal is to provide students and families with a model reading of the texts you want them to rehearse. When you have developed a packet of performance texts, post them on your classroom website so that students and family members will have access to them throughout the summer. Follow these additional steps to finalize the packet and prepare students and families for summer reading.

1. Create and post on your classroom website a podcast of you reading or singing each text. Each podcast should contain
   a. A brief introduction to the text.
   b. Your portrayal of each text, reading or singing with an expressive voice, emphasizing reading in appropriate phrases and with good expression.
   c. Your explanation of how you read or sang the text, again emphasizing phrasing and expression.
   d. A discussion of the content of the text itself.
2. Include a sampling of songs, poems, speeches, and scripts in the packet. You can find examples here in this lesson, in the previous lessons on fluency, and in other related texts online.
3. Have an end-of-the-year conference with parents on the importance of summer reading and the value of avoiding a summer reading slide.
4. Invite parents to make their Fourth of July celebration a bit more special by adding reading and singing of patriotic texts that they will find in the packet of performance texts.
   a. Suggest to parents that they find time on the Fourth of July to perform the texts. A great time might be before or after the main meal or picnic. Have individual family members recite the full text or portions of it in their best voices. The readers theater script can be performed by various family members. Songs can be sung chorally by everyone.
   b. Remind parents that any good performance requires rehearsal. Therefore, they should assign various texts to family members (or call for volunteers). Through that week, family members should be expected to rehearse their assigned parts so that when they perform, they are able to

read with confidence, expression, and meaning. Songs can be rehearsed in family groupings whenever possible. Remind parents that when rehearsing, all members of the family should have a copy of the assigned text.

STEP 6: REFLECTION

Oral or Written Response

Have students and parents respond on your classroom website to their Independence Day performances. Invite them to describe their performances and answer the following questions:

- How did the audience react?
- Was it successful?
- Any surprises?
- Any difficulties?
- Suggestions for future family performances?
- Have them respond in their Word Journals to the essential question: "What do I need to do to make my reading of a performance text meaningful to an audience?"

ADAPTATION AND EXTENSION

Many performance texts can be found in online searches related to other holidays, celebrations, or commemorations such as Labor Day, Flag Day, Veterans Day, and Martin Luther King Jr. Day. Students may also be asked to create their own performance texts (e.g., poems, songs, scripts, speeches) for each holiday that can then be performed. Extend the notion of holiday text performances into your own English language arts curriculum throughout the school year and vacation months.

- *Small-Group Instruction:* Assign selected songs or other texts (or portions of songs and other texts) for students to perform in small groups. Or, play Wordo or other word games with selected words from texts read and performed.
- *Parents and Tutors:* Write a letter to be delivered to parents a few days before the holiday, reminding them of the celebration and sharing ideas on how to make the celebration rich with reading and performing.
- *Independent Work:* Read books appropriate for children on the topic of Independence Day. One example is *Don't Know Much About American History* by Ken Davis.

- *English Language Learner Suggestion:* Encourage students (and parents) to find poetry, songs and other texts that reflect their own celebrations, cultures, and traditions. After students learn to read and perform these texts at home, they should be encouraged to bring them into the classroom to share with their classmates.

- *Struggling Reader Suggestion:* Repeated reading is an established method for improving the reading of struggling readers. Suggest to parents and students that they read and sing the texts students learned, throughout the year. Remind parents that students should be tracking the texts visually even if they have the text memorized. Reading occurs only when the reader has his or her eyes on the words in the text.

EVALUATION

"I can . . ." Statements

- I can read the words in my assigned texts with ease.
- I can read my assigned text with expression that reflects and amplifies its meaning.
- I can read and perform my script with good volume and confidence.
- I can read and perform my text aloud with good posture.
- I can understand the meaning of the words in the text I read.
- I can understand the content of the text that I and my family members read.
- I can rehearse my part of a text to the point where I can read it fluently.
- I can work cooperatively with my family members to produce a fluent and meaningful performance of texts related to Independence Day.
- I can listen attentively to texts being performed by my family members and offer positive feedback to the group.

Behavior Indicators

- Demonstrates enthusiasm to be able to rehearse and perform assigned texts.
- Works cooperatively and positively with family members and provides positive feedback as they rehearse and perform their assigned texts.
- Exhibits attentive and positive behavior as an audience member.
- Finds and chooses texts to rehearse and perform for others.

Performance Passages for Independence Day

Note that songs can also be read and performed as poems.

America, the Beautiful

O beautiful for spacious skies,
For amber waves of grain,
For purple mountain majesties
Above the fruited plain!
America! America!
God shed his grace on thee
And crown thy good with brotherhood
From sea to shining sea!

Grand Old Flag

You're a grand old flag,
You're a high flying flag
And forever in peace may you wave.
You're the emblem of
The land I love.
The home of the free and the brave.
Every heart beats true
Beneath the Red, White and Blue,
Where there's never a boast or brag.
Should auld acquaintance be forgot,
Keep your eye on the grand old flag.

Yankee Doodle

Yankee Doodle went to town
A-riding on a pony
He stuck a feather in his hat
And called it macaroni
[Chorus:]
Yankee Doodle, keep it up
Yankee Doodle dandy
Mind the music and the step
and with the girls be handy!
Father and I went down to camp
Along with Captain Gooding
And there we saw the men and boys
As thick as hasty pudding.
Chorus
And there was Captain Washington
And gentle folks about him
They say he's grown so tarnal proud
He will not ride without them.
Chorus

Patriotic poetry and other songs can be found online. Here are a few more titles: "God Bless America," "This Land Is Your Land," and "America (My Country Tis of Thee)."

A Speech

Excerpts from Ronald Reagan's First Inaugural Address

It is time for us to realize that we are too great a nation to limit ourselves to small dreams. We're not, as some would have us believe, doomed to an inevitable decline. I do not believe in a fate that will fall on us no matter what we do. I do believe in a fate that will fall on us if we do nothing.

So with all the creative energy at our command, let us begin an era of national renewal. Let us renew our determination, our courage, and our strength. And let us renew our faith and our hope. We have every right to dream heroic dreams.

Those who say that we're in a time when there are no heroes—they just don't know where to look. You can see heroes every day going in and out of factory gates. Others, a handful in number, produce enough food to feed all of us and then the world beyond. You meet heroes across a counter—and they're on both sides of that counter. There are entrepreneurs with faith in themselves and faith in an idea who create new jobs, new wealth, and opportunity.

There are individuals and families whose taxes support the Government and whose voluntary gifts support church, charity, culture, art, and education. Their patriotism is quiet but deep. Their values sustain our national life.

Now I have used the words "they" and "their" in speaking of these heroes. I could say "you" and "your" because I'm addressing the heroes of whom I speak—you, the citizens of this blessed land. Your dreams, your hopes, your goals are going to be the dreams, the hopes, and the goals of this Administration, so help me God.

We shall reflect the compassion that is so much a part of your make-up. How can we love our country and not love our countrymen—and loving them reach out a hand when they fall, heal them when they're sick, and provide opportunity to make them self-sufficient so they will be equal in fact and not just in theory? Can we solve the problems confronting us? Well, the answer is an unequivocal and emphatic "Yes."

Well, I believe we, the Americans of today, are ready to act worthy of ourselves, ready to do what must be done to insure happiness and liberty for ourselves, our children, and our children's children. And as we renew ourselves here in our own land, we will be seen as having greater strength throughout the world. We will again be the exemplar of freedom and a beacon of hope for those who do not now have freedom.

Source: Ronald Reagan: "Inaugural Address," January 20, 1981. Online by Gerhard Peters and John T. Woolley, *The American Presidency Project.* Available: www.presidency.ucsb.edu/ws/?pid=43130.

FIGURE 4.13

Readers Theater Script: *The Declaration of Independence*

Directions: Assign students to read aloud parts: three Narrators (N1–3) and three Declarers (D1–3). At All, ask the other students to read the part as a chorus.

N1: This is the story

N2: of the birth of

All: **the United States of America.**

N2: At one time the United States were colonies of England. However, people in the colonies began to feel that the King of England was exerting more control over them than they felt was warranted.

All: **Colonists began to call for a separation of the North American colonies from England,**

N1: they began to call for independence.

N3: The King had imposed on the colonies laws and taxes that the colonists felt were unfair.

All: **The King had also ignored petitions or requests from the colonies that their grievances be heard.**

N1: And so, one by one, the various colonies began to demand independence from England. By May 1776, eight colonies had decided that they would support independence.

N2: On May 15, 1776, two months before July 4, the largest colony, Virginia, resolved that

All: **the delegates appointed to represent this colony be instructed to propose to declare the United Colonies free and independent states.**

N3: The Continental Congress, the governing body of the 13 colonies, met a few weeks later in Philadelphia and on the 7th day of June, Richard Henry Lee of Virginia read this resolution to the Congress

N1: "Be it resolved: That these United Colonies are, and of right ought to be, free and independent States, that they are absolved from all allegiance to the British Crown, and that all political connection between them and the State of Great Britain is, and ought to be, totally dissolved."

N2: A committee of five members of the Congress was then formed to create a written statement declaring the freedom of the colonies from England.

N3: The members of this committee were two men from New England: John Adams from Massachusetts and Roger Sherman from Connecticut.

N1: Two representatives were from the middle colonies: Robert Livingston of New York and Benjamin Franklin from Pennsylvania.

N2: And one was from the South: Thomas Jefferson from Virginia.

N3: Jefferson was given the primary task of writing the document.

N1: By the end of June he had completed his declaration. It was sent to the Continental Congress on July 1.

N2: After much discussion and heated argument, the declaration was revised and revised again.

N3: And, although the independence that the colonies sought was not totally realized until several years later at the end of the Revolutionary War . . .

N1: this declaration began a new country whose history is still being written today—our country,

All: The United States of America.

N2: On July 4, 1776, after much further debate, the Declaration was adopted by all the colonies in the Continental Congress. Church bells throughout Philadelphia rang out in celebration as the Declaration was proclaimed to the people.

All: **In Congress, July 4, 1776. The Unanimous Declaration of the thirteen united States of America.**

FIGURE 4.13 (*continued*)

D2 (slowly and deliberately): When in the course of human events, it becomes necessary for one people to dissolve the political bands which have connected them with another, and to assume among the powers of the earth, the separate and equal station to which the Laws of Nature and of Nature's God entitle them,

D3: a decent respect to the opinions of mankind requires that they should declare the causes which impel them to the separation.

D1: We hold these truths to be self-evident, that all men are created equal, that they are endowed by their Creator with certain unalienable Rights

All: **That among these are**

D1: Life,

D2: Liberty,

D3: and the pursuit of Happiness.

D2: That to secure these rights, Governments are instituted among Men, deriving their just powers from the consent of the governed.

D1: That whenever any Form of Government becomes destructive of these ends, it is the Right of the People to alter or abolish it and institute a new Government, laying its foundation on principles and organizing itself in a way that to them shall seem most likely to bring their Safety and Happiness.

D3: Prudence, indeed, will dictate that long established governments should not be changed for light and transient causes;

D2: But, when a long train of abuses reduces and oppresses the people, it is their right, it is their duty, to throw off such Government, and provide a new government for their future security.

D1: Such has been how the Colonies have suffered.

D2: And such is now the necessity which forces them to alter their Government.

D3: The history of the present King of Great Britain is a history of repeated injuries and taking of rights and liberties, all done to establish an absolute Tyranny over these States…

D1: In every stage of these Oppressions, we have petitioned for redress in the most humble terms from the King.

D2: Our repeated petitions have been answered only by repeated injury.

D3: A Prince whose character is thus marked by acts that define a Tyrant, is unfit to be the ruler of a free people . . .

D1: We, therefore, the Representatives of the United States of America, in General Congress, assembled here,

D2: Appealing to the Supreme Judge of the world, do, in the Name, and by Authority of the good People of these Colonies, solemnly publish and declare

D3: That these United Colonies are, and of Right ought to be Free and Independent States,

D2: That they are absolved from all Allegiance to the British Crown,

D1: And that all political connection between them and the State of Great Britain, is and ought to be totally dissolved.

D3: And that as Free and Independent States, they have full Power to levy War,

D1: conclude Peace,

D2: contract Alliances,

D3: establish Commerce,

continued

FIGURE 4.13 (*continued*)

D2: and to do all other Acts and Things which Independent States may of right do.

D1: And for the support of this Declaration, with a firm reliance on the protection of divine Providence, we mutually pledge to each other

D2, 3: our Lives,

N1, 2, 3: our Fortunes,

All: **and our sacred Honor.**

D1: This is the story of the birth of our Country–

All: **The United States of America.**

All: (Sing):

> My country, 'tis of thee,
> Sweet land of liberty,
> Of thee I sing;
> Land where my fathers died,
> Land of the pilgrims' pride,
> From every mountainside,
> Let freedom ring!

LESSON 6. COMPREHENSION: PREVIEWING

Title PREVIEW POWER

Trailer Summer is the time for lazy barefoot days, blockbuster movies, road trips, and of course great books! Watch student reading motivation and skills grow as students tap into "preview power" by applying the preview strategies in this lesson during lively small-group lessons, partner sessions, and book club activities. *Sneak Preview 1-2-3, Informational Text Features Tour,* and *Text Trip Maps* all join in to make summer learning fun and rewarding. Students learn to strengthen their predictions and dig deeper for text evidence (Oczkus, 2018). Watch out—as the preview party begins, student motivation to read will take off!

Literacy Enhancer Comprehension: Previewing—Text Structures, Text Features

Key Academic Vocabulary
(Terms spiraled from previous lessons)

Author: Person who wrote the text

Author's Point of View: In nonfiction, the opinion or feelings the author has toward the topic; in fiction, point of view also means who is telling the story

Author's Purpose: The reason the author wrote the text, usually to inform, entertain, or persuade the reader

Caption: A text feature used to give a brief explanation to an article, illustration, or photo

Chart: A form of a table, graph, or diagram used to capture information

Graph: A diagram showing the relation between variable quantities

Heading: Divides the text into sections and tells the main idea of each section; high-lighted in bold or larger type, it helps the reader locate information in the text

Illustrator: The person who draws or paints the artwork to accompany the text

Index: An alphabetical list of content with references to the places where they occur

Map: A text feature used as representation of an area showing spatial arrangement

Photograph: Image captured using a camera

Predict: To make an educated logical guess, or inference, about what will happen next in the text using clues from the text and one's own background knowledge

Prediction: An educated guess about what may happen in a story or other text about to be read

Preview: To look over the text before reading to predict what it will be about and to see what text features the author has included

Table of Contents: A listing of the text's sections, chapter titles, and page numbers so the reader can locate information and see how the text is organized

Text Features: The tools an author uses to help the reader navigate the text to locate and access meaning from the text; may contain a table of contents, headings, photographs, bold words, maps, graphs, charts, index, and glossary

Text Structure: The organizational structure of the information in the text: fiction might consist of a problem and solution, and a beginning, middle, and end; nonfiction may be organized around a main idea and details, a cause and effect, a problem and solution, a sequence of ideas, or a compare and contrast of ideas

Theme: The life's lesson, author's message, or moral of the story; usually not directly stated

Learning Objectives

- Preview fiction texts by studying the title and covers and by flipping through the text to predict what the story will be about and the author's purpose.
- Preview fiction texts to predict the fiction elements of setting, characters, problem, events, and theme.
- Preview nonfiction texts by studying the title, covers, and text features to predict what the text will be about and the author's purpose.
- Recognize that nonfiction texts have different text structures such as a main idea and detail, a cause and effect, a sequence, a compare and contrast, and a problem and solution.
- Create text maps for fiction and nonfiction for previewing text and to fill in after reading.

Essential Questions

- What predictions can be made by using the title, covers, and flipping through a fiction or nonfiction text?
- How can you use a fiction text feature map to preview a text?
- How can you use a nonfiction map to preview a text and keep track of what you are learning in a nonfiction text?
- How can you use the text features of a nonfiction text to help you preview and predict what you will learn?

STEP 1: PREPARATION

Organize Materials

- *Sneak Preview 1-2-3 Bookmarks* reproducible (Figure 1.9)
- *Informational Text Tours* reproducible (Figure 2.10)
- *Text Trip Maps for Fiction and Nonfiction* reproducible (Figure 3.12)
- *Song Parodies for Text Maps* reproducible
- Fiction and nonfiction texts to use to model
- Texts for book clubs
- Texts for guided reading
- Texts to read to little buddies
- Poster paper and markers
- Parent letters
- Literacy Notebooks

STEP 2: INITIATION

Preview Summer Fun Activities

Share with students that summer is a great time to travel to parks and attractions, to go to movies, and to read great books. Note that we use previewing skills to get the most out of these activities. When someone suggests, "Hey, let's go to the park or to a movie" in the summer, the invitation is always followed by a preview. The person extending the invitation usually says something exciting to entice us to go. Then, as participants, we often search for more details online, such as a map of the park or a movie review to help us preview the activity. Ask students to share examples of movies and places they've previewed lately. Just like going somewhere fun in the summer, we preview the text we are about to read. Then, we dig deeper by studying the covers, the inside, and even reviews, to help motivate us and to strengthen our comprehension. Previewing power works to make our reading better!

STEP 3: DEMONSTRATION

Try modeling fiction and nonfiction texts using student texts or your own reading or both! Modeling with your own texts can be very powerful (Oczkus, 2018). Students perk up and listen when we share tidbits from our personal lives. Tell students that before reading, good readers begin to predict what the story will be about and how the author has organized the text.

1. Model with Your Fiction

Model briefly with a novel you have read that is appropriate to share. Begin by showing the cover of the book, and then show the *Sneak Preview 1-2-3 Bookmark for Fiction* reproducible (Figure 1.9) as you think aloud. For example, you might say:

> When I read, I use the same strategies we are learning. For example, I use the Sneak Preview 1-2-3. First, I tried "That Covers It." When I first saw Jodi Picoult's book *Leaving Time*, I read the title, back cover, and a few online reviews. I predicted the story is about a girl who lives with her grandma because her mother has been missing for many years. The mom was a scientist who studied elephants. Her disappearance is a mystery, so that is the main problem. Then I tried "Page Flip Through," or step number two. I flipped through the book and noticed that every chapter is told in the voice of one of the characters—the mom, the girl, and the detective. I have read other books that switch character voices every chapter. This means I have to pay attention to who is talking and telling the story. I flipped through and saw flashbacks to the mom's work with elephants. I think that has something to do with her disappearance. Lastly, I thought about our third step, "Puzzle, Purpose, POV." I know it is a mystery and that the author wrote it to entertain me. The story is told from several points of view. I learned all that just by previewing the book while thinking about the fiction map!

2. Model with a Mentor Text for Fiction

Select a chapter book, a picture book, or even a basal story to model how to use the *Sneak Preview 1-2-3 Bookmark for Fiction* reproducible or the *Fiction Text Map* reproducible.

3. Model with Your Nonfiction

Select a news article or book with a nonfiction topic you are reading about to use as a model for students. For example, if you are training your new puppy to fetch or sit, perhaps choose an online article about puppy training to model. Try showing how you preview the text using the text features found on the *Informational Text Tours* reproducible. Also, discuss the use of a *Nonfiction Text Map* reproducible.

4. Model with a Mentor Text for Nonfiction

Select a news article, a picture book, or a chapter from a content-area reading book to model how to preview nonfiction text. Show and think aloud using the *Sneak Preview 1-2-3 Bookmark for Nonfiction* reproducible, the *Informational Text Tours* reproducible, or the *Nonfiction Text Map* reproducible.

STEP 4: COLLABORATION

Fiction and Nonfiction Map Songs

To reinforce the concepts, sing or chant "The Fiction Map Song" or "The Nonfiction Map Song" on the *Song Parodies for Text Maps* reproducible in Figure 4.14. Play or hum the original "I've Been Workin' on the Railroad" melody for students to hear the tune before singing the adapted verses. Try singing "The Fiction Map Song" all together, and then split up the lines for different groups to join in. Invite students to practice reading the verses as a poem with partners and teams.

Small-Group Instruction

Conduct a series of small-group instruction lessons using the three previewing reproducibles and either fiction or nonfiction texts (Figures 1.9, 2.10, and 3.12).

As students fill in the maps and use the bookmarks, encourage them to respond using the academic language found on each. Have them turn to partners to discuss, and then share with the group to encourage more discussion.

STEP 5: APPLICATION

Set up a partner reading station in the classroom where students use the *Sneak Preview 1-2-3 Bookmarks* and *Nonfiction Text Map* reproducibles with books that the pairs select to read together.

Provide the class with several book choices to read in book clubs of four to five students. Invite the book clubs to use the *Sneak Preview* reproducible to preview their text. Encourage students to read the text in pairs or independently. After reading, ask the group to create a giant colorful text map using the *Text Map* reproducible as a guide for either fiction or nonfiction, depending upon the text choice. Display the giant maps in the hallway or library for all to see! Ask students to include a summary and book review of the text.

FIGURE 4.14

Song Parodies for Text Maps

The Fiction Map Song
(To the tune of "I've Been Working on the Railroad")

Fiction books start with a setting

And a story along the way.

Fiction stories have a problem

With characters just like a play.

Can you figure out the trouble

Rising up so often on the page?

Can you figure out the theme too?

Reader, follow the clues!

Follow your fiction map,

Follow your fiction map.

Reader, won't you follow the clues?

Follow your fiction map,

Follow your fiction map,

Reader, won't you follow the clues?

Someone's got the resolution,

Someone's got the theme I know.

Someone's got the resolution,

It's the ending, let's go!

Singin' fee, fie, fiddly-i-o

Fee, fie, fiddly-i-o-o-o-o

Fee, fie, fiddly-i-o

It's the ending, let's go!

The Nonfiction Map Song
(To the tune of "I've Been Working on the Railroad")

Nonfiction texts start with information

And an author's purpose with facts.

Nonfiction books start with information

Organized to keep us on the tracks.

Can you figure out which text map

The author chose to plug in?

Can you figure out the main ideas?

Reader, won't you try again?

Reader, compare, contrast,

Reader, sequence it,

Reader, try problem and solution.

Reader, won't you try?

Reader, won't you try?

Reader, won't you read it again?

Someone's got the main idea

Someone's got the point of view

Someone's got the main idea

Read it closely, let's go

Singin' fee, fie, fiddly-i-o

Fee, fie, fiddly-i-o-o-o-o

Fee, fie, fiddly-i-o

Read it closely, let's go!

STEP 6: REFLECTION

Oral or Written Response

Ask students to write a paragraph using the prompts from any of the reproducibles featured in this lesson. Invite students to create *Text Maps* in their literacy journals for a favorite book they've read independently.

ADAPTATION AND EXTENSION

- Send home any of the reproducibles mentioned in this lesson and the parent letter (see Figure 4.15) to invite parents to preview texts with their children at home. Encourage children to teach their parents how to use the reproducibles and bookmarks to preview a variety of texts.

- *Small-Group Instruction:* Conduct small-group lessons in guided reading and with student-run book clubs using fiction and nonfiction texts and the *Sneak Preview 1-2-3 Bookmark, Text Features Tour,* and *Text Trip Maps.*

- *Parents and Tutors:* Copy the reproducibles so that students can use them with their parents with a variety of fiction and nonfiction texts.

- *Independent Work:* Copy the reproducibles so students can use them with partners and alone.

- *English Language Learner Suggestion:* Invite students to write reviews of books they've read to try to entice other students to read them also. Use a microphone and conduct a show in the format of a commercial or talk show with one student posing as the preview show host. Videotape the show and post on the school or classroom website.

- *Struggling Readers Suggestion:* Students may wish to create instructional "How to Preview" videos for various kinds of books to help other students or younger children. Post on the school website or show to a younger class.

FIGURE 4.15

Parent Letters for Previewing and Reading Texts

Dear Parents and Family,

Here are some suggestions for ways you can help your child better understand **stories, or fiction texts.** When you and your child read stories together, rather than just starting to read at the beginning of the book, it is important to first preview the text. Previewing is what good readers naturally do! Good readers look a text over and think about what the reading will be about before they begin reading.

1. Study the cover of the text.
- Talk about the title of the book. What do each of you think it will be about?
- Read the name of the author and illustrator. Do you know any books written by this author or drawn by this illustrator?
- Look at the cover art. What clues help you figure out what the story is about?
- Look at the back cover. What do you see that helps you predict what this story is about?

2. Flip through the pages of the book.
- When you flip around in the book, what do you notice?
- How is the book organized?
- What clues do the illustrations provide to help you figure out who the characters are and details about the setting? Do you know what the problem in the book might be?

3. Discuss your predictions.
- Take turns sharing what you think will happen in the book based on your preview.

4. Read the book!
- Read in a variety of ways, including reading aloud to your child, reading together, or taking turns reading.

5. Discuss after reading.
- Return to your original preview ideas and predictions. Was the text about what you thought it was going to be about?
- Discuss the setting, characters, problem, and events that happened along the way.
- What was the author trying to teach us? Was there a moral?

Enjoy discussing books with your child. Take turns and share your ideas too. Make the experience more like a discussion than a test.

Sincerely,

Your Child's Teacher

FIGURE 4.15 (*continued*)

Dear Parents and Family,

Here are some suggestions for ways you can help your child better understand **informa-tional (nonfiction) texts.** When you and your child read nonfiction books or articles, it is important to preview the text before reading it. Instead of just starting at the beginning of the text and reading it, invite your child to look it over first and consider what might be learned. Try making this a fun discussion when you read nonfiction together.

1. Study the cover of the text.
- Talk about the title of the book, article, or chapter in a textbook. What do you both think it will be about?
- Read the name of the author and illustrator if they are listed. Do you know any books written by this author or drawn by this illustrator?
- Look at the cover art. What do you think you will learn by reading this text?
- What does the author want you to know?
- Look at the back cover. What do you see that helps you predict what this is about?

2. Flip through the pages of the book.
- How is the book organized?
- Read the table of contents if there is one.
- What clues do the illustrations, charts, maps, and other graphics provide?
- Read the headings as you flip through the book.
- What do you think you will learn? What does the author want you to know?

3. Discuss your predictions.
- Take turns sharing what you think you will learn in the reading based on your preview.

4. Read the text!
- Read in a variety of ways including reading aloud to your child, reading together, or taking turns reading.

5. Discuss after reading.
- Return to your original preview of ideas and predictions. Was the text about what you thought it was going to be about? What did you learn?
- Discuss the text features such as illustrations, maps, and charts. What did you learn from them?

Enjoy discussing books with your child. Take turns and share your ideas, too. Make the expe-rience more like a discussion rather than a test.

Sincerely,

Your Child's Teacher

LESSON 7. COMPREHENSION: INFERRING AND DRAWING CONCLUSIONS

Title SUMMER BOOK BUDDIES

Trailer Throughout the school year, students have learned how to make inferences and to draw conclusions about what they are reading. These approaches include making predictions before and during reading, creating mental images while reading, and using our own bodies to create tableaux that represent the meaning of texts we are reading. The summer months are now a chance for students to put these methods into practice in their own independent reading. Summer is a time for students to have fun. Through Summer Book Buddies, students can learn that reading itself is an enjoyable activity, especially when they can share their reading with a friend.

Literacy Enhancer Reading Comprehension: Making Inferences—Imagery, Predictions, Tableaux

Key Academic Vocabulary
(Terms spiraled from previous lessons)

Background Knowledge (Schema): The existing knowledge a person has about a topic

Imagery: The creation of an internal representation of meaning based on something that is read; can include the sight, sound, smells, movements, and feelings associated with a scene from a text

Inference: An educated guess or prediction about some aspect of the content of a text that is not specifically mentioned; a sophisticated form of reading comprehension

Prediction: An educated guess about what may happen in a story or other text about to be read

Tableau(x): A living picture; a depiction of a scene usually presented by silent and motionless participants

Learning Objectives

- Engage in independent reading of a book over summer vacation.
- Collaborate with a book buddy in reading the book.
- Productively use the inference methods learned through the year in interaction with a book buddy.

Essential Questions

- What is an inference?
- Am I able to make and share predictions based on a book I am reading with a book buddy?

- Am I able to develop and share images that represent meanings of a book I am reading with a book buddy?
- Am I able to develop and share tableaux that represent characters or scenes from the book I am reading with a book buddy?
- Am I able to discuss with my book buddy the predictions, images, and tableaux that we generate in our reading of our shared book?

STEP 1: PREPARATION

Organize Materials

- Interest-based, developmental set of books
- Picture of a tableau
- Questions for a student survey

STEP 2: INITIATION

Book Buddies

A week before the end of the school year, talk with your students about the Book Buddies project that they will be expected to engage in over the summer.

- Students are assigned a partner or two.
- Each group of students will be assigned or can choose one book to read as book buddies.
- Book buddies will preview the book during the last week of school and develop a weekly schedule for reading the book (e.g., number of pages per week, a minimum of four weeks).
- Book buddies will be required to do the following tasks for each week of the project and share their work with their book buddy:
  - A paragraph summary of what they have read.
  - An image or description of an image that represents a selected scene from the section they have read.
  - A picture of a tableau that they create based on the section they have read.
  - A prediction of what each reader thinks will likely happen in the next section of the book.
  - In a final year-end meeting with parents, describe the book buddies project. Provide parents with the protocol students are expected to engage in with their book buddy over the course of reading the book. Explain that the project is an activity required by their child's new teacher. Type up a description and protocol for the Book Buddies project. Post the

document on your classroom website and send copies home to parents and children.

STEP 3: DEMONSTRATION

Book Buddy Share

1. Identify a set of books that you feel will appeal to the developmental level and interest of your students. Be sure that your students will be able to gain access to the books through the school book room or community library.

2. Identify pairs of students in your classroom who you feel would be good partners or book buddies (you may also wish to place students into groups of three). Be sure that students have a way of communicating with their assigned book buddy (e.g., snail-mail or e-mail address, phone number).

3. Connect with the teachers in the next grade level to describe the project and ask them to make it a requirement for the incoming group of students (i.e., your students for the current year).

4. During the last week of school, read a picture book that can be read to students in one sitting.

5. Find a parent or other adult who is willing to work with you in the classroom as a book buddy for this picture book. After presenting the title and a brief introduction, develop a prediction for the book and ask your volunteer to do the same. Share your predictions and talk with your buddy about how your predictions are alike or different.

6. Determine a logical stopping place midway through the book. At this point, you and your book buddy should develop and share an image and a tableau that each of you developed from the first part of the book. Discuss your images and tableaux. Then you and your book buddy should make and share your predictions for the remainder of the book. When you have finished reading the book, you and your book buddy should again develop and share images and tableaux from the second portion. Discuss the images and tableaux with your book buddy and the extent to which your predictions were confirmed.

7. Tell your students that this demonstration of sharing thoughts, images, tableaux, and predictions is a powerful way to increase engagement in and understanding of the book. In the following days, you will ask your students to do the same with a book that you will read to them in school.

STEP 4: COLLABORATION

During the last week of school, read a book to your students that can be finished in five days. Have students work with their book buddies to listen as you read. After sharing the title and a brief introduction, have book buddies share their own predictions for the book. With each chapter or section read, have book buddies make and share an image and a tableau with one another, and then make a prediction about the next chapter or section of the book. Remind students that this process of sharing thoughts, images, tableaux, and predictions is what you will expect them to be doing during the summer.

STEP 5: APPLICATION

Confirm that you have e-mail and snail-mail contact information for your students and their parents. Set a date for the beginning of the Book Buddies program and a schedule for the reading of the assigned books. Send out a reminder that it is time for students to begin the program and send weekly reminders to your students (and parents) to engage in their assigned reading and to communicate with their book buddies. As students communicate with their book buddies, you may have them copy you on their communications so that you have a record of their work.

STEP 6: REFLECTION

Oral or Written Response

Develop a survey that you can send electronically to students at the end of the project. Ask students to respond to the questions and return the survey to you so you can evaluate the program and make improvements for the following year. The survey may ask students to rate various dimensions of the program or to provide written commentary. A similar survey could also be developed and shared with parents to get their perceptions of the program. Here are some options for student survey questions:

1. Did you participate regularly in the Book Buddies program as it was scheduled?

    ☐ Yes, very much
    ☐ Yes, somewhat
    ☐ No, not at all
    Comments:

2. Did you find reading with a book buddy enjoyable?

☐ Yes, very much

☐ Yes, somewhat

☐ No, not at all

Comments:

3. Did making and sharing predictions, images, and tableaux improve your reading of the book?

☐ Yes, very much

☐ Yes, somewhat

☐ No, not at all

Comments:

4. What suggestions do you have for improving the Book Buddies program next year?

Comments:

At the beginning of the next school year, you can invite participants from the Book Buddies program to visit you at a mutually convenient time. You may wish to do this meeting over lunch and bring pizza or some other treat to share with your students. Ask this focus group to simply talk about how the Book Buddies program played out for them. Ask them to honestly share their likes and dislikes about the program and to make recommendations for improving the program in the coming year.

ADAPTATION AND EXTENSION

- If it is difficult to pair students as book buddies who will regularly communicate with one another, you can find other buddies for your students. Many parents would love to partner with their children in sharing a book over the summer. You could ask for volunteer adults in your school to take on one or more students. You could be a book buddy for several of your students, especially those whose progress and participation most worries you. The concept of book buddies can be applied throughout the school year and can be used in the classroom or as an at-home program in conjunction with the comprehension strategies presented in this section.
  - *Beginning of the Year (Autumn):* Book buddies are formed and read a book together. At appropriate stopping points (chapters), buddies share predictions about the next section of the book.

- *Middle of the Year (Winter):* Students are paired as new book buddies and read a new book together. At appropriate stopping points (chapters), buddies share their images of the next section of the book. The images can be shared either in drawings, discussion, or both.
- *End of the Year (Spring):* Students are matched with new book buddies and read a third book. At appropriate stopping points (chapters), buddies create and share their individual tableaux of the next section of the book. Buddies then can create new tableaux in which they both participate, and these collaborative tableaux can be shared with the larger class.

- *Small-Group Instruction:* Have book buddies take and share photographs of tableaux they made over the summer (along with captions that describe the tableaux). Display the pictures, captions, and book titles in your classroom or hallway for a great way to welcome students to another year of reading.
- *Parents and Tutors:* Send home a list of "can't miss" books for children to read that are available at the local library.
- *Independent Work:* Have students make a collection of 20–50 interesting words they found in their book buddy reading and explain why they felt the words were interesting.
- *English Language Learner Suggestion*: Pair ELLs with book buddies you feel can provide support and encouragement.
- *Struggling Reader Suggestion*: Pair your struggling readers with adult volunteers (including yourself) or responsible older students who are willing to provide additional support in terms of word recognition, vocabulary, and comprehension through the summer months.

EVALUATION
"I can . . ." Statements

- I can read a book independently at home during vacation.
- I can communicate and share my response to my reading with a book buddy.

Behavior Indicators

- Engages in reading an age-appropriate book over the summer vacation.
- Communicates and shares various types of responses to the reading via email (or other form of communication) with a book buddy.
- Discusses the content of the book with a book buddy.

LESSON 8. COMPREHENSION: QUESTIONING FOR CLOSE READING

Title QUESTION GENERATOR

Trailer Beach balls are for fun in the sun as you toss them around in the air! Beach Ball Boogie and Hula Hoop Catch are just a few of the many games that include a beach ball. The goal is always to keep the ball in the air. This lesson incorporates a beach ball and the concept of "lifting up." We will be trying to lift our level of thinking by using the beach ball to generate questions from a continuum that will lead to higher-order and more divergent thinking. [*Blow whistle*] PLAY BALL!

Literacy Enhancer Comprehension—Questioning

Key Academic Vocabulary
(Terms spiraled from previous lessons)

Anticipate: To expect or predict

Cite: Quote from a specified source as evidence for or justification of an argument or statement

Close Read: To determine purpose and notice features and language used by the author so readers can think thoughtfully and methodically about the details in the text and why they were used

Inference: A conclusion (i.e., interpretation, judgment, opinion, prediction) based on text evidence and reasoning merged with personal background knowledge

Interpretation: Explanation of the meaning of something

Interrogate: To examine with questions, looking for answers

Judgment: Ability to make decisions or come to logical conclusions

Opinion: A view or judgment formed about something, not necessarily based on facts

Question–Answer Relationship (QAR): A tool to ask and answer questions considering both information in the text and the reader's background knowledge

Quote: Direct words from a text; to repeat what someone said

Reasoning: Thinking and processing information in a logical way

Speculative Talk: Making an inference by suggesting or hinting at connections and conclusions; elements of imaginative thinking to support understanding

Text-Based Evidence: Evidence derived from key facts and details in the text

Text-Dependent Questions: Sentences in interrogative form that can only be answered by referring explicitly back to the text being read

Learning Objectives

- Provide a framework for creating divergent and convergent questions on a specific topic.
- Demonstrate the relationship between questions and answers.
- Use explicitly stated information, background knowledge, and connections to the text to ask and answer questions.

Essential Questions

- What is the relationship between questions and answers?
- Why is it important to ask questions and make predictions before reading a text?
- Why is it important to ask questions during reading?
- Why do readers generate questions after reading a text?
- What is the difference between convergent and divergent types of questions?

STEP 1: PREPARATION

Organize Materials

- Inflatable beach ball
- Whistle (optional)
- *Interrogating the Text Chart* reproducible in Figure 1.12
- *Question Generator Chart* reproducible
- Chart paper or display device for color-coded list
- Multimodal text

STEP 2: INITIATION

Hot Potato

Ask students if they have ever played the game "hot potato," and discuss procedures for playing. Hold up the beach ball and explain that since it's summer fun time, we are going to use a beach ball instead of a potato to toss around while playing summertime music. In advance, create a color-coded list based on the ball's color strips (green = who, red = why, yellow = what, blue = when and where, white = now). Or, align the colors with discussion prompts (i.e., question words, story elements, vocabulary words) or directly write on the ball with a permanent or dry-erase marker. Begin playing the music as students toss the ball around. Stop the music periodically, and the student who has the ball at that moment looks to see which color or question word is closest to his right thumb. Have him share a response to the discussion prompt. Record the students' responses on a chart. You may wish to use the *Interrogating the Text Chart* reproducible to provide a springboard for a group summary discussion.

STEP 3: DEMONSTRATION

Question Summary Ball

1. Review the *Interrogating the Text Chart* in Chapter 1, Lesson 8. Discuss the importance of asking questions before, during, and after reading.
2. Read the selected text and generate questions using the ball to activate the color codes for the *Question Generator Chart* reproducible (see Figure 4.16) as students ask and answer questions relating to the text read. Create questions by using one question word from the color-coded ball and one word from the Question Generator word choices that aligns to the specific color.
3. Explain how this *Question Generator Chart* reproducible will provide students with a visual framework for developing a range of meaningful questions, encompassing both closed-ended, more factual-convergent questions, and divergent-open-ended questions. The farther up you go on the chart, the more complex and high-level the questions.

STEP 4: COLLABORATION

Ask partners to generate two to three questions about the text from each section and use text evidence to answer the questions. Engage students in conversational coaching by examining the essential questions:

- Why is it important to ask questions and make predictions before reading a text?
- Why is it important to ask questions during reading?
- Why do readers generate questions after reading a text?

STEP 5: APPLICATION

Before, during, or after reading a text or viewing a movie, have the students create questions by using one word from the first column on the *Question Generator Chart* reproducible and one word from the top row. Have them record their questions on the chart in the Generated Questions column. Challenge students to write questions for as many of the Levels of Questioning sections as possible and be ready to share with collaborative partners.

FIGURE 4.16

Question Generator Chart

Levels of Questioning	Color Coding and Question Words	Question Generators	Generated Questions
Extended Thinking Creating and Evaluating	**RED** **How** means **Why** reason	can, could will, would shall, should may, might	
Strategic Thinking Analyzing	**WHITE** **Which** choice **Why** reason	can, could will, would shall, should may, might	
	YELLOW **Which** choice **Why** reason **How** means	is, are have, has did, does, do	
Skills and Concepts Understanding and Applying	**BLUE** **Where, When** time, setting **What** event, situation **Who** person	can, could will, would shall, should may, might	
Recall Remembering and Understanding	**GREEN** **Where, When** time, setting **What** event, situation **Who** person	is, are have, has did, does, do	

STEP 6: REFLECTION

Oral or Written Response

Ask students to practice identifying and answering the different types of questions. Have students determine the question–answer relationship of each question and record and justify their answers in their notebooks. How does questioning support comprehension? How does a reader find answers to questions presented?

ADAPTATION AND EXTENSION

Revisit the "Questioning for Close Reading" lessons and the accompanying Adaptation and Extension sections for a variety of examples for strengthening students' ability to close-read using the questioning strategy:

- Top Five Interrogative *W* Words for Speculative Talk in Chapter 1
- Inference Dance Moves in Chapter 2
- "*Anticipating, Reacting,* and *Evaluating*" in Chapter 3
- *Small-Group Instruction:* After reading a text, post the *Question Generator Chart* and assign different groups a color. Have each group work together to create a question in each section and a separate answer guide to complete the chart. Have groups practice answering the generated questions.
- *Parents and Tutors:* Select predetermined questions from the *Question Generator Chart* and record them on cards. Have a blank *Question Generator Chart* and read the question with the student to determine best placement on the chart for the selected question. Explain justification for the placement.
- *Independent Work:* Students can write questions and answers for each section.
- *English Language Learner Suggestion*: Pair ELLs with students who can provide support and encouragement on how to ask and answer questions.
- *Struggling Reader Suggestion*: Have students think about a movie they recently saw. Have them create questions for the "Top Five Interrogative *W* Words" and then use the answers to practice giving a summary that describes the movie.

EVALUATION

"I can . . ." Statements

- I can ask and answer questions to establish a purpose for reading.
- I can gather facts from the text; develop questions based on the facts, background knowledge, or connections; and find the answer to my question within the text.
- I can determine the author's message by asking and answering questions about the text.

Behavior Indicators

- Answers literal and inferential questions and identifies how and where the answers were found.
- Demonstrates the relationship between questions and answers.
- Quotes accurately from a text when explaining what the text explicitly says and when drawing inferences.
- Generates questions to discover new information.
- Uses questions for clarification and problem solving.

LESSON 9. COMPREHENSION: DETERMINING IMPORTANCE AND SUMMARIZING

Title MOVIE MESSAGE MADNESS

Trailer Lights. Camera. Action! Get your tickets now for Movie Message Madness! This featured show will be a lesson on finding the important details. We will sift through the information presented and determine what will make the cut for the final clip of our Central Message Movie. To find the message, we will recount what is happening in chronological order for each scene of our movie. Finally, we will splice all the scenes together to get the gist of this author's message—in this case, the director of the featured film.

Literacy Enhancer Comprehension—Determining Importance and Summarizing: Recount Key Details, Main Idea

Key Academic Vocabulary

(Terms spiraled from previous lessons)

Cause and Effect: A relationship between actions in which one event (the cause) makes another event happen (effect)

Central Message: The gist, main thought, or principal theme the author is trying to tell or teach

Chronological: Organized within a sequential order of time

Compare and Contrast: To analyze two or more objects on similarities and differences

Contribute: To help achieve or provide something; bring about the sequence of events

Fable: A story passed down among generations that teaches a lesson, using animals that personify people, plants, or forces of nature; demonstrates different cultures and teaches about morals and valuable lessons learned from the details in the text

Gist: The main topic, idea, or central message of a text

Main Idea: The gist, important information, or central thought that tells about the overall idea of a paragraph or section of text

Moral: The teaching or practical lesson contained in a story

Recount: A detailed retelling that describes in past tense an account of an event or experience in chronological order, including precise word choice to convey the main idea

Summarize: To state the main points of a text using fewer words and concise form

Text-Based Evidence: Evidence derived from key facts and details in the text

Learning Objectives

- Describe in depth the characters, setting, events, or procedures using key details from the text.
- Identify similarities and differences among characters, settings, and events.
- Sequence story elements through a detailed recount of what was read.
- Analyze how a character's actions and reactions contribute to the sequence of events in a story.
- Determine the main ideas within a text and explain how they are supported by key details.
- Summarize and determine the central message of the text.

Essential Questions

- How do authors convey cause-and-effect relationships through characters, setting, and events?
- What are the essential story elements needed to determine the main idea of the text?
- How does comparing and contrasting elements of a story provide deeper insight into the text?
- Why is it important to be able to recount a text in chronological order?
- What is the relationship between the key details and the main idea in a text?
- What are the characteristics of an effective summary?

STEP 1: PREPARATION

Organize Materials

- Materials from Chapters 1 to 3, Lesson 9: Determining Importance and Summarizing
- *Sifting the Details,* Figure 1.14
- *Recount Recipe,* Figure 2.17
- *Circling Around the Main Idea,* reproducible, Figure 3.19
- Three movie clips with the same theme
- *Narrative Rubric* reproducible, Figure 4.17
- *Informational Rubric* reproducible, Figure 4.18
- Book: *The Invisible Boy* (optional)

STEP 2: INITIATION

Summertime at the Movies

Discuss everything that is connected with summertime (e.g., swimming, refreshing, reading for pleasure, playing baseball, going to the movies). Make a list of students' favorite movies and ask, "What are some of the movies you hope to see this summer?" Have them think about the movies *Charlotte's Web*, *Toy Story*, and *Zootopia*, and ask, "What do they all have in common?" The message of each movie is friendship. Share how in this lesson we will have a movie theme and will be reviewing many of the concepts we know about sifting details, recounting the story, and being able to get the gist out of what we read using a movie theme.

STEP 3: DEMONSTRATION

Sifting Details

1. Review the Sifting the Details lesson from Chapter 1. Point out that a story is told in sequential order, like the steps used for the rock demonstration. The cause-and-effect structure gives the sequence of events like scenes from a movie. Key details contribute to the meaning the author wishes to convey.

2. Remind students about the Recount Recipe lesson from Chapter 2. The main character, setting, key details, and events of the story relate to one another in a chronological order and contribute to the central message. Share how the characters' words and actions in *Charlotte's Web*, *Toy Story*, and *Zootopia* in relationship to the other characters are important ingredients to convey the friendship theme.

3. Review the Getting the Gist lesson from Chapter 3 by pointing out how using your fingers and snapping is equal to pointing out the key details in each scene to get the gist—the main idea of what is being presented.

4. Model the process of the *Circling Around the Main Idea* from Chapter 3 with a current movie.

5. Create or use the *Narrative Rubric* or *Informational Rubric* in this lesson to analyze and evaluate an effective summary. See Figures 4.17 and 4.18.

STEP 4: COLLABORATION

Tell students that they will review some of the concepts they have learned about how to identify the theme, summary, main idea, and central message. Engage in conversational coaching by asking students to discuss the following questions with diverse partners using a story like *The Invisible Boy* as their text:

- How did the author use cause and effect to help create the author's central message?
- What is the relationship between the key details and the main idea in a text?

FIGURE 4.17

Narrative Rubric Reproducible

4 Exemplary	3 Proficient	2 Emerging	1 Striving
Describes characters, settings, and major events in the story using key details, such as who, what, where, when, and why, and explains how the characters respond to major events and challenges.	Identifies characters, settings, and major events in a story, using key details such as who, what, where, when, and why to identify main topic.	Identifies characters, settings, and major events in a story using few key details, but with prompting and support.	Offers responses unrelated to the text; unable to retell familiar stories; no setting or wrong setting recalled.
Chronologically sequences major events from beginning, middle, and end using transition words to identify main topic.	Identifies some main events in the beginning, middle, and end using some transition words.	Recount has little evidence of events in the beginning, middle, and end.	Provides no evidence of story sequencing.
Identifies and elaborates upon the problem.	Identifies problem in story.	With prompting, identifies problem.	No problem is given.
Identifies and elaborates upon the solution.	Identifies the solution.	With prompting, identifies the solution.	No solution is given.

FIGURE 4.18

Informational Rubric Reproducible

4 Exemplary	3 Proficient	2 Emerging	1 Striving
Identifies and elaborates on the main concept to determine the main topic.	Identifies most of the main concept or theme to determine the main topic.	With prompting and support, identifies the main concept.	Offers responses unrelated to the text.
Describes the location in detail, if applicable.	Identifies some details about the location.	With prompting, identifies few key details about the location.	No setting or wrong location recalled.
Sequences major events from the beginning, middle, and end, clearly stating transition words.	Identifies some main events in the beginning, middle, and end, using some transition words.	Retell has little evidence of events in the beginning, middle, and end.	Random sequencing and unrelated events.
Identifies and elaborates upon the problem or conflict.	Identifies the problem or conflict.	With prompting, identifies the problem or conflict.	No problem or conflict given.
Identifies and elaborates upon the solution.	Identifies the solution.	With prompting, identifies solution.	No solution is given.

STEP 5: APPLICATION

Have students recount events from a book and produce a movie, beginning with independently creating main idea illustrations using key details to summarize the story. Use cause and effect, compare and contrast, and chronological order to recount the author's message. Students can illustrate scenes from a movie or use picture clips and then arrange them in chronological order and orally recount or record the story with a partner or a parent.

STEP 6: REFLECTION

Oral or Written Response

Using the sequenced illustrations students created, have them independently summarize the story in writing. Invite students to use the *Narrative Rubric* or *Informational Rubric* reproducibles to evaluate the script and their created summary.

ADAPTATION AND EXTENSION

Revisit previous Adaptation and Extension sections for a variety of examples for Determining Importance and Summarizing:

- Sifting Details in Chapter 1
- Recount Recipe in Chapter 2
- Getting the Gist in Chapter 3
- *Small-Group Instruction:* Illustrate scenes from a movie or use picture clips, and then arrange them in chronological order and orally recount or record the story with a partner.
- *Parents and Tutors:* Review transition words (*first, next, last*) and help students to practice inserting these words as they recount text they are reading.
- *Independent Work:* Have students write a summary for a text they are reading and use the Narrative Rubric to score it.
- *English Language Learner Suggestion:* Have the student work with a partner to use the *Recount Recipe* to practice the steps to creating a recount.
- *Struggling Reader Suggestion:* Use a garden glove as an example to create a Story Glove (Ellery, 2014). Have each finger represent a story element (e.g., the thumb = who/characters, pointer finger = where/setting, middle finger = what/problem, ring finger = how/solutions, pinky = why it all comes together/summary).

EVALUATION

"I can . . ." Statements

- I can describe a story's character, setting, or events using specific details from the text.
- I can explain how a character's action contributes to the events in the story.
- I can describe steps in a procedure in the order they should happen.
- I can recount a fable using key details from the text.
- I can convey how information presented helps me interpret the text around it.
- I can compare and contrast important relationships between information presented using specific details based on the text.
- I can determine the central message using specific details based on the text.
- I can use details to summarize the main idea in a text.
- I can explain how the main idea is supported by key details to summarize the text.
- I can explain the relationships between two or more individuals, events, ideas, or concepts in an informational text.
- I can use specific information from the text to support my explanation of the relationships and interactions between two or more individuals, events, ideas, or concepts in historical, scientific, or technical text.

Behavior Indicators

- Identifies the story's characters, setting, events, or procedures for the key details (e.g., big rocks), and any actions, traits, feelings, or motivations for the supporting and causal details (e.g., smaller stones).
- Analyzes how a character's actions and words contribute to the sequence of events and central message in a story.
- Describes the relationships of events, ideas, or concepts in a text.
- Identifies similarities and differences of the important relationships between information presented using specific details based on the text.
- Sequences story elements through a detailed recount of what was read.

LESSON 10. COMPREHENSION: MOTIVATING READERS

Title SPLASH INTO SUMMER READING!

Trailer Make sure that *reading* lands on your students' summer list of fun activities! Research shows that when students choose their own reading material they are more likely to be motivated to finish reading books (Scholastic, 2017). Provide plenty of opportunities to motivate students by allowing them to choose their own books and to determine their summer reading rituals. Whether they read under a tree, in a makeshift tent made from an old sheet, in a cardboard box fort, or under the covers with a flashlight, students need to figure out where and when they will read. Offer enticing summer book club options that will increase comprehension and motivation to read. Help students build their reading self-images as they dive into books to escape and to learn about the exciting world around them. Invite students to splash into summer reading!

Literacy Enhancer Comprehension: Motivating Readers—Improving Comprehension with Discussions in Book Clubs

Key Academic Vocabulary

(Terms spiraled from previous lessons)

Author: The person who wrote the book

Connect: To share what the text reminds you of: your experiences, texts, or the world around you

Evaluate: To rate a text, assign a score, and give reasons for the rating

Fiction: The genre that includes stories that are make-believe; may also include poetry

Nonfiction: The genre that includes factual or real information that is portrayed to answer, explain, or describe

Summarize: To tell what has happened in the text by sharing important points and details

Learning Objectives

- Set goals for reading at home and at school that include what to read, where to read, when to read, and who to read with.
- Maintain class reading logs and individual reading logs at home and school.
- Participate in class book talks, discussions, and book clubs.

- Discuss summaries, evaluations of texts, connections, and points such as good writing and funny and favorite parts.
- Ask relevant questions.

Essential Questions

- How can you set goals and routines for reading that include what to read, where to read, whom to read with, and when to read?
- How can you keep track of your summer reading with a book log?
- How can you figure out what to read next?
- How can you participate in discussions with partners, classmates, and book clubs in the classroom and online as you share your ideas about your reading?
- What can you say about a book to share it with others?

STEP 1: PREPARATION

Organize Materials

- *Summer Reading Plan* reproducible
- *Anytime Book Clubs* reproducible
- *Parent Letter for Motivating Students to Read* reproducible
- Stack of books the teacher is reading to share
- Fiction and nonfiction books (We used *Sea Turtles* by Frank Staub.)
- Articles
- Chart paper and markers
- Sticky notes

STEP 2: INITIATION

Summer Goals for Activities and Reading

Ask students to work in teams to list fun summer activities and goals. For example, students may want to learn to swim across the pool or improve their basketball dribbling skills. Encourage students to dramatize their summer goals as each team shares. Tell students that for their summer reading, they can set goals for where, when, and with whom to read. Give each team a topic to brainstorm—places to read, times, or people to read with. Encourage teams to make a quick sketch to go with their ideas to share with the class.

Poetry and Quotes

Share your favorite poems and inspirational quotes related to reading or search online for new options. Try reading aloud poems from a collection such as *Book*

Speak! Poems About Books by Laura Purdie Salas, or *I Am the Book* by Lee Bennett Hopkins. When sharing quotes about reading, ask students to discuss what the quotes mean to them. Quotes are valuable to share because they often contain the literary devices of simile and metaphor, as in these two examples: "Books are a uniquely portable magic" (Stephen King) and "A book is like a garden carried in the pocket" (Chinese proverb).

"Musical Books" to Introduce Books

Share book titles using a spin-off of the game musical chairs, but do not remove chairs as the game continues. Arrange six or more pairs of chairs in a row back-to-back and place a book under each chair. Model appropriate behaviors for sitting in the chairs. Invite students (one for each chair) to come up and walk around the chairs while the music plays. When you stop the music, the walkers sit in the chair closest to them, retrieve the book from under the chair, and preview it to see if they'd like to read it. Signal players to place books back under the chairs and walk around to the music again to repeat the activity. After several turns, invite students to discuss the titles. Run several of the chair formations at the same time so all students may participate.

STEP 3: DEMONSTRATION

Read-Aloud and Model Goals: Teacher as Reader

1. Bring in a stack of books that you plan to read over the summer, including fiction, cookbooks, travel guides, and manuals for hobbies. For fun, reveal one at a time from a bag or box and tell why you've selected each text. You may want to share where you like to read and photograph yourself reading inside or outside your home, on a lounge chair, or on a picnic blanket. Discuss when you like to read and explain that good readers have set times as well as spontaneous times for reading. Also, share if you read alone or with a family member or a book club. Use the *Summer Reading Plan* reproducible (see Figure 4.19) to share your summer reading goals.

2. Invite a student to fill out the *Summer Reading Plan* reproducible in front of the class as you guide and interview the student. Invite classmates to ask the student questions as well. Talk about the importance of variety in reading material and help the student to list both fiction and nonfiction reading ideas.

FIGURE 4.19

Summer Reading Plan Reproducible

Splash into Summer Reading
What to Read

- ☐ fairy tales; folktales
- ☐ adventure
- ☐ science fiction
- ☐ biography, autobiography
- ☐ historical fiction
- ☐ mysteries
- ☐ realistic fiction
- ☐ humor
- ☐ poetry
- ☐ nonfiction

Topics

_animals   _cooking   _famous people

_natural disasters _crafts   _sports

_rocks   _dinosaurs   _art

_music   _space

Other topics I want to read about include:_____

_____

_____

_____

_____

_____

_____

_____

When to Read

Show the times of day you will read.

I will read at _____ and _____.

I will read for _____ (minutes or hours).

Where to Read

Sketch two places where you plan to read.
Ideas: *under a tree, front porch, blanket, tent*

Who to Read With

I will read _____ by myself

I will read with

_a parent   _other adult

_a younger sibling   _older sibling

_book club   _animal

Sketch yourself reading with someone.

List of books I want to read.

1._____

2._____

3._____

4._____

5._____

6 _____

7._____

3. Distribute the *Summer Reading Plan* reproducible and ask students to fill in the what, where, and when portions. Call on student volunteers to act out some of the information they wrote on the reproducible (e.g., reading under a tree, in a tent).

Model Anytime Book Clubs!

1. Invite students to discuss what they know about book clubs and share your experiences or thoughts (e.g., club members read and discuss the same titles and eat treats related to the book). Gather high-interest books to establish a book club for students. Use the book club experience to introduce the class to authors, genres, and topics they may wish to read on their own. Choose books in the same genre (e.g., mysteries, fairy tales, humor), by the same author, or on the same topic (e.g., volcanoes, pets, friendships). You will need to have multiple copies of different books—a minimum of two or three copies of titles for small groups of two or three students. As alternatives, the entire class can read one book title but break into smaller discussion groups, or students can choose short articles on the same topic.

2. Model how to use the *Anytime Book Clubs* reproducible (see Figure 4.20) by selecting a book or article that all students have available, or use a read-aloud book and show it on the document camera or whiteboard. Also, provide a copy of the reproducible for all students and project a copy as you demonstrate filling it in.

3. Using any book or excerpt available to your class, model going through the steps in Figure 4.20. We used Chapter 2 from the book *Sea Turtles* by Frank Staub for a demonstration.

   a. **Model a Connection:** Say, "This chapter reminds me of another book I read about turtles where I learned how the mother turtle lays over 100 eggs in the sand." Students turn to partners and discuss your connection and add their own.

   b. **Model Points to Discuss:** Say, "I will put a sticky note on page 22 with a question mark on it because I want to discuss the caption about the sea turtle following the city lights and heading the wrong way. There are other dangers, too, that turtles and eggs face in the sand." Students talk to partners about your point to discuss and then add their own.

   c. **Model My Evaluation of the Text:** Say, "I give the chapter a 2 for *good* on the scale of 1 to 4. I think the author should have included more information about poachers and how people can help. Good thing the last

FIGURE 4.20

Anytime Book Clubs Reproducible

Name _____ **Date** _____

Book Title _____ **Author** _____

My Summary	**My Evaluation of the Text**
Write a few sentences telling what happened in the text.	I rate the text
	1 GREAT 2 GOOD 3 OK 4 POOR
	because _____
	_____.
	I liked the character_____
	because _____.
	Or
	I learned_____
	_____.
	What else I enjoyed:
Draw a picture to go with your writing.	___ art ___ writing style ___ the story ___ (other)
	_____
	Explain why:_____
	_____.

My Connections: This book reminds me of	**Points to Discuss**
_____	Mark these spots with sticky notes or record the page numbers.
[something I know or have done, another book I read, something I saw on TV] because _____	**A+** favorite part or sentence!
_____.	**LOL** funny part
	? question about a part, word, other
	Sketch one of your favorite parts or a funny part.

Book Celebration Activity: Choose a way to present your book to the class or group.

___   Make a poster to advertise your book.

___   Write an online review of the book for the class website or blog.

___   Make a skit about your book. Act out a scene.

___   Write a book talk and tell the class why they should read the book.

___   Write a poem about the book.

chapter we will read is about Save the Sea Turtles." Students discuss your evaluation and then write their own.

    d. **Model My Summary:** Say, "Female sea turtles crawl through the dry sand to dig a nest and lay 100 eggs. Many of them will not hatch or live long. She buries the eggs and heads back to the water. The eggs have to face many dangers, including animals, insects, heavy rains, big waves, even people." Students work together to share their summaries after discussing yours.

STEP 4: COLLABORATION

Social Skills: Encourage students to listen actively by looking at one another and leaning in. Show them how to agree or add to one another's comments, and how to disagree or share another idea. Invite students to create a chart or poster with symbols or drawings for the class to use to show agree, add on, disagree, or question.

Jigsaw: Cut apart the *Anytime Book Clubs* forms. Give each student at a group table one section of the form: My Summary, My Evaluation of the Book, My Connections, or Points to Discuss. Ask students to move to different parts of the classroom to join other students who have the same section. When students finish reading the text and filling out their portion of the form, they return to their original groups to share.

STEP 5: APPLICATION

Small-Group Lesson

Using the *Anytime Book Clubs* reproducible, teach a guided reading group using an appropriate text for the students' instructional reading level. In place of the form, create a large chart and give students sticky notes to write down their summaries, evaluations, connections, and discussion questions as they read. Share and discuss as a group.

Parents Read with Their Children

Make copies of the *Parent Letter for Motivating Students to Read* reproducible (Figure 4.21) to send home along with one or more books that the student has selected to read.

STEP 6: REFLECTION

Troubleshooting Chart

Ask students to discuss problems they may have figuring out what to read as well as when, where, and with whom. What are some solutions to these common pitfalls? See Figure 4.20 for some examples and options for troubleshooting.

ADAPTATION AND EXTENSION

- *Small-Group Instruction:* Teacher as reader demonstration, musical books, *Anytime Book Clubs* reproducible
- *Parents and Tutors:* Share the *Parent Letter for Motivating Students to Read* reproducible (Figure 4.21) and *My Reading Book Log* (Figure 1.17)
- *Independent Work:* Silent sustained reading, *Summer Reading Plan* reproducible, and *Anytime Book: Clubs* reproducible
- Revisit earlier lessons on motivation for more ideas:
  - Chapter 1: The Class Book Club: Motivation with Book Logs!
  - Chapter 2: Take Off and Partner Talk Bookmarks
  - Chapter 3: Ready, Set Goals, Read!
- *English Language Learner Suggestion:* Students read with partners and write on a shared copy of the *Anytime Book Club* form, filling it out together. To remove writing from the requirements, ask students to use sticky notes to mark their thoughts in the text and use the form as a guide for their discussions.
- *Struggling Reader Suggestion*: Students can share books with a younger class of buddies using the *Anytime Book Club* format for a discussion guide. Guide students as they practice reading the book three times before sharing with the younger reading buddy. Use sticky notes to mark where to stop to discuss the text with the younger child.

EVALUATION

"I can . . ." Statements

- I can find appropriate books that I want to read using a variety of resources in the library and online.
- I can share a plan and goals for my daily reading that include what I will read, where I will read, and when I will read.
- I can discuss books with others at school and at home.
- I can participate in a book club discussion and share my ideas.
- I can follow rules for book club discussions that include taking turns, looking at each other, and agreeing or disagreeing politely.

Behavior Indicators

- Identifies books to read over the summer.
- Identifies a plan and sets goals for daily reading that includes what to read, where to read, who to read with, and when to read.
- Participates in class book clubs using the *Anytime Book Club* reproducible.
- Follows rules for book club discussions.

FIGURE 4.21

Parent Letter for Motivating Students to Read

Dear Parents,

Summer brings warm weather, fun outdoor activities, and reading for pleasure. Make sure that your children do not take a break from reading in the summer! Research shows that students who *do not* read in the summer fall behind when school starts. Some students lose up to three months of reading achievement over the summer. The good news is that students who *do read* for 30 minutes or longer every day throughout the summer will maintain and even improve their reading. How can you help your child with their reading over the summer?

Ways to Motivate Your Child to Read

1. What to read:
- Ask your child to make a list of favorite topics and personal interests.
- Go to the local library and request suggestions from the children's librarian.
- Borrow age-level books from school.
- Check online for book suggestions for your child's age group.
- Sign up for the Scholastic Summer Reading Challenge. Find more information at www.scholastic.com/ups/campaigns/src-2017.
- Search online for reviews of children's books. Try the Spaghetti Book Club, which features book reviews for kids by kids!
- Keep track of summer reading by making a list of the books your child finishes.

2. Where to read:
- Encourage your child to read in various spots inside and outside the house.
- Read in bed with a flashlight under the covers.
- Read in a cozy chair.
- Read in a tent (real or made with blankets) in the yard or house.
- Read outside under a tree, on the porch, or on a blanket.

3. When to read:
- Read every day at a set time for 30 minutes or more, if possible.
- Choose to read while waiting in line or before a meal.

4. Who to read with:
- Read with a parent, grandparent, or other adult.
- Read with a younger or older sibling.
- Read to a pet!

continued

FIGURE 4.21 (*continued*)

Read to Your Child	Read aloud to your child even if he or she knows how to read. Let your child select the books. Discuss the reading rather than making it sound like an oral test. Take the time to talk about your favorite parts and what you wonder will happen next.
Take Turns Reading Together	Take turns reading by pages or parts. Read parts of the text in unison.
Your Child Reads	Encourage your child to read silently for 30 minutes a day. Discuss reading in a joyful manner. Help your child find interesting topics, but let your child choose the reading material and books.

Thank you for helping your child spend the summer growing and learning in literacy!

Sincerely,

Your Child's Teacher

Study Guide

This guide is designed to enhance your understanding and application of the information contained in *Literacy Strong All Year Long: Powerful Lessons for Grades 3–5*.

You can use this study guide before or after you have read the book, or as you finish each chapter. The questions provided are not meant to cover all aspects addressed in the book, but, rather, to address specific ideas that might warrant further reflection.

Most of the questions contained in this study guide are ones you can think about on your own, but you might consider pairing with a colleague or forming a study group with others who have read this book.

Objectives for individual or group book studies of *Literacy Strong All Year Long: Powerful Strategies for Grades 3–5:*

- To encourage student growth in literacy to become literacy strong.
- To adopt strategies that spiral across the year to strengthen student growth and close the achievement gap.
- To reflect on student needs and adjust practice to differentiate instruction for all students, including struggling readers and English language learners.
- To explore, discuss, and reflect on research-based lesson design to increase student achievement in the following areas of literacy: phonics and phonemic awareness, fluency, comprehension, vocabulary, and motivation.
- To increase student achievement using an interactive lesson design that engages and supports students as they become strong, independent, and motivated readers.

Study Guide: Introduction

1. Prioritize Effective Intermediate Grade Approaches. What are some effective research-based approaches that educators can use to keep literacy strong and promote growth in the intermediate grades? Why do these practices matter? Which are most important for the population you serve?

2. Spiral Instruction to Promote Growth. How does literacy growth for intermediate students change throughout the school year? How does instruction need to increase in complexity and spiral to meet student needs?

3. Teach Important Skills and Strategies. How does the development of skills and strategies in the areas of word study, fluency, comprehension, vocabulary, and motivation affect intermediate student achievement? Prioritize this list for your students. Explain.

4. Select and Rank Lessons. Study Figure 1, page xvii, that lists the 40 lessons in this book. Notice the progression of lessons across the seasons of the school year. Identify and note the lessons or strands your students need the most. Discuss with your group. How will you monitor growth in these areas?

5. Differentiate Instruction with Lesson Features
Study and discuss the lesson design features found in every lesson (listed here for your convenience). Discuss how help students become independent and literacy-strong learners.

> Preparation (Before Teaching)
> - Lesson Trailer
> - Literacy Enhancer
> - Materials
>
> Gradual Release Steps
> - Initiation
> - Demonstration
> - Collaboration
> - Application
> - Reflection
>
> Differentiation and Evaluation Options
> - Adaptation and Extension
> - Evaluation

6. Select and Teach Lessons. Select a lesson to teach to your students or select and plan a lesson as a group. Be prepared to share your students' response after teaching the lesson. Discuss what you learned and what you'd like to do next to further student progress and understanding.

Study Guide: Chapter 1. Starting the School Year Literacy Strong

1. Prioritize Beginning-of-the-Year Must-Do's. Brainstorm a list of must do's for the beginning of the school year. Compare your list to those listed in the chapter opener. Which ideas appeal most to you? How do such literacy routines help develop independence in your students?

2. Gather Initial Formative Assessment. Discuss which informal and formative assessment procedures are most helpful to you at the start of the school year. How can you gather literacy baselines quickly, and how will you use the information to design instruction?

3. Set Up Procedures for Read-Aloud and Independent Reading. What are the benefits of reading aloud to students in the first day or days of school? Which titles work well for reading aloud at your grade level? How can you engage students during read alouds to promote better comprehension? Discuss the importance of independent reading and practical ways to encourage students to read on their own.

4. Promote Student Independence. How can you structure lessons so that students are doing the heavy lifting? What does the gradual release of responsibility look like in your classroom and why does it matter in the intermediate grades?

5. Differentiate Instruction. Discuss the role of small-group instruction and formative assessment in the intermediate grades. Look through the lessons. How can you differentiate instruction by delivering instruction in small groups? As a group, choose one lesson and work together to discuss ways to teach the lesson or parts of it to small groups. Which students will you target and why?

6. Match Lessons to Your Curriculum. Select and rank the lessons in the order that you wish to teach them at the beginning of the year. Think about or discuss why you've selected these particular lessons and how you will deliver them to your class. How do the lessons mesh with your district's curriculum? Explain how you use the lessons to supplement or supplant the curriculum you teach.

7. Select and Teach Lessons. Work with a group to select one lesson to study, plan, and deliver to students. Report back and share how students responded. Discuss and share your findings. What do you need to do next to meet student needs?

Study Guide: Chapter 2. Beating the Midyear Blahs

1. Prioritize Midyear Must-Do's. Brainstorm a list of literacy must do's as you enter the middle of the school year. Compare your list to the list you made at the beginning of the year. How have things changed? Where do you need to focus instructional attention that will most strengthen students' literacy capacity?

2. Review the Literacy Scenarios. Read over the Take Off and Partner Talks bookmarks and Text Feature Tours scenarios at the beginning of the chapter. Do either of these scenarios appeal to you to promote how students should navigate a text? Read the Like What? Similes and Metaphor Galore scenario and think about how you use similes and metaphors in your classroom. What will you need to share with your students so that they can implement the techniques from these scenarios?

3. Establish Book Clubs Based on Choice. Explore various options for creating book clubs in your classroom or school. Create some sample book commercials to get started. Determine when and where the book clubs will meet. Create a few open-ended questions for the book clubs to use to start the discussion. How many groups will you have? What book titles will you have available?

4. Select and Teach Lessons. Work with a group to select several lessons from Chapter 2 to study, plan, and deliver to students. Report back and share how students responded. Discuss and share your findings. What do you need to do next to meet student needs?

5. Spiral Lessons and Align Them to Your Curriculum. Review the lessons that you implemented from Chapter 1. Notice the Literacy Enhancement Strategy and identify how the next lesson in the same strategy spirals from it. Identify the standards being addressed in the lessons in Chapter 2. How do the lessons align with your district curriculum? Explain how you use the lessons to supplement or supplant the curriculum you teach.

6. Gauge Student Response to Literacy Lessons. Reflect on your students' word journals and other written and oral responses. Were there any lessons or features of lessons that they particularly enjoyed or that you discovered were particularly effective? How will you use student response to change and improve your literacy instruction?

Study Guide: Chapter 3. Ending the School Year Literacy Strong

1. Prioritize End of the Year Must Do's. Brainstorm a list of literacy must do's as you enter the final months of the school year. Compare your list to the list you made at the beginning of the year. How have things changed? To end the year literacy strong, where do you need to focus instructional attention?

2. Review the Literacy Scenarios. Read the literacy scenarios at the beginning of the chapter. Which one appeals most to you (and your students)? Do you plan to use Earth Day to teach literacy? How do you think your students will respond as statues to texts that they read? Is it time to put on a show in your classroom using poetry, song, scripts, and other performance texts? Create a plan to make a special scenario work in your classroom.

3. Assess Students You Are Most Worried About. Use the informal formative assessment procedures you chose at the beginning of the school year to check on the progress of the students who need the most help. Have they made sufficient progress from your baseline assessment? If not, what will you do to meet these students' literacy needs?

4. Maintain a Parent Connection. As the end of the school year approaches, it is easy for parents to drift away from the practices that strengthen literacy. How might you help parents continue working with and supporting their children at home in reading? Consider an end-of-the-year parent conference in which you share ideas and book titles to keep literacy going strong into summer. How else might you communicate with parents? What ideas would you want to share with parents?

5. Continue to Promote Student Independence. As the school year ends, students should be well engaged in independent reading at school and at home. How can you reinforce the importance and significance of independent reading in those last few months of the school year?

6. Gauge Student Response to Literacy Strong Lessons. As the school year ends, ask students to respond to the literacy lessons that you have implemented. Will you ask students to respond in writing or, perhaps, in focus groups? Were there any lessons or features of lessons that they particularly enjoyed and found effective? How will you use student responses to change and improve your literacy instruction?

7. Move Beyond the Lessons. The lessons in this book are meant to act as models for your own lessons. Choose a lesson in this book that you will teach in the final months of the school year. Describe and plan a lesson that you can design to spiral from that lesson and dig deeper into the content.

Chapter 4. Stopping the Summer Slide

1. Review the Literacy Scenarios. Read the Family Games and Parent Partner Reading scenarios at the beginning of Chapter 4. Consider and discuss with your group these and other summer literacy scenarios that you can recommend to parents. What will you need to share with parents to implement a summer literacy effort?

2. Assess Students One More Time. Just before vacation begins, assess your students informally to determine the progress they made during the school year. Analyze the data to determine recommendations you can make to students' parents and next year's teachers. Are there any literacy competencies that you need to give additional attention in your curriculum?

3. Keep in Touch with Parents and Families. Gather and share contact information as well as articles about the importance of reading. Recommend books and texts, summer reading programs, and send letters of thanks and encouragement.

4. Send a Book Home. How might you acquire books to give to your students? Based on each student's interests, recommend books. Perhaps pair students with the same interests to read the same book. Make a list of activities that students can do over the summer in response to reading their books.

5. Review the School Year and Anticipate the Next. Take stock of your students' success in strengthening their literacy skills. How can you help next year's students do even better? What changes can you make to ensure that the concerns will turn into success next year?

6. Choose Lessons Wisely. It is unlikely that all the lessons in Chapter 4 will or can be used by families. With that in mind, list the lessons that will have the greatest positive effects on your students. Then, plan how you will deliver these lessons to parents.

7. Monitor Summer Lessons. The lessons for the summer months are designed for families. Still, it is a good idea to monitor the lessons. Perhaps send reminders to parents or ask students to respond to the lessons.

8. Connect to the Coming School Year. The lessons in Chapter 4 segue into the next school year. For example, patriotic songs and poetry may lead to other songs and poetry. Review the summer lessons and brainstorm recommendations for next year's teachers on how they may continue the summer literacy activities.

References

Allington, R. L., & McGill-Franzen, A. (Eds.). (2013). *Summer reading: Closing the rich/poor reading achievement gap.* New York: Teachers College Press.

Anderson, O. R. (2009). The role of knowledge network structures in learning scientific habits of mind: Higher order thinking and inquiry skills. In I. M. Saleh & M. S. Khine (Eds.), *Fostering scientific habits of mind: Pedagogical knowledge and best practices in science education* (pp. 59–82). Rotterdam, Netherlands: Sense.

Avi. (2005). *Poppy.* New York: HarperCollins.

Beck, I. L., Perfetti, C. A., & McKeown, M. G. (1982). The effects of long-term vocabulary instruction on lexical access and reading comprehension. *Journal of Educational Psychology, 74*(4), 506–521.

Beers, K. (2003). *When kids can't read, what teachers can do: A guide for teachers, 6–12.* Portsmouth, NH: Heinemann.

Blachowicz, C., & Ogle, D. (2001). *Reading comprehension: Strategies for independent learners.* New York: Guilford.

Block, C. C., & Dellamura, R. J. (2000). Better book buddies. *The Reading Teacher, 54*(4), 364–370. Retrieved from http://www.jstor.org/stable/20204921

Bolt Simons, L. M. (2015). *Cinquain poems.* North Mankato, MN: Child's World.

Boushey, G., & Moser, J. (2014). *The Daily Five: Fostering literacy independence in the elementary grades* (2nd ed.). Portland, ME: Stenhouse.

Bradley, T. (2012). *Animal architects.* Huntington Beach, CA: Teacher Created Materials.

Brassell, D., & Rasinski, T. V. (2008). *Comprehension that works: Taking students beyond ordinary understanding to deep comprehension.* Huntington Beach, CA: Shell Education.

Bridges, L. (2015). *The joy and power of reading: A summary of research and expert opinion.* New York: Scholastic.

Bromley, K., Winters, D., & Schlimmer, K. (1994). Book buddies: Creating enthusiasm for literacy learning. *The Reading Teacher, 47*(5), 392–400. Retrieved from http://www.jstor.org/stable/20201274

Caine, R. N., & Caine, G. (2013). The brain/mind principles of natural learning. In T. B. Jones (Ed.), *Education for the human brain: A road map to natural learning in schools* (pp. 43–62). Lanham, MD: Rowman & Littlefield.

Carlo, M. S., August, D., McLaughlin, B., Snow, C. E., Dressler, C., Lippman, D., et al. (2004). Closing the gap: Addressing the vocabulary needs for English-language learners in bilingual and mainstream classrooms. *Reading Research Quarterly, 39*(2), 188–215.

Clay, M. M. (2000). *An observation survey of early literacy achievement.* Portsmouth, NH: Heinemann.

Cunningham, P. M., & Allington, R. L. (2010). *Classrooms that work: They can all read and write* (5th ed.). Boston: Allyn & Bacon.

Cunningham, P. M., & Cunningham, J. W. (1992). Making words: Enhancing the invented spelling-decoding connection. *The Reading Teacher, 46*(2), 106–115.

Dweck, C. S. (2006). *Mindset: The new psychology of success.* New York: Ballantine Books.

Ellery, V. (2014). *Creating strategic readers: Techniques for supporting rigorous literacy instruction* (3rd ed.). Huntington Beach, CA: Shell Education.

Ellery, V., & Rosenboom, J. L. (2011). *Sustaining strategic readers: Techniques for supporting content literacy in grades 6–12.* Newark, DE: International Reading Association.

Fitzhugh, L. (1968). *Harriet the spy.* New York: Harper and Row.

Flanagan, K. R., Hayes, L., Templeton, S. R., Bear, D. R., Invernizzi, M., & Johnston, F. R. (2010). *Words their way with struggling readers: Word study for reading, vocabulary, and spelling instruction, grades 4–12.* New York: Pearson.

Harvey, S. (1998). *Nonfiction matters: Reading, writing, and research in grades 3–8.* Portland, ME: Stenhouse.

Herber, H. L. (1984). *Teaching reading in the content areas* (2nd ed.). Englewood Cliffs, NJ: Prentice Hall.

Hiebert, E. H., & Taylor, B. M. (Eds.). (1994). *Getting reading right from the start: Effective early literacy interventions.* Boston: Allyn & Bacon.

Hoyt, L. (2002). *Make it real: Strategies for success with informational texts.* Portsmouth, NH: Heinemann.

Invernizzi, M., Johnston, F. R., Bear, D. R., & Templeton, S. R. (2017). *Words their way: Word sorts for within word pattern spellers* (3rd ed.). New York: Pearson.

Irwin, J. W., & Baker, I. (1989). *Promoting active reading comprehension strategies: A resource book for teachers.* Englewood Cliffs, NJ: Prentice Hall.

Jensen, E. (2009). *Teaching with poverty in mind: What being poor does to kids' brains and what schools can do about it.* Alexandria, VA: ASCD.

Johnston, F., Invernezzi, M., Bear, D. R., & Templeton, S. R. (2018). *Words their way: Word sorts for syllables and affixes spellers* (3rd ed.). New York: Pearson.

Kelley, M. J., & Clausen-Grace, N. (2008). *R5 in your classroom: A guide to differentiating independent reading and developing avid readers.* Newark, DE: International Literacy Association.

Kim, J. S., & White, T. G. (2011). Solving the problem of summer reading loss. *Phi Delta Kappan, 92*(7), 64–67.

Kozubek, S. M. (2016). *Beyond the shore: Haiku, tanka and other poems.* North Charleston, SC: Create Space.

Lanning, L. A. (2013). *Designing a concept-based curriculum for English language arts: Meeting the common core with intellectual integrity, K–12.* Thousand Oaks, CA: Corwin.

Lapp, D., Flood, J., Ranck-Buhr, W., Van Dyke, J., & Spacek, S. (1997). "Do you really just want us to talk about the books?" A closer look at book clubs as an instructional tool. In J. R. Paratore & R. L. McCormack (Eds.), *Peer talk in the classroom: Learning from research* (pp. 6–23). Newark, DE: International Reading Association.

Ludwig, J. (2013). *The invisible boy.* New York: Knopf.

McEwan-Adkins, E. K. (2012). *Collaborative teacher literacy teams, K-6: Connecting teacher literacy to student achievement.* Bloomington, IN: Solution Tree.

Miller, D. (2009). *The book whisperer: Awakening the inner reader in every child.* San Francisco: Jossey-Bass.

Mraz, M., & Rasinski, T. V. (2007). Summer reading loss. *The Reading Teacher, 60*(8), 784–789.

National Governors Association Center for Best Practices & Council of Chief State School Officers. (2010). *Common core state standards for English language arts.* Available at www.corestandards.org

National Research Council. (2012). *Education for life and work: Developing transferable knowledge and skills in the 21st century.* Washington, DC: National Academies Press.

Oczkus, L. D. (2004). *Super six comprehension strategies: 35 lessons and more for reading success.* Lanham, MD: Rowman & Littlefield.

Oczkus, L. D. (2009). *Interactive think-aloud lessons: 25 surefire ways to engage students and improve comprehension.* New York: Scholastic.

Oczkus, L. D. (2012). *Best ever literacy survival tips: 72 lessons you can't teach without.* Newark, DE: International Literacy Association.

Oczkus, L. D. (2014). *Just the facts: Close reading and comprehension of informational text.* Huntington Beach, CA: Shell Education.

Oczkus, L. D. (2018). *Reciprocal teaching at work: Powerful strategies and lessons for improving reading and comprehension.* (3rd ed). Alexandria, VA: ASCD.

Oczkus, L. D., & Rasinski, T. V. (2015). *Close reading with paired text, level 5.* Huntington Beach, CA: Shell Education.

Piven, H. (2007). *My dog is as smelly as dirty socks and other funny family portraits.* New York: Dragonfly Books.

Polacco, P. (1993). *The bee tree.* New York: Philomel.

Polacco, P. (1998). *Thank you, Mr. Falker.* New York: Philomel.

Raphael, T. E. (1986). Teaching question answer relationships, revisited. *The Reading Teacher 39,*(6): 516–522.

Rasinski, T. V. (1999). Making and writing words. *Reading online.* International Reading Association.

Rasinski, T. V. (2010). *The fluent reader: Oral and silent reading strategies for building word recognition, fluency, and comprehension* (2nd ed.). New York: Scholastic.

Rasinski, T. V., & Griffith, L. (2011). *Building fluency through practice and performance.* Huntington Beach, CA: Shell Education.

Rasinski, T. V., & Oczkus, L. (2015a). *Close reading with paired text levels 1.* Huntington Beach, CA: Shell Education.

Rasinski, T. V., & Oczkus, L. (2015b). *Close reading with paired text levels 2.* Huntington Beach, CA: Shell Education.

Rasinski, T. V., & Oczkus, L. (2015c). *Close reading with paired text levels 3.* Huntington Beach, CA: Shell Education.

Rasinski, T. V., & Padak, N. (2005). *3-minute reading assessments: Word recognition, fluency, and comprehension.* New York: Scholastic.

Rasinski, T. V., Padak, N. D., & Fawcett, G. (2009). *Teaching children who find reading difficult* (4th ed.). New York: Pearson.

Rasinski, T. V., Padak, N. D., Newton, E., & Newton, R. (2007). *Building vocabulary from word roots* (grades K–11). Huntington Beach, CA: Teacher Created Materials.

Rasinski, T. V., Padak, N. D., Newton, R. M., & Newton, E. (2008). *Greek and Latin roots: Keys to building vocabulary.* Huntington Beach, CA: Shell Education.

Rasinski, T., & Smith, M. C. (2018). *The megabook of fluency: Strategies and texts to engage all readers.* New York: Scholastic.

Reutzel, D. R., & Clark, S. (2011). Organizing literacy classrooms for effective instruction. *The Reading Teacher, 65*(2), 96–109. doi:10.1002/TRTR.01013

Reutzel, D. R., & Fawson, P. C. (2002). *Your classroom library: New ways to give it more teaching power.* New York: Scholastic.

Roth, L. (2012). *Brain-powered strategies to engage all learners.* Huntington Beach, CA: Shell Education.

Routman, R. (2003). *Reading essentials: The specifics you need to teach reading well.* Portsmouth, NH: Heinemann.

Scholastic. (2017). *Kids and family reading report* (6th ed.). New York: AU. Retrieved from http://www.scholastic.com/readingreport/files/Scholastic-KFRR-6ed-2017.pdf

Simons, L., & Petelinski, K. (2015). *Cinquain poems.* North Mankato, MN: Child's World.

Small, M. (2010, September). Beyond one right answer. *Educational Leadership, 68*(1), 28–32.

Sousa, D. A. (2011). *How the brain learns* (4th ed.). Thousand Oaks, CA: Corwin.

Strobel, J., & van Barneveld, A. (2009). When is PBL more effective? A meta-synthesis of meta-analyses comparing PBL to conventional classrooms. *Interdisciplinary Journal of Problem-Based Learning, 3*(1), 44–58.

Thayer, E. L. (1888, June 3). Casey at the bat. *The Daily Examiner*, p. 4.

Tomlinson, C. A. (2017). *How to differentiate instruction in academically diverse classrooms* (3rd ed.). Alexandria, VA: ASCD.

Topping, K. J. (2005). Trends in peer learning. *Educational Psychology, 25*(6), 631–645. doi: 10.1080/01443410500345172

Torgesen, J. K. (2005). Recent discoveries from research on remedial interventions for children with dyslexia. In M. J. Snowling & C. Hulme (Eds.), *The science of reading: A handbook* (pp. 521–537). Malden, MA: Blackwell.

Wiederhold, C. W. (1997). *Cooperative learning and higher-level thinking: The q-matrix.* San Clemente, CA: Kagan.

Wiggins, G., & McTighe, J. (2011). *The Understanding by Design guide to creating high-quality units.* Alexandria, VA: ASCD.

Wilhelm, J. D. (2002). *Action strategies for deepening comprehension.* New York: Scholastic.

Wolfe, P. (2010). *Brain matters: Translating research into classroom practice* (2nd ed.). Alexandria, VA: ASCD.

Wong, H. K., & Wong, R. T. (2009). *The first days of school: How to be an effective teacher.* Mountain View, CA: Harry K. Wong Publications.

Wood, K. D., Lapp, D., & Flood, J. (1992). *Guiding readers through text: A review of study guides.* Newark, DE: International Reading Association.

About the Authors

Valerie Ellery has dedicated 30 years to the field of education in various roles as a National Board Certified Teacher, curriculum specialist, mentor, reading coach, international educational consultant, and best-selling author for 10 years. Her books *Creating Strategic Readers* and *Sustaining Strategic Readers* have been used internationally in classrooms and universities to inspire educators to motivate and engage today's learners. She authored 10 student readers for Saint Mary's Press with guiding questions, vocabulary, and retell it cards. In addition, she coauthored two secondary curriculums in the area of self-worth and human trafficking, *Bodies Are Not Commodities* and *Shine Hope* (A21 campaign.org and Hillsong.com), which will be used to influence young adults in 37 nations. Using innovative, interactive, and informative methods, Valerie models best practices in classrooms and motivates staffs globally to create strategic thinkers and readers. She lives in Florida with husband Gregg and has four adult children and two beautiful grandchildren. For more information or to reach Valerie for professional development, visit http://www.ValerieEllery.com.

Lori Oczkus is a literacy coach, best-selling author, and popular international speaker. Tens of thousands of teachers have attended her motivating, fast-paced workshops and read her practical, research-based professional books and articles. Lori has experience working as a bilingual elementary teacher, intervention specialist, staff developer, and literacy coach. She works with students in classrooms every week and knows the challenges that teachers face in teaching students to read. Lori has been inducted into the California Reading Association Hall of Fame for her many contributions to the field of reading. Her travels to provide literacy trainings in other countries include trips to Canada, London, and Trinidad. Lori is the author of seven best-selling professional books. Her latest publications include *Just the Facts: Close Reading and Comprehension of Informational Text* and *Close Reading with Paired Texts,* a K–5 series coauthored with Tim Rasinski. Lori's *Reciprocal Teaching at Work: Strategies for Improving Reading Comprehension* is a best seller. She also is coauthor of several reading programs, including *Talk About Books*, a K–2 guided reading series and *Exploring Reading*, a K–8 intervention kit for Teacher Created Materials. Lori lives in California with her husband, Mark, and has three young adult children. For more information or to reach Lori for professional development, visit http://www.LoriOczkus.com.

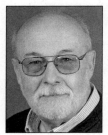 **Timothy Rasinski** is a professor of literacy education at Kent State University. He has written more than 200 articles and has authored, coauthored, or edited more than 50 books or curriculum programs on reading education. His best-selling book on reading fluency, *The Fluent Reader*, is now in its second edition. His scholarly interests include reading fluency, word study, and readers who struggle. His research on reading has been cited by the National Reading Panel and has been published in journals such as *Reading Research Quarterly, The Reading Teacher, Reading Psychology,* and the *Journal of Educational Research*. Tim is the lead author of the fluency chapter for the *Handbook of Reading Research*. Tim has served on the board of directors of the International Reading Association and was coeditor of *The Reading Teacher*, the world's most widely read journal of literacy education. He has also served as coeditor of the *Journal of Literacy Research*. Tim is past president of the College Reading Association and was inducted into the International Reading Hall of Fame in 2010. Prior to coming to Kent State, Tim taught literacy education at the University of Georgia. He taught for several years as an elementary and middle school classroom and Title I teacher in Nebraska. For more information or to reach Tim for professional development, visit http://www.timrasinski.com or e-mail at trasinsk@kent.edu.

Related ASCD Resources: Literacy

At the time of publication, the following resources were available (ASCD stock numbers in parentheses).

Print Products

Achieving Next Generation Literacy: Using the Tests (You Think) You Hate to Help the Students You Love by Maureen Connolly and Vicky Giouroukakis (#116023)

Building Student Literacy Through Sustained Silent Reading by Steve Gardiner (#105027)

A Close Look at Close Reading: Teaching Students to Analyze Complex Texts, Grades K–5 by Diane Lapp, Barbara Moss, Maria Grant, and Kelly Johnson (#114008)

Effective Literacy Coaching: Building Expertise and a Culture of Literacy by Shari Frost, Roberta Buhle, and Camille Blachowicz (#109044)

Engaging Minds in English Language Arts Classrooms: The Surprising Power of Joy by Mary Jo Fresch, Michael F. Opitz, and Michael P. Ford (#113021)

Literacy Leadership for Grades 5–12 by Rosemarye Taylor and Valerie Doyle Collins (#103022)

Literacy Strategies for Grades 4–12: Reinforcing the Threads of Reading by Karen Tankersley (#104428)

Literacy Unleashed: Fostering Excellent Reading Instruction Through Classroom Visits by Bonnie D. Houck and Sandi Novak (#116042)

Read, Write, Lead: Breakthrough Strategies for Schoolwide Literacy Success by Regie Routman (#113016)

Research-Based Methods of Reading Instruction, Grades K–3 by Sharon Vaughn and Sylvia Linan-Thompson (#104134)

Tools for Teaching Writing: Strategies and Interventions for Diverse Learners in Grades 3–8 by David Campos and Kathleen Fad (#114051)

Total Literacy Techniques: Tools to Help Students Analyze Literature and Informational Texts by Pérsida Himmele, William Himmele, and Keely Potter (#114009)

Vocab Rehab: How do I teach vocabulary effectively with limited time? (ASCD Arias) by Marilee Sprenger (#SF114047)

For up-to-date information about ASCD resources, go to *www.ascd.org*. You can search the complete archives of *Educational Leadership* at *www.ascd.org/el*.

ASCD myTeachSource®

Download resources from a professional learning platform with hundreds of research-based best practices and tools for your classroom at http://myteachsource.ascd.org/

For more information, send an e-mail to member@ascd.org; call 1-800-933-2723 or 703-578-9600; send a fax to 703-575-5400; or write to Information Services, ASCD, 1703 N. Beauregard St., Alexandria, VA 22311-1714 USA.

THE WHOLE CHILD

The ASCD Whole Child approach is an effort to transition from a focus on narrowly defined academic achievement to one that promotes the long-term development and success of all children. Through this approach, ASCD supports educators, families, community members, and policymakers as they move from a vision about educating the whole child to sustainable, collaborative actions.

Literacy Strong All Year Long: Powerful Lessons for Grades 3–5 relates to the **engaged**, **supported**, and **challenged** tenets. For more about the ASCD Whole Child approach, visit ***www.ascd.org/wholechild***.

WHOLE CHILD TENETS

1 HEALTHY
Each student enters school healthy and learns about and practices a healthy lifestyle.

2 SAFE
Each student learns in an environment that is physically and emotionally safe for students and adults.

3 ENGAGED
Each student is actively engaged in learning and is connected to the school and broader community.

4 SUPPORTED
Each student has access to personalized learning and is supported by qualified, caring adults.

5 CHALLENGED
Each student is challenged academically and prepared for success in college or further study and for employment and participation in a global environment.